Scripting the Black Masculine Body

SUNY SERIES, NEGOTIATING IDENTITY:
DISCOURSES, POLITICS, PROCESSES, AND PRAXES

---

Ronald L. Jackson II, editor

# SCRIPTING THE BLACK MASCULINE BODY

## Identity, Discourse, and Racial Politics in Popular Media

RONALD L. JACKSON II

STATE UNIVERSITY OF NEW YORK PRESS

Poet Bridget Gray's poem "My Letter to Hip Hop" is used here by permission.

Chapter 5 is used here by permission from International Thomson Publishing/Wadsworth and Celnisha Dangerfield. It is an expanded version of the following article: Jackson, R. L. & Dangerfield, C. (2002). Defining Black Masculinity as Cultural Property: An Identity Negotiation Paradigm. In L. Samovar & R. Porter (Eds.), *Intercultural Communication: A Reader* (pp. 120–130). Belmont, CA: Wadsworth.

Published by
STATE UNIVERSITY OF NEW YORK PRESS
ALBANY

© 2006  State University of New York

For information, address
State University of New York Press
194 Washington Avenue, Suite 305, Albany, NY 12210-2384

Production, Laurie Searl
Marketing, Susan Petrie

**Library of Congress Cataloging-in-Publication Data**

Jackson, Ronald L., 1970–
    Scripting the Black masculine body : identity, discourse, and racial politics in popular media / Ronald L. Jackson II.
      v.  cm. — (SUNY series, the negotiation of identity)
    Includes bibliographical references and index.
    Contents: Introduction : origins of Black body politics — Scripting the Black body in popular media : exploring process — Black masculine scripts — "If it feels this good gettin' used" : exploring the hypertext of sexuality — Towards an integrated theory of Black masculinity — Epilogue : the revolution will not be televised.
    ISBN-13: 978-0-7914-6625-4 (hardcover : alk. paper)
    ISBN-10: 0-7914-6625-6 (hardcover : alk. paper)
    ISBN-13: 978-0-7914-6626-1 (pbk. : alk. paper)
    ISBN-10: 0-7914-6626-4 (pbk. : alk. paper)
    1. African American men—Social conditions. 2. Masculinity—Political aspects—United States. 3. Body, Human—Social aspects—United States. 4. Body, Human—Political aspects—United States. 5. African Americans—Race identity. 6. African Americans in popular culture. 7. African Americans and mass media. 8. Mass media—Political aspects—United States. 9. Discourse analysis—Political aspects—United States. 10. United States—Race relations. I. Title. II. Series
    E185.86.J334 2005
    305.38'896073—dc22

                                                            2005002385

10   9   8   7   6   5   4   3   2   1

*To my brother Bruce, my son Niles,*
*my nephew Miles, and all the other men in my family—*
*my father, father-in-law, little brother, uncles, and close male friends—*
*that you may seek, find, and develop in yourself the most loving and*
*spiritually imbued manhood you can. May God bless you on this journey!*

# Contents

# Acknowledgments

First, all honor for making this book possible goes to God, who has continually expanded my life. Moreover, I am thankful for my family, and especially for my mother Sharon Prather who has taught me more about being a man than any man ever has. Other strong women in my life who have influenced my manhood are my wife, Ricci Jackson, my late grandmother Thelma Gross, as well as Phyllis Gross, Georgie Jackson, Vanessa Carter, Baola Gould, Mary Haiman, and Mary G. R. Gordon. I am also grateful for the influential men in my life: my father, Ronald L. Jackson, Sr., my brothers Bruce and Tishaun Jackson, as well as Bob Wilson, Brad Hogue, Keith Wilson, Ramone Ford, Carlos Morrison, Maurice Hall, Eric Watts, Shaun Gabbidon, Wayne Gersie, Michael Hecht and the men of Omega Psi Phi Fraternity, Inc. Additionally, a special thanks goes to James Peltz, Laurie Searl, and Susan Petrie for the acquisition, copyediting, production, and marketing of the book, respectively. I am also grateful to the indexer of this book, David Prout. A special note of gratitude goes to the Africana Research Collaborative for their support toward completion of this book.

INTRODUCTION

# Race and Corporeal Politics

Ideology is a representation of the imaginary relationship of individuals to their real conditions of existence.

—Althusser, 1994

No one would deny that race, as a cultural and social phenomenon, continues to retain its vitality and centrality in American life. Race clearly matters.

—Miller, 1993

Opening a magazine or book, turning on the television set, watching a film, or looking at photographs in public spaces, we are most likely to see images of Black people that reinforce and reinscribe White supremacy. Clearly, those of us committed to Black liberation struggle, to the freedom and determination of all Black people, must face daily the tragic reality that we have collectively made few, if any, revolutionary interventions in the area of race and representations.

—hooks, 1992

Much of the literature on the social construction of race, including the works excerpted above, has convincingly argued that the body is the primary site and surface of race and representation (Baker-Fletcher, 1996; Bordo, 1994; Dyson, 1994; Hall, 1997; hooks, 1995b). Certainly, the interpretations of mass-mediated inscriptions[1] of the body reveal the hidden contours of psychic and institutional investitures that drive, indeed motivate, the producers of the inscriptions. Socially, the body facilitates the perpetuation of ascriptive devices used to assign meanings to ingroups and outgroups; it also serves to jog the personal memories of cultural interactants, to remind them visually of the constitutive discourses that provide form and structure to their social cognitions about racialized bodies.

1

The terms inscription, scripting, scripts, inscriptive, and inscribing are used interchangeably throughout to mean figuratively that the body is socially understood and treated as a discursive text that is read by interactants. There are various racial meanings attached to bodily texts that can inspire individuals to behave differently toward foreign or unfamiliar bodies when encountering them in public and private spaces. In this book, I argue that mass-mediated depictions of culturally and racially different human beings encourage people to respond to the differences rather than the similarities. There is a hyperawareness, for example, of the negative inscriptions associated with the Black masculine body as criminal, angry, and incapacitated (Belton, 1996; Jackson, 1997; McCall, 1995; Orbe, 1998; Orbe & Hopson, 2002). These scripts are exacerbated by popular cultural portrayals of Black males, which make it almost impossible to retrieve custody of the meanings associated with blackness and Black males. Because mass media and popular culture are predominantly littered with these negative images, it appears they are unwilling to see Black bodies positively, and this affects everyday looking relations (Dent, 1992). Essentially, as human beings we are all involuted in a sort of Foucauldian "panopticism," in which, as Evans (1999) puts it, "The visual [becomes] construed as an object for power/knowledge" (p. 15), which makes the body political—hence the term "body politics."

The construction of the Black body² as a public and popularly mediated spectacle is evident in everyday televisual and cinematic images, as well as in routine interpersonal encounters between Blacks and non-Blacks (Bogle, 2001; Dixon & Linz, 2000; Ellis, 1982; Entman & Rojecki, 2000; Gandy, 1999; Watts & Orbe, 2002). Perhaps what is not so clear is how the Black body is discursively bound to an ideological matrix propagated by a socially preponderate whiteness. Although assigning the Black body in a "discursively bound" juxtaposition to whiteness ideology seems to place unimaginatively whiteness in sinister opposition to blackness, and blackness in inescapable subordination to whiteness, it is critical to note that the I–Other racial dialectic is pervasive and instructive in our present-day postmodern context. It is also extremely relevant to how we may come to understand multiple and sometimes devastating inscriptions of the Black body.

Within the field of communication, systematic analyses of the body (and its politics) have been most often situated in performance and media studies, as well as in critical-theoretic work accomplished primarily by feminists and researchers of whiteness with scant attention paid to the total confluence of race, gender, discourse, identity, ideology, and corporeal politics. The infrequent analysis of this full convergence leaves a conspicuous void in interdisciplinary studies in general, and in the field of communication in particular. As the title conveys (Scripting the Black Masculine Body: Identity, Discourse and Racial Politics in Popular Media), this book seeks to fill that void partially and it does so without localizing the exploration to communication studies; hence it is admittedly and unashamedly interdisciplinary. The principle focus is on the Black body, and the varied literatures are synthesized to facilitate critical theoretic and social scientific analysis of race and body politics.

## WHY STUDY U.S. BLACK BODY POLITICS?

Inevitably, some readers will be disgusted that the principal concern of this book is the Black-White dialectic in the United States rather than what they believe to be the more sophisticated analysis of interracial dialectics including native Africans, Spanish-speaking peoples, and Asians. It is highly unlikely that one can rightfully and intensively examine all of these continental and diasporic perspectives in one volume. It is much more heuristic, in my opinion, to explore and deconstruct systematically ontological challenges to one set of racialized bodies than to commit the disservice of presenting a haphazard and lopsided treatment of multiple perspectives without much depth. So, it is the intent of this volume, as its title suggests, to concentrate solely on how the Black masculine body has been and still is inscribed in popular culture. I urge the reader not to miss the point, which is that both Black male and female bodies have been ontologically rearranged, displaced, and economized. It is virtually impossible to speak of male masculinities without at least insinuating femaleness or femininity, so there will be frequent mention of women as the book progresses. Also, "Black" has been situated in direct opposition to "White" for centuries (Harris, 1993). It is precisely this situation that deserves further commentary within the context of interdisciplinary body politics discourses.

The vast array of research on whiteness has taught us the Black–White dialectic is preserved by an undeniable hegemonic whiteness. Consequently, I do not disengage, absolve, or acquit whiteness from Whites, as some scholars would prefer. Keating (1995), for example, argues vehemently for separating the two, since allowing them to be contiguous permits the faulty presumption that all Whites prescribe to whiteness ideology. Barthes (1977), a structuralist-semiologist, would agree, and would add that the temporal moment, no matter how disparaging of Black bodies, should not be delivered from the entire historical text, which may otherwise be good. That is, the text is partially a response to what has preceded it; therefore, its meaning is merely a composite of other meanings and is in no way singular or tied to an instance. Although Keating's and Barthes's claims are both intriguing, and tactically relativistic, it is at our own peril that we allow polemics to stand between sound reason and lived experience.

The fact is Whites are the inventors and primary proprietors of race and its social construction in the United States (West, 1993). As Tierney and Jackson (2002) assert, "It would be cowardly not to place and name that dominance." This is not to say that all Whites are racist, patriarchal, or hegemonic, but that

*Whites + whiteness separation*

there are numerous historical and contemporary sets of discourses in place that offer very compelling evidence contrary to Keating's and Barthes's intuition concerning the separation of the two. Even more significant to this book is that it is irresponsible to separate the authors of whiteness ideology from the race-intensive text the authors produced, lest we lose our grounding for an examination of scripting or inscription of the Black body. Nonetheless, in a parallel semiological exercise, Barthes's (1999) trilateral construction of signifying practices holds true for scripting; he contends, "[there is] the signifier, the signified and the sign, which . . . is the associative total of the first two terms" (p. 52). Within this book, the scripter, the scripted (Black body), and the inscription are the constituent parts of the social equation that compromises corporeal politics. The point of unraveling or deconstructing the verbal signifiers of race and its double entendres via Black body politics is to figure out who produced the initially inscribed text on the Black body, in what context it was produced, how this production was accomplished, and how it sustains itself even today. That requires recognition of racial inscription as process, historically and in situ. Whites *and* Blacks facilitate the present-day perpetuation of race and racism via their active complicity with daily institutional racial inscriptions (Harris, 1993). McPhail (1994b; 1996) maintains that complicity is a collaborative act in which two or more parties sustain the essence of a construct by adhering to and enacting its essentialist premises. For example, one popular inscription is that Black males are angry and volatile (Orbe & Hopson, 2002). One iteration of this can be observed in contemporary rap music. If the prophecy is that Black males express themselves with an angry or hostile tone, then the prophecy is likely to be fulfilled if one observes even a few rap music videos. Although this example is simplistic, it does illustrate how inscriptions can become real during a limited set of observations and how complicity to inscriptions will likely lead to more inscriptions. Personal prejudices naturally expand to institutional prejudices, especially in cases when individuals in decision-making media positions already hold racial presuppositions (Entman & Rojecki, 2000; Gandy, 1999).

Although this book could be misread as a reinitiation of the "blame game" in which all Whites are allegedly moral criminals, it will become increasingly clear that this is not entirely the case. Nonetheless, the savvy reader will recognize the historical truths recounted here, and will acknowledge the importance of deconstructing corporeal politics in U.S. popular media as an emancipatory act. Again, the purpose is not to "point fingers," but to locate a displaced agency and discover the source of inscriptions existent on Black bodies and prominent in popular media.

American popular culture, inclusive of music, television, and film, is fixated on representations of a pathologized blackness, how it is constituted and embodied (Guerrero, 1993). The vast majority of social interpretations of race are predicated on difference and devaluation, and the body is often conceived as a mere physical vessel that links human beings and their differences to the social world; however, the body, in and of itself, contains its own discourse, its own scripts, which are often utilized as an apparatus to secure racial and cultural capital. It is what those scripts say, how they are inscribed, and what we do with them that are my principal concerns in *Scripting the Black Masculine Body*.

Twentieth- and twenty-first century representations of Black bodies have powerfully debilitating possibilities because of their negative denotations and connotations. With the emergence of new media transducing racialized information from multiple popular cultural constituencies and mass-mediated news sources, and through the steady climb of hate group prosyletization via the Internet, Black bodies are being socially reconstituted and redefined on a daily basis. Besides this, American citizens are also witnessing documented cases of racial-profiling practices at every level of law enforcement, as well as racially disproportionate technological access, healthcare coverage, infant mortality and poverty rates, home ownership, unemployment, and education (Hecht, Jackson, & Ribeau, 2003; K. Wilson, 2000). Although the Clinton administration initiated dialogue about racial disparities, countless reports have indicated modest gains (Pinar, 2001; Smelser et al., 2001). Martin Luther King Jr. was noted for eloquently articulating the plight of marginalized groups, particularly Blacks, and he once indicated that the prescription for the cure lies in the accurate diagnosis of the disease. It is the intent of this book to diagnose and deconstruct the politics of racial representation by focusing on the nature of racialized bodies in the public sphere. In approaching this task, it is necessary to introduce three premises foundational to my analysis of race and corporeal politics in *Scripting the Black Masculine Body*: (1) bodies are inscriptive surfaces that are discursive texts, which can be rewritten after acts of struggle toward emancipation, though still not fully divested of prior inscriptions; (2) body politics is the lifeline for race and racism; and (3) corporeal inscriptions stimulate the negotiation of racial identities.

## SUMMARY OF BOOK BY CHAPTERS

With these three premises in mind, I have divided the book into five chapters plus an epilogue. In chapter 1 I present a critical-historical sketch of Black body politics in the United States, concentrating on slavery and its mass-mediated counterparts of minstrel theater and early blackface cinema. The social construction of a racialized blackness in the United States began with the inception of slavery in the "New World" in the late 1500s. This is evidenced by historical accounts of the dehumanizing effects of slavery and the concomitant social and artificial inscriptions of Black bodies that appeared on paraphernalia (i.e., posters, ceramic figurines, games, etc.) and also on theater stages.

In chapter 2, I explain the scripting process and offer a few examples of how it is contemporarily deployed via popular culture. I also explore the ideological underpinnings of scripting before examining several instances of hegemonic inscriptions in televised commercial advertising and film. One such endeavor, for example, is my examination of distinctive economies assigned to Black male and female bodies in film.

In chapter 3 I discuss the various stereotypes that have been projected onto the inscriptive canvas of the Black masculine body. Unlike chapter 2, where I generally explore scripting in popular culture, chapter 3 is the first time I devote full attention to one gendered perspective rather than discussing the composite Black body composed of male and female, masculine and feminine. This chapter also sets the precedent for the remainder of the book, which almost exclusively attends to negative inscriptions of Black masculinity.

By this point, I will have presented the origins, definitions, processes, and stereotypes of Black bodies. In chapter 4 I continue the deductive sequence already in place by discussing how some Black hip-hop musical artists and Black film directors have been complicit with stereotypes of Black bodies, as evidenced by sex-laden popular cultural corporeal inscriptions. More specifically, I talk about how Black male and female thugs as well as pimp film producers, who have seized at least some agency to define how their bodies will be publicly understood, have valorized and showcased the Black body as a sexually perverse and fragmented entity. They have resurrected the pimp–whore complex, and this has instigated celebration of a paternally driven, misogynistic narcissism.

In chapter 5 I present a paradigm that seeks to offer a corrective envisioning of the often surreal and imagined portrayals of Black masculine bodies. Realizing that Black identities are centrally confounded by struggle—struggle to achieve, to be heard and understood, to be loved, recognized, and valued, and to survive—the Black Masculine Identity paradigm is introduced as a mandala composed of four "needs" that orbit around struggle. According to Hall (1983), "mandalas are particularly useful when one is dealing with paradoxical relationships, dissimilar pairs or clusters of activities which one's intuition indicates are related but which have not been previously associated, linked or combined into a comprehensive system" (p. 15). The four elements of the Black masculine identity theory mandala are as follows: recognition, independence, achievement, and community (all revolving around the center, which is struggle).

The final segment of the book is not a chapter, but rather an epilogue entitled "The revolution will not be televised," a phrase borrowed from activist and poet Gil Scott Heron. In this brief commentary, I explore a few directions that proclaim and avouch the possibilities for liberation, an escape from the often ineffectual representations of blackness that paralyze race relations in the United States.

My goal in *Scripting the Black Masculine Body* is to call attention to the spontaneous objectification of Black bodies still present in contemporary media by exploring origins, definitions, processes, inherent stereotypes, and complicity with negative inscriptions that all confound Black body politics in the United States (i.e., societal strategies). Subsequently, I offer a remedial paradigm that explains variegated Black masculine behaviors. Finally, I leave the reader with encouragement to pursue healthy reinscriptions of Black bodies that will recognize their plurality (i.e., personal strategies).

Please keep in mind that it is the intention of this book to briefly trace the history of stereotypes followed by an application of the scripting paradigm to explore the stereotypical representation of Black bodies in popular media. I am not simply claiming that stereotypes about Black masculine persons involve Black masculine bodies. That claim, alone, would not necessitate a book. Instead, I am arguing that constituents of popular media have historically and irresponsibly scripted Black masculine bodies in multiple ways. These ways must be identified and the analysis of scripting must be consistently situated in an ethical discourse of character and responsibility.

Though not always explicitly addressed as such, the examination of racialized bodily discourse is the centerpiece of this book. The body is a social instrument that figuratively holds the projections of others in the confines of its texts. Those projections are what I refer to as the *inscriptions*, the impositional writings of others on bodies that are not their own. With each new pejorative iteration, as promulgated via popular culture as well as other public and private vehicles, the body is burdened by another set of ideologies and ideas. It is not that the body passively accepts these negative inscriptions, but that even in its strongest resistance to them, if this image-making is institutionally sanctioned and fortified via electronically and digitally reproduced omnipresent stereotypes that are accepted and consumed en mass, it becomes virtually impossible to interrupt the cycle of despair unless we are able to unravel systematically the psychical structures emplaced by this machinery. These same structures provide the circuitry necessary to regulate "looking relations," representational gazes, and disciplined surveillance of Black bodies, and, ultimately, to retrieve agency. With access to agency, which defines one's own reality, the instruments and apparatus used to facilitate the cyclical inscription of Black bodies become inapplicable and eventually defunct. For Blacks, liberation from the colonizing discursive and political practices binding their corporeal inscriptions is necessary, lest their identities be perpetually entrapped in a matrix of race relations that only grants subjugation (Jackson & Richardson, 2003). Our lives depend on it!

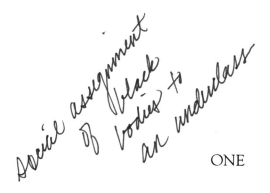
*Social assignment of Black bodies to an underclass*

# ONE

# Origins of Black Body Politics

The notion that Black people are human beings is a relatively new discovery in the modern west.

—West, 1982

To the real question, how does it feel to be a problem? I seldom answer a word.

—DuBois, 1903

DuBois asks, "How does it feel to be a problem?" The question I will ask and answer in this chapter is, "How did Black bodies become a problem in the first place?" The social assignment of Black bodies to an underclass is a historical conundrum that has multiple origins, two of which are the institutions of slavery and the mass media. This chapter will explain how a set of racial projections became concretized in the American landscape via the development of meanings that were eventually fortified in many aspects of American life. In other words, Black bodies were inscribed with a set of meanings, which helped to perpetuate the scripter's racial ideology. Through these scripts, race gradually became its own corporeal politics. Essentially, this book is an un-muting of DuBois's reply to the question, "How does it feel to be a problem?" Also, it inevitably offers a discussion of West's assertion that Black people's humanity is a fairly new discovery.

Although it is clear, as Foucault (1972) announces, "that everything is never said," it is important to engage the historicity of the concept of Black body politics and the scripting of the Black body[1] for what they reveal about embedded racially xenophobic tendencies that are redistributed and recycled in mass-mediated cultural practices. The selected vehicle for doing so is critical-historical analysis, which recounts the genesis of a phenomenon while mapping contemporary parallels and grappling with age-old problems revisited. This mode of inquiry has become valuable and transitive for its ability to support social reformulations and reconstructions of knowledge in addition to the sociopolitical machinery that functions to perpetuate historically concomitant ideologies. Critical-historical analysis is necessarily an emancipatory act of reasoning through historical problems while elevating an analysis that calls for an end to a kind of domination characteristic as evidenced in the Manichean dialectic of psyche (mind) and colonialism (coercive control). This social and philosophical dualism, as implied by the word "Manichean," suggests an inescapable commitment to power relations. My lifelong concern for the liberation of Black bodies, and therefore Black people, is conspicuous and unapologetic. Black bodies are not discussed here as a way to objectify, reconfigure, or disfigure Blacks and Black lives. Instead, the aim is to theorize how race is currently enacted at the moment of the gaze, and how this spectatorial surveillance complicates social relations because of how it is historically and inextricably situated and lodged in the US collective consciousness and the American ethos via popular media.

The gaze, as Wiegman (1995) describes it, is a specular event, a tool for examining sites of obsessive desire that admit the visibility of difference, but remain troubled by it. The gaze can certainly be impartial or nonobligatory, but within the interplay of race relations, corporeal zones such as that of skin color and hair texture automatically evoke feelings, thoughts, perhaps anxieties, if they are already resident or dormant. The gaze suggests that there must be the presence of an Other. The Other can be a self-reflection, or it can be an unfamiliar or distanced Other. Either way, the Other functions to affirm the Self within this I–Other dialectical arrangement (Hitchcock, 1993). The Self is more than the "I" since the Self involves self-consciousness, self-esteem, and a personhood influenced by society and culture (Grosz, 1994; Hall, 1997). Anticolonialist Frantz Fanon (1967) was clear about this when he wrote, "To speak is to exist absolutely for the Other" (p. 17). Writer-scholar Ralph Ellison (1952) also lucidly addressed this matter when he asserted, "I am an invisible man . . . I am invisible, understand, simply because people refuse to see me" (p. 3). It has become ordinary to talk about the I-versus-Other dialectic, but it is also possible to be Self *and* Other, though Homi Bhabha (1986) rearticulates this equation as follows: "[it is] not Self and Other, but the Otherness of the self inscribed in the perverse palimpsest of colonial identity" (p. xv). That is, the sickly nature of hegemonic inscriptions may influence an individual to begin to view the self as a stranger, as an obscure Otherized corporeal object, rather than as a familiar subject. So then, it is both the Other and the Other's formulated inscription that are at work in Bhabha's "Self and Other" equation. There is a matrix within the present investigation that involves three parts: personal perceptions that accompany the gaze, institutional inscriptions, and the social consequences of institutional inscriptions. I cannot emphasize enough, as filmmaker Isaac Julien puts it, "it's the look—the act of looking—that we want to challenge" (p. 169). The act of looking involves the gaze, but is not restricted to or by it. The gaze, as Mercer (1999) allows, is spectatorial. It presumes there is a visually noticeable object that is dialectically connected to a codified and signified subject. Scripting, in this book, includes the gaze and also the social prescriptions that disprivilege racialized, politicized, and commodified Black bodies.

Blacks can endlessly participate in self-healing exercises in an effort to retrieve custody over the total inscription of their bodies and the debilitating social conditions that attempt redefinition and confinement of their corporeality, but this analysis will reveal that inscriptions of race and racism are not entirely a Black problem; hence, Blacks cannot expunge them alone. All North American cultural groups must participate in deconstructive processes, deciphering the origins and precincts of racist and socially corrupt images, and one way this can be initiated and achieved is by understanding the practice I call "scripting the Black body." This must be done before racial healing may begin. One way this can be accomplished is via a critical-historical method.

Nietzsche's version of genealogical criticism with emphasis on metaphor and metonymy is often credited as the progenitor of the genealogical method, one of the most frequently explored critical-historical approaches. I agree with West (1993) that Nietzsche demonstrated a symbol-driven, "deep historical consciousness" (p. 266) and pragmatism deserving of adoption in contemporary analyses of race; yet his perspective alone does not account for the confluence of power, discourse, and the body. Being equally impressed with Foucault's historical-materialist refinement of this technique found within his genealogical criticism of institutional structures and power/knowledge formations, I recommend a merger of the two approaches. Foucault's (1980) treatises on power/knowledge teach us that patriarchal and essentialist epistemologies and ideologies sometimes have ambiguities and contradictions that inhabit the logic of oppressive representational politics. Furthermore, we are informed by his later work that the body functions as a signifier of meanings imposed on them by subjectivities (Foucault, 1984). These subjectivities discipline the body by policing and regulating its ontological modalities, and then by reconstituting the body in conformity with institutionally derived regimes of truth.

I am aware of the dialectical tensions between Nietzsche's and Foucault's critical-historical perspectives, both of which were either–or perspectives. They suggested that bodies were burdened because of either themselves or institutions. In concert with McPhail's complicity theory, I have adopted a "both–and" rather than an "either–or" perspective of body politics. Nietzsche, as Grosz (1994) explains, was most interested in proving that bodies are subjects rather than objects in their own scripture. On the other hand,

Foucault asserted a poststructuralist stance that suggested bodies are instruments of institutions that only want to propagate their ideological viewpoints. In an effort to explain Foucault's propositions, Grosz insightfully adds: "The body functions almost as a 'black box' in this account: it is acted upon, inscribed, peered into; information is extracted from it and disciplinary regimes are imposed on it; yet its materiality also entails a resilience, and thus also (potential) modes of resistance to power's capillary alignments" (p. 146).

I believe Black corporeal inscriptions are infused iterations of whiteness ideology embodied as Black corporeal objects, but complicated by the irregularities subsumed in a profound matrix of desire and control. So, it is not simply that there are personal and social influences on bodily inscriptions, but that the personal is the social. At first glance, this seems contradictory. Pinar (2001) points out that even when White supremacists appear singly interested in proclaiming the innate inferiority of Black bodies, it is possible that contradictory impulses of these Whites overwhelm the situation, as in the case of White slave owners' rapes of Black women. Hence, desire and repulsion operate on dialectic poles, accenting the complexity of politicizing racial bodies. Yet the most critical aspect of this is that the body is forced to hold the contradictions and anxieties laced within the inscribed meanings because it inescapably exists in a social habitat preoccupied with these meanings.

Together, the Nietzschean and Foucauldian versions of the critical method for accomplishing a genealogical criticism present an assistive model and conceptually undergird the analysis found in the following brief sketch of Black body politics in popular media, which is presented as contemporaneous with slavery. Part of what I intend to explore in this chapter appears as a rudimentary recounting of facts and ideas that have been presented in pieces throughout extant literature. The purpose of this re-presentation of ideas is to allow the reader to see how the politicization and scripting of Black bodies has been a common thread of American life since at least the seventeenth century forward. So, for advanced readers, this first chapter may seem elementary, but it provides a necessary foundation for the remainder of the book. It should also be understood that scripting, as a paradigm, is not just about stereotypes and negative images; it is about how the treatment of Black *bodies* as commodities has persisted for hundreds of years and continues today. Implicitly, this exploration of scripting suggests that bodies are canvases on which figurative scripts or writings are inscribed. Since the emergence of race as a social construct, Black bodies have become surfaces of racial representation. To say it bluntly, race is about bodies that have been assigned social meanings. So, it is only logical that any attempt to divorce the concept of race from body politics leaves the analysis incomplete. In order to demonstrate this, I present a two-fold mirror in which the horrid racial past is compared to the much-improved, but still debilitated, present conditions and the central focus is popular media.

Beginning with the jovial character Sambo in the late 1700s theatrical production *The Divorce*, the docile and obsequious film character Uncle Tom in Edwin Porter's *Uncle Tom's Cabin*, and the villainous bucks and mulattoes in D. W. Griffith's *Birth of a Nation*, I will generally trace the historical stock images of Black bodies throughout mass media until the present day while discussing how they are commodified. This genealogy is only a cursory glance at images in popular media with a particular emphasis on minstrelsy as one of the early popular cultural forms; hence, there will certainly be omissions. Several well-known volumes are much more explicative than I intend to be here.[2] The purpose of this critical-historical analysis is to pinpoint the origin of the debasement of Black bodies in U.S. popular media while examining the politics that accompanied it.

## DEHUMANIZATION OF THE BLACK BODY

It is certainly imperative to contextualize the beginnings of Black racial representation,[3] on stage and elsewhere, with the conterminous "peculiar institution" of slavery (Karenga, 2002) in the United States. Although I will neither specifically examine indentured servitude nor explore the system whereby Blacks became slave owners, I do acknowledge that such systems existed alongside the much more expansive system of slavery discussed here. American presidents such as George Washington, Abraham Lincoln, and Thomas Jefferson owned several slaves. Appiah and Gates (2003) maintain that "most of the founding fathers were large-scale slaveholders, as were eight of the first twelve presidents of the United States" (p. 850). In fact, the extended kin of Jefferson, beginning with his enslaved mistress Sallie Mae Hemings, remains a matter of public speculation (Khamit-Kush, 1999; Vivian, 2002). As Means-Coleman notes (2000), "the importation of foreign slaves," which began in 1517, "ended in 1807 with more than enough, approximately three million slaves [still] on American soil" (p. 37), but by that time estimates that suggest as many as twenty million slaves and perpetual indentured servants, foreign and domestic, existed throughout the period some euphemistically called "The Middle Passage" (Franklin & Moss, 1988).

The maafa or holocaust of enslavement was one of the most tragic events in the history of the world. Multiple historical accounts all agree on the atrocious details of the transportation of African slaves to the New World (Franklin & Moss, 1988; Karenga, 2002). A minimum of two slaves' hands and feet were chained together and fastened to the boat. Many of the three- or four-ton boats were packed with hundreds of auctionable slaves to the extent that bodies were sandwiched together with little interstices left open for breathing, disemboguing, and defecating. Slave auctioneers knew they could maximize profits if they brought as many Blacks as possible, risking the slaves' lives in the process for no other reason than the perception that Black bodies were dispensable. Naturally, before the vessel reached its destination, some dehydrated and starved slaves who were barely able to move did not survive the pathogenic conditions that were unfit for any human. The deceased and diseased Black bodies were jettisoned. They were considered ruined, spoiled goods, and, since they were mere property, there was no need to hold a funeral or perform a ceremonial burial. This is among the most gruesome examples of gross maltreatment related to race and economy in the world. It could be argued that Western traders and slave owners did not have any sense of what race was at that time, and perhaps that is true, but the beginning of slavery was the direct and immediate antecedent to a concept said to have been conceptualized only decades later in 1684 by French physician Francois Bernier (West, 1993). He developed the term to classify dead bodies, and his catalogue of races inspired centuries of racial labeling and pseudoscience. At one point, the number of racial labels amounted to three to five races. Later, as many as three hundred races were counted. The term became diluted, but still was considered useful as a logical device. Seventeenth-, eighteenth-, and nineteenth-century eugenicists, many of whom were esteemed intellectuals and founders of academic disciplines such as paleontology, astronomy, and anthropology, discovered that racial logic helped to demonstrate what would become uncontested truth claims: that Blacks were intellectually, behaviorally, interpersonally, and physically inferior and should be treated as objects (Jackson, 1999). This devaluation and objectification of Black bodies arrested any agency to define the Black self, but also intercepted any public valuation of Blacks as subject. Subjectivity was owned by Whites; they were self-authorized to see themselves as pure, good, competent, and deserving of privilege. They devised the essence of racial particularity by averting their gaze away from Blacks and applying injunctive pressure on them to behave in ways that complied with their own modernist obsessions. As Bhabha (1986) asserts, Otherness is an *episteme* in White colonialist discourses used to mark socioeconomic boundaries of racial difference and announce the superiority of the hegemonic subject—in this case, whiteness and White bodies.

Brought here in chains, Blacks and particularly Black bodies, in what we now know as the United States, never had the chance to be valued, celebrated, or even considered a citizen until 1863, well over 300 years after the first African slaves arrived in the New World. They were property or possessions whose foreign and physical bodies were literally considered tools for labor and procreation that were evacuated of thought and culture. It was practically unimportant whether they could think beyond accomplishing a series of menial tasks demanded of them.

Of course, the literature is replete with examples of how their cogent and strategic thinking led to insurgencies, the most well known of which were those of Denmark Vesey and Nat Turner. For example, the discursive strategies of indirection and signifying assisted escapees. These techniques were laced in the lyrics of plantation songs such as "Steal Away Jesus" and "Wade in the Water."

When the slaves at the plantation sung the first song, for example, that meant the master was not around and now was the appropriate time to attempt escape. If the master discovered a slave was missing, he would get his bloodhounds, his rifles, and his entourage and hunt for the slave. Then, they would sing the second song, "Wade in the Water," in order to warn the escapees that the master was in pursuit with dogs who could not detect the slaves' presence when in the water. The use of these lyrics demonstrated cunning and adroit planning. Rarely acknowledged for their intellect, slaves were purposefully dejected and dehumanized in an effort to preserve control over their minds, bodies, and spirits. If the slave was not found immediately, the slave owner would post an advertisement in the runaway listings with painstaking details about the missing slave such as personal habits, musical skills, behavioral inclinations, and physical characteristics, often including a notation that the slave's cheeks had been branded with the master's initials (Southern, 1983).

Psychically, slave owners fostered a climate of separation that would not allow communion of slave and slave master as human beings. The civilized–savage and human–inhuman dichotomies were intentionally arranged by the owner to maintain distance and disdain, to prove to his self that Black bodies were devoid of interiority or basic thinking and reasoning skills. Though illogical, it seemed the slave's exteriority was all that was of concern. It was that which facilitated the slave master's detachment from seeing the Black body as human. The body was legibly encoded and scripted as an object of specularity and, consequently, became its own discursively bound identity politic. This politic is embedded in white supremacist ideology and Black corporeal inscription. That is, ideology, as Gray (1989) and Althusser (1994) suggest, becomes a concrete, taken-for-granted fact, moving from ideology to axiology in sometimes unnoticeable ways. If properly designed, social participants, in this case White social participants, see ideology not as a version of truth, but *the* only truth worth knowing. The body can be said to be political because it, as an immediately identifiable and visible marker of difference, accounted for the distribution of material, spatial, temporal resources Black bodies were not allowed to share. It was discursively bound because, although it was polysemic, the primary meaning the Black body conveyed was its correspondence to an object believed to be a subhuman, heathenish utility. The body was needed to perform labor and generate revenue; therefore, as long as the slave appeared happy-go-lucky, his or her physicality and physical readiness were of the utmost importance. It is no mistake that most of the literature examining social reproductions and proscriptions of the body speak primarily of visual interpretations of exteriority (Johnson, 1994; Levinas, 1969; Pinar, 2001; Wiegman, 1993, 1995). The epistemic violence that augments and is concomitant with the social construction of race and racism is shuttled principally by the recognition of visible racial markers or corporeal zones rather than by its interiority composed of organs, glands, bones, and so on.

In imagining difference between himself as human and the slave as equivalent to cattle, the slave master was able to convince himself of the slaves' alterity, the foreignness of their Black bodies. However, even though he wanted Black bodies that were large, strong brutes to toil the land and plant crops and wanted slaves who could resist all kinds of inclement weather, those individuals were the ones he feared the most, insofar as they were potentially more dangerous. All the evidence concerning the maltreatment and exploitation of Black bodies points to an undeniable conclusion: it was during the period of enslavement that Whites developed many of their greatest fears and anxieties toward Blacks, particularly toward Black males, and established safeguards for rationalizing their vulnerability and unacceptable activities as slave owners. Whites' patriarchal domination and racial supremacist ideology were publicly unquestioned. Although it began with anxiety generally associated with Black men's bodies, Black preverbal communicative aspects such as darker-than-White skin color, wide noses, and thick lips, or what I call corporeal zones,[4] were eventually enough to trigger xenophobic reactions and remain sufficient cause for chronic racist behaviors among Whites and non-Whites today. Later, in chapter 3, I will briefly explain how police brutality is inextricably linked to racial xenophobia. Present-day racism evolves from systemically validated demoralized practices and crude conventions begun during slavery.

## STRANGE FRUIT: LYNCHINGS OF THE BLACK BODY

The public trading, auctioning, and ownership of slaves was commonplace and well documented. Every area of the mass media has commented on it, and when slaves allegedly became disobedient, they were penalized severely, often times lynched. Gaines (2001), in her critique of lynching narratives, opines that "the act of lynching . . . is a classic displacement, that highly charged adjustment in which something of peripheral importance comes to occupy a central position" (p. 167). In the vein of Cornel West (1993), bell hooks (1995), and others' perennial arguments about the juxtaposition of market and nonmarket values, economy and love, commodified and consumerist representation versus privatized and relational looking, Gaines assigns herself a task she leaves incomplete. Mentioning but not addressing the critical cultural issues surrounding class, race, and sexuality as well as corporeal and specular politics can lead one to dismiss her assertions as merely elliptical. Gaines is correct to suggest that lynching was foundationally tied to economics, but not necessarily more so than desire, sexual, racial, or otherwise. Despite its legalistic subterfuge, lynching was about Black prohibition and White privilege. It was a "looking exercise" articulated and captured within the framework of dominance (Allen, Als, Lewis, & Litwack, 2000). It seems to me what is critical about analyzing the act of lynching is not its displacement, but rather its historical contiguity with present-day epistemic violence inflicted via inscription of the Black body in popular media. Equally significant is the conspicuous dialectic between White xenophobia and voyeurism.

In fact, the lynched victims came to be known as "strange fruit," later the title of one of Billie Holiday's most popular songs, written by White poet Lewis Allan (a pseudonym of Abel Meeropol) (Katz, 2002). Allan accented the paradoxical nature of lynching with the metaphor "strange fruit," which refers to a foreign Black body. Immediately, without knowing the reference, one is inclined to think that fruit is healthy, beautiful, tasty, and sweet, but then this image is juxtaposed to the adjectival signifier "strange," which implies something that is foreign, weird, out of the ordinary, and unpredictable. Besides the fact that the Black body is starkly contrasted to that of Whites, you cannot trust the fruit to be what you expect it to be or to function as you may anticipate it will. As the strange fruit hangs from the poplar tree, its Southern surroundings are comfortable, pleasant, and utopic, yet the fruit is being burned and mangled. Even though it is almost ripe, almost perfect, its possibilities are interrupted, and it is no one's fault, but the elements'. The fruit just could not bear the conditions and so now it is ready to be plucked and dissolved. The Black body as "fruit," shackled and hoisted in the air, was not seen as being complicitous with White supremacist laws forbidding the body to move freely. Stifled by the conditions, the abnormal Black body becomes a detestable symbol of deviance, a brute that must be tamed, an inscriptive surface that signifies one who is bereft of loyalty to whiteness and, therefore, any ability to behave appropriately. The terrorization of the body in the form of lynching became an act of deterrence and, for Whites, a source of voyeuristic entertainment (Allen, Als, Lewis, & Litwack, 2000).

Pinar (2001) estimates that nearly 4,900 lynchings occurred in the United States between 1882 and 1927. Blacks were lynched for charges that were very minute such as acting suspicious, being obnoxious, unpopularity, frightening a White woman, and arguing with a White man. As many as 15,000 people attended these lynchings; however, quite often attendance was much lower. Black bodies were hung as objects of the White voyeuristic gaze. Many pictures were taken and families were gathered. This was an event celebrated like a carnival. Families would even bring food for a picnic. One nine-year-old boy enjoyed himself so much that he remarked, "I have seen a man hanged," he told his mother, "now I wish I could see one burned" (Allen, Als, Lewis, & Litwack, 2000, p. 14). Many of the photographs of lynching ceremonies picture some White audience members with snapshot cameras, with others posing for the picture next to the hanging, lifeless body. Other photographs became postcards sent to relatives. It was a public spectacle, horrific and violent (Marriott, 2000). Perhaps, as Marriott opines, the most fascinating part of this "racial scopophilia" (p. 32), as he calls it, was the bizarre self-inverted gaze that occurred as a result of being able to view photographs in which Whites were both spectators and participants.

Essentially, they were enwrapped in a performance of race as both audience and actors, repulsed and attracted, all of which orbited around the inscribed surface—the Black body. Marriott intuits a perverted matrix of desire, disassociation, and narcissism confounded within the act of lynching and its photographic capture as Whites in attendance marveled at the product of their inscription. With this, I am reminded of Bakhtin's (1981) notion of the vulgar because of how it resonates with this grotesque hypervigilant fascination with Black bodies, even as corpses. In explaining the subject/object duality inherent in discursive utterances, Bakhtin suggests that there are definable moments during which the speech act becomes dialogized, situated between I and Other, center and periphery, as well as subject and object. In this case, the "speech act" or utterance is the inscription on the Black body. The inscribed body serves as its own discursive set that can be read—if the body remains agent or subject—or written on—if the body becomes Otherized or object. The relationship between the lynch mob and the Black body is a power-infused dialogic. The racially encoded inscription of the Black body, especially during lynching, represents a refereed boundary between Blacks and Whites, a prohibition that annuls any possibility of the Black body becoming subject (Harris, 1993).

If not lynched, some Black males were castrated for having an association with White women, whether simply greeting them or having intimate relations. Without the possibility for reproduction, the slave likely would be killed or auctioned as damaged goods, since he would no longer be useful for siring more children (Pinar, 2001). This heinous act of castration also has been argued as an act of emasculation, a way of attempting to strip the slave completely of his dignity and pride beyond the limitations placed on him to be a fully attentive father and husband (Staples, 1982). Naturally, this reduced, if not totally eliminated, his ability to experience sexual pleasure. This was unquestionably the master's notice that the castrated man be perpetually reminded that his was a life of misery, not happiness. Dyson (2001) also contends that castration served the purpose of expelling any threat that Black men would retaliate against White men's raping of Black women by raping *his* women—White women. The castrato fantasy signifies a powerful and profound set of White male fears, ones that would symbolically and literally jettison Black male bodies into an ectopic sphere, a foreign location in which they would be asked to live on the periphery of their own existence.

Black men were not treated as men. As Staples (2001) explains, and I paraphrase, Black male slavehands had no formal or legal linkage to their families. Family members could not adopt the native surname of the male and enslaved women were not legally married to the enslaved men. They performed a ritualistic practice known as "jumping the broom" in order to signify a formal nuptial arrangement. This was one of the earliest examples of structural prohibition of Black bodies. These concerns for convention were far outweighed by the slave master's well-known tendency to rape Black female slavehands. His corruptive debauchery, though seemingly contraposed to his beliefs about the natural inferiority of "negroes," was rationalized as all of his repugnantly hateful acts were. He claimed, in order to exculpate his self, that the Black woman was sexually charged and seductive, and that she, of course, needed the slavemaster to tame her animalistic and savage sexual urges and desires. So, while the White male had full access to Black female bodies, despite her nonconsensuality, Black males could be killed for appearing too friendly with a White woman (even if the attraction was mutual) or saying anything to her that could be interpreted as negative.

This was merely one among many types of regulative governance that facilitated a climate of overt tempered servility and an implosive private hostility. The slaves, who were not formally trained and educated, were taught what they knew within their community enclaves. The primary predominant public displays of Black cultural expression were minstrel show songs and religious services. Virtually every other area of cultural expression was privately practiced outside of the master's presence. Naturally, this led to the slave master's very limited view of the behaviors of Blacks. They were considered chattel, movable property likened to cattle, and, as mere apparatus, were constitutionally considered three-fifths of a human (Franklin & Moss, 1988; Karenga, 2002; Pinar, 2001). Slaves were trained like the chattel they were thought to be: to be obedient, servile, and docile, or else be penalized. Furthermore, Black males were restricted from being fathers constantly attendant to the needs of the family, since he had to accommodate the slave master first. Out of necessity for the survival of the family, Black females became the matriarchs of the household. They were mostly field workers like men and shared the same horrors of enslavement. They were even lynched like the men were. Davis (1983) reminds us that the most popular accounts of slave women's roles suggest they were house servants such as cooks, maids, and mammies who reared the master's children. The narrative is told that after the White child was asleep, she was allowed to go home to spend time with her husband and tend to her own children, which is why younger kin and extended kinship networks were critical for family survival. While this was true for some Black female slavehands in border states, this was a limited and romanticized purview of the harsh reality of the majority of female slaves who resided in the deep south. The slave with a family did what the master required of him in order to survive, though some of them plotted to escape in order to avoid further misery of enslavement (Franklin & Moss, 1988).

## EMANCIPATED BODIES, SHACKLED MINDS

Lynchings and overall enslaved conditions were very prominent until the late 1800s. Some scholars would like to believe that all slaves were set free January 1, 1863, with President Abraham Lincoln's signing of the Emancipation Proclamation, but history teaches us that Lincoln only freed three-fourths of the slaves, while another one-quarter were retained as a gesture of sensitivity to soldiers of the Civil War. This is not to mention the fact that some slaves in the District of Columbia were set free earlier as part of an 1862 emancipation law President Lincoln signed, a precursor to the Emancipation Proclamation. Those slave owners who did surrender their slaves were compensated no more than $300 per slave by the federal government (Franklin & Moss, 1988). A few confederate states, including parts of Virginia, Louisiana, and West Virginia, were allowed to keep their slave laborers. Franklin and Moss (1988) estimate that over a million slaves were unaffected by the Emancipation Proclamation. The government even used the possibility of emancipation to entice slaves to enlist in the Union army and fight in the war. Although not paid the same remuneration as Whites, thousands took advantage of this offer to be full-fledged citizens rather than chattel, and eventually the Confederate army surrendered. It was not until 1865, two years later, that Confederate slave owners conceded their slaves. Even after slavery officially ended and reconstruction began, very little initial support was given to support these neophyte citizens. Slaves who found work earned a modest living, and still were not treated as equal.

Contemporaneous with the last 100 years of slavery was theatrical representations of Black bodies. As early as 1769 in *The Padlock*, Mungo, a Black character, was introduced as a loud, buffoonish character who would spew off a series of quick, yet non-witty one-liners. Mungo was a flop and did not receive much attention, except as a precursor to a more perfected minstrel character, Sambo, who was White. The irony in that is thick—Whites were convinced that Blacks could not adequately depict Blacks, only Whites could. One can only speculate the reasons for this shift. Perhaps Mungo was not exaggerated enough. Nonetheless, in 1781 and 1795, respectively, plays such as *The Divorce* and *Triumph of Love* emerged, and the jovial, though shiftless, gibberish-talking, huge red-lipped caricature Sambo dressed in rags, played by white actors in blackface, became a prominent and well-liked stage figure. This was the beginning of the success of minstrelsy and the character Sambo was a live image of how whites perceived Blacks. Though his facial features were exaggerated by black makeup all over the face with red paint orbiting around the lips, extending inches beyond the mouth, he was not seen by Whites as a caricature as much as a true depiction of the obedient, servile, and docile slaves they owned (Pinar, 2001).

Slavery would not be over for another eighty-plus years, even though around the late 1700s prominent clergy and antislavery advocates like Richard

Allen, Benjamin Banneker, and Prince Hall actively and publicly denounced slavery, and other Black men began asking, "Am I not a man and a brother," while Black women, particularly Sojourner Truth, would ask, "Aren't I a woman" (hooks, 1981). Slave insurrections were increasing with the advent of the fugitive-assisting "underground railroad" around 1815. Meanwhile, the abolitionist discourse produced by slaves was mounting, and appeared in leaflets like David Walker's *Appeal to the Colored People of the World* (1829) and in newspapers like Samuel Cornish and John Russwurm's *Freedom's Journal* (1829), and, eventually, Frederick Douglass' *North Star* (1847).

So, despite revolts and political upheaval among slaves during the time the Sambo character was introduced, they were not nearly enough to stave off denigrating stage depictions of Black bodies. Sambo was one, among few, of the most wicked, scornful, and psychically injurious representations of blackness, one from which Blacks are still recovering even today as those comedic images of inadequacy, nonintellectuality, and incompetence are deeply lodged in the American psyche. One simply needs to take note of the only recent surge of noncomedic popular cultural representations of Black life to understand that producers of American mass media either lack imagination or do not want to see positive, healthy, complete, and salvatory images of blackness presented frequently and dramatically. Instead, current films and television situation-comedies, especially with predominately Black casts, often portray Blacks as fragmented, aloof humorists, sometimes even as buffoons. Perhaps *Bernie Mac* and *Cedric the Entertainer Presents* are among the few that do not revert to the minstrel formula. Spike Lee's inflammatory cinematic parody of this phenomenon entitled *Bamboozled* was executed with powerful resonance to what is uncovered in the present analysis of minstrelsy.

Over the course of 150 years from 1769 to about 1927, minstrelsy would become an institution, revered by Whites for its dehumanizing yet somehow entertaining characterization of Blacks as darkies and Whites as ordinary, normal, and cultured ladies and gentlemen. This was not strange to Whites; it was indicative of both their attitudes about Blacks and their own self-perceptions. During the early 1800s, slaves such as Caesar Thompson Wharton would appear in novels like James Fenimore Cooper's *The Spy*, yet minstrelsy would dominate the growing entertainment industry. Minstrel shows would become detailed stage and even cinematic performances that would pack theater houses, by sticking to a formula proven to evoke laughter (Means-Coleman, 2000). For over half of that huge time span from 1781 to 1927, Blacks were still enslaved; this may have been another reason, besides the perception that Whites were more competent thespians, that Blacks were seldom stage actors. Blacks also made great strides toward civil rights with the work of outspoken activists and organizers.

As mentioned previously, in 1863, most slaves were freed and entered a time in which their citizenship and concomitant constitutional rights were questioned on a daily basis. President Lincoln reasoned that both Whites and Blacks were the bane of one another's existence, so they should be segregated (Franklin & Moss, 1988). Therefore, although Blacks could now be formally educated, they had to attend segregated schools and use segregated facilities, thereby keeping Whites' racial xenophobia intact via limited contact with Blacks. Blacks-only schools were initiated and established by the Freedmen's Bureau in the 1870s.

By 1900, many Black universities such as Cheyney, Howard, Tuskegee, and Fisk, were in full operation. Fisk established a traveling entourage of singers in the 1870s and the group had become rather famous as the "Fisk Jubilee Singers" well into the 1900s. They performed spirituals and slave songs for Black and White audiences. Many Blacks much preferred this group instead of watching minstrel shows; later, ragtime would be added in the 1890s as an entertainment alternative. Throughout the 1920s and 1930s, the Lincoln Motion Picture Company became one of many independent film production companies that championed comparably more positive represen-tations of Blacks, although larger companies, of course, had bigger budgets and more resources to reach larger audiences.

In 1927, one such major company, Universal Pictures finally brought *Uncle Tom's Cabin* to cinema. The cinematic version of Harriett Beecher Stowe's famous novel was adapted and directed by former mechanic Edwin Porter, with the lead acting role given to a Black man by the name of Charles Gilpin, who had won acclaim for his role in Eugene O'Neill's *Emperor Jones*. Gilpin refused to play a completely obsequious and placated stock Uncle Tom character and was soon replaced by James Lowe, another Black actor. Gilpin's defiance marked his association with a period of conscious resistance by Black actors to negative representation. I will discuss the character of Uncle Tom later in this chapter.

Gradual change of attitudes toward segregation came after years of protesting and, when brave organizers, protestors of segregation, and advo-cates of civil rights like James Meredith attempted to actually enter segre-gated schools despite laws prohibiting it, the U.S. federal government became interested in changing the legislation. In 1954, the *Brown v. Board of Education* decision legalized the desegregation of schools, a joyous moment of victory, especially since Blacks-only schools were known for being dilapi-dated and poorly funded. In 1955, James Meredith stood at the door of Uni-versity of Mississippi and attempted admittance and was met with violent protests by Whites. Almost a year later, in 1956, Autherine Lucy attempted to enter the University of Alabama after the state of Alabama ordered the University to admit her, and she was met with an equal if not more harsh resistance and rioting, which caused her to be expelled by the board of regents for disruption. By denying Meredith and Lucy admittance, due to no fault of their own, the university was saying to them that their black bodies were despicable and disturbing, that the mere fact of their racial existence was reason enough to justify horrid treatment. It is important to remember that these White protestors and administrators were the children and grandchildren of slave owners. They were only a generation or two removed from slavery and so it was still commonplace to behave this way toward Blacks, without liberal guilt, because the protestors were not liberal and did not come from liberalist backgrounds. That is, their reactions to desegregation were sickening, though not completely surprising, given their family histories.

## FROM MINSTREL PARAPHERNALIA
## AND GAMES TO MINSTREL SHOWS

The paraphernalia of the late 1800s and early 1900s did not just reinforce an orthodoxy infused with negative stereotypes of Blacks, but also accented Whites' sentiments that the entire existence of Blacks was dissimilar to Whites. Turner (2002) in her insightful book *Ceramic Uncles & Celluloid Mammies* discusses the various exoticized collectible items that were available during this period to signify the attitudes toward and imagistic representations of Black bodies. One such item worth noting is a game introduced in 1890 by Milton Bradley Company called "Jolly Darkie Target Game," in which the object was to "score bulls-eyes by throwing a ball into the gaping mouth of a Black male figure" (p. 11). In fact, Turner (2002) reports having heard about a fairly regular recurrence of a Black male sitting outside a theater house immediately before the showing, with his mouth open, orally receiving balls thrown by little kids who decided to make this an entertaining activity. Perhaps this was the inspiration for the "Jolly Darkie Target Game." Assuming this was true, it was apparently either not seen as inhumane, or simply acceptable behavior even among adult onlookers; after all, this type of denigrated blackness was the point of the minstrel show they were headed to see inside the theater.

The exaggerated physiognomic features of minstrel figures and their collectible counterparts speak volumes about the nature of early racial scripting processes developed in the interests of the polity. Billboards, theatrical performance announcements, and posters, as well as sheet music displayed huge facial images of minstrel figures, usually "darkies," a label that accurately described the blackened faces of even dark-skinned Black actors. The faces were with bulging eyes, and cosmetically altered huge red lips accented on a completely blackened facial surface. I agree with Means-Coleman's (2000) assertion, "blackface was about much more than the degradation of African Americans; it too was a mask for Whites' obsessive curiosity and envy over blackness" (p. 41) and I would add that blackface was a public spectacle that displayed the deeply entrenched subconscious iterations of a malicious whiteness ideology trying to justify its immoral posture. Mapp (1972, pp. 30–31) recalls and enumerates nineteen stereotypes about Blacks that could be found within stage and film performances:

1. The savage African
2. The happy slave
3. The devoted servant
4. The corrupt politician
5. The irresponsible citizen
6. The petty thief
7. The social delinquent
8. The vicious criminal
9. The sexual superman
10. The superior athlete
11. The unhappy non-White
12. The natural-born cook
13. The natural-born musician
14. The perfect entertainer
15. The superstitious churchgoer
16. The chicken and watermelon eater
17. The razor and knife "toter"
18. The uninhibited expressionist
19. The mental inferior

Given that slave masters were rarely an integral part of the slaves' private lives, much of the dialogue and interactional behaviors involving two Blacks was a fictive part of the White playwright's imagination, yet the important task of the playwright was always to depict White characters as righteous, honest Christians who innocently possessed slaves as property in order to make money to support their families. During and perhaps even after slavery, White theatergoers could leave the stage play feeling assured that they were behaving respectably in the eyes of God and that the playwright was simply portraying Black and White lives exactly as they existed with a slight exaggeration of Black facial features just for fun (Bogle, 1996). The darkened face, created from the moistened debris of burnt and crushed champagne corks, insolently signified that Whites did not want to see Blacks for who they really were culturally, but, instead, as an altercast, an iconographic image, a scripted racial body inscribed with meanings and messages Whites enjoyed seeing, ones that were self-affirming and insular.

In the post-emancipation period, Blacks could also attend minstrel shows, but tended not to do so. If they did elect to attend, they had to sit in the balcony during the show and wait for White theatergoers to exit before walking down from the balcony and leaving the building. Until the early 1900s, White stage actors like Christians Ben Cotton, George Nichols, and the most-favored Jewish actor Al Jolson often played White and Black characters, with few exceptions, like Mungo. As an aside, each blackface musical included a very significant segment showing the minstrel blacking up for the part by applying burnt cork to the face. This process heightened the xeno-phobic effect of the film or show (Cripps, 1977, 1993; Rogin, 1996). It was not until 1903 (with the emergence of the Uncle Tom character) that five major stereotypical Black minstrel figures (played by Blacks) began to be introduced, starting with Sambo, the coon stock character. Bogle (1996) identifies this five-part stock minstrel charactery as the pantheon: coon, Uncle Tom, tragic mulatto, mammy, and buck. Although it was evident that these characters were stereotypical and degrading depictions of Blacks designed to make a mockery of Black life, there were many Blacks who were proud to play the roles and use the wages to support their families. It is also important to recognize, as Rogin (1996) reminds us, that blackface marked the entrée of Black actors in the entertainment industry, particularly in the early days of filmmaking. So, this analysis does not seek to devalue their pres-ence, but rather to point out how their presence *in blackface* created long-last-ing effects on Black identities in the United States and served as a visual foundation for the present perpetuation of Black corporeal inscription. I, along with many others, would like to be able to say that we have completely exserted the imagery associated with minstrelsy from our filmic repertoire, but the reality is we are continually plagued by this charactery even today. The five characters of the pantheon currently exist in varying forms, still with condescending effects, although so suppressed and implicit that many television viewers and moviegoers (Black and White) would argue they do not exist. Few would argue that the social construction of race has been purged from the American ethos, but how it is presently manifested in popu-lar culture is still ambiguous in the minds of some American citizens. In the next section, I will explain the original characters and also their present-day manifestations. *representation*

## COONS, UNCLE TOMS, TRAGIC MULATTOES, MAMMIES, AND BUCKS

The five pantheon stock characters were introduced during the era of silent filmmaking. With no sound and a burgeoning motion picture industry, films were exciting because they were new and innovative. Bogle (1989) says it best:

> In its initial stages, during the period of silent films, from the early 1900s to the late 1920s, from the days of *Uncle Tom's Cabin* (1903) through *The Birth of a Nation* (1915) and afterwards, black film history looks simply like a study in stereotypes: a crew of gentle Toms, doomed mulattoes, comic coons, overstuffed mammies, and mean, menacing violent black bucks. (p. 1)

The resemblance of Bogle's character descriptions to the present-day stereo-types of African American males as lazy, comical, non-intellectual, promis-cuous, violent, and deviant, alongside stereotypes of African American females as stoic and overweight or highly sexualized with pronounced gluteal features (like Hottentot Venus, otherwise known as Sarah Bartmann)[5] is frightening when we consider many of these images created over a century ago still haunt us. We still find images of Black women who are presented as sexually charged, sometimes-uppity automatons (like the strong-willed, domineering-wife, *Amos n Andy* radio show character Sapphire). I will discuss this further in chapter 4.

In this long line of caricature images, the Mungo character can be considered the first portrayal of Blacks by Blacks in a stage play. Remember that the film industry did not begin until the 1900s, and Blacks were among the first to be represented cinematically. They were mostly depicted as foot-shuffling, wide-smiling idiots who had a propensity for malapropisms. There were certainly distinctions among the coon, Uncle Tom, mulatto, mammy, and buck, yet they are all a part of the pantheon, insofar as they are each sophisticated scripts of the Black body that have transcended time.

## COONS

The terms coon and Sambo are often used interchangeably. The Sambo character was introduced first in the late 1700s in the stage play *The Divorce* (1781). He was a cheerful and contented individual who was loved by Whites for his complacent faithfulness and unquestionable loyalty to Whites. Later, he would be depicted prominently in minstrel shows as well as aurally via radio and songs. For example, by 1900, over 600 coon songs had been written and performed, the most popular of which are probably "All Coons Look Alike to Me" and "Mammy's Little Pickaninny" (Toll, 1974).

There were many names for the coon stock character. He has been referred to as the urban zip coon, dancing dandy, and, most notably, Sambo, the happy slave. Bogle (1996) points to four famous coon characters: the pickaninny, Rastus, Stepin Fetchit, and Uncle Remus. Each protagonist manifesting these types played the coon character differently. As the pickaninny, adolescent actors played the coon role; he or she was silly and aloof. As Rastus and Stepin Fetchit, he was known as a jovial sluggard and raconteur who kept the audience "in stitches" because of his perpetual antics. As Uncle Remus, he was Tom's cousin, and he shared Tom's heightened modesty and complacent spirit.

*The Pickaninny as Coon.* The pickaninny, which came to be defined in the dictionary as a negative label for a young Black child, was indeed played by Black children, as in the case of the literary figure *Little Black Sambo*. At the time, the idea of including them was thought to be innovative, since they had not been used before and it seemed to offer a much more complete and compelling portrait of the pathologized composite Black family. Dispersed throughout various films, the family was never presented as aunts, uncles, and children in a happy community setting. Bogle explains, "The pickaninny was the first of the coon types to make its screen debut. It gave the Negro child actor his place in the black pantheon. Generally, he was a harmless little screwball creation whose eyes popped, whose hair stood on end with the least excitement, and whose antics were pleasant and diverting" (p. 7). The Pickaninny, like all coon stock types, could be seen on posters, sheet music, cigarette lighters, clothes patches, and other memorabilia. In movies and memorabilia related to Thomas A. Edison's *Pickaninnies* (1894), the title character was often shown gaping while holding a watermelon, and looking around with overdilated pupils. Subsequent to the emergence of the pickaninny in nineteenth-century advertisements and early 1900s movies was one of the most popular pickaninny motion pictures—Hal Roach's *Our Gang* (1938). Produced by Metro-Goldwyn Pictures, this is the film that later evolved and became known as *The Little Rascals*. *Our Gang* had one Black character—Farina, played by Ernie Morrison, who was a cute little boy with twisted ponytails that would stand straight in the air at any moment of surprise. Farina was unwittingly the butt of all the kids' jokes, so he would simply laugh when they laughed. *The Little Rascals*, the televisual progeny of *Our Gang*, had reruns that were still being shown into the 1970s and 1980s, and were clearly a carryover on television from the minstrel period and early days of cinema and sound.

Initially, pickaninnies were rarely given speaking parts; they were just shown acting silly. In *The Little Rascals*, the Black characters Farina, Stymie, and Buckwheat were generously allowed an occasional line or two as part of a group of mischievous schoolchildren. Bogle (1996) describes the characters as follows:

> While Farina was given to heroics (except when there were ghosts about— at which time he was quick to head for the hills), Stymie was noted for his nonchalance and detached shrewdness. Usually he saw straight through any sham . . . Little Buckwheat was the last but certainly not the least of the important Black children appearing in the series. With a round chocolate moon face and enormous eyes, Buckwheat always came across as a quiet, odd-ball type, the perfect little dum-dum tag-along. (p. 23)

At first sight, it seems laudatory that at least the group was integrated, but, on closer examination, one finds that the personality profiles of the Black characters were far from desirable. Among most Americans today, Buckwheat is probably the most well known, among the three Little Rascals, because of Eddie Murphy's enlivened portrayal of the character on *Saturday Night Live* in the 1980s and in syndicated reruns played in the early 1990s. Murphy's tragicomical mockery of the character was actually true to form. Murphy's Buckwheat wore an Afro, talked loudly, and spoke in Black dialect. It was clear that the full-grown Buckwheat was still puerile and ignorant.

Perhaps the most obvious examples of coon pickaninnies still on the air are the cacophonous title characters of Nickelodeon's show *Keenan & Kel* directed by Howard Storm. After viewing one episode of this *Teen Nick Series* show, it is easy to be convinced that these slapstick comedic characters, presented often in close-up camera shots that zoom in on their wide grins and bulging eyes, do not know what to do with themselves. They are objects of hysteria; they sporadically speak nonsensical lines, apparently in homage to *Abbott & Costello* routines (but without the impeccable timing and formula), which are indicative of ignorance; however, to their credit, it is clear they are intelligent youngsters who are scripted to do nothing more than embody extreme buffoonish hilarity. Despite what I can observe as intelligence, they often do behave as though they are stupid. For example, in one episode, Kel was enticed to participate in a grocery-bagging contest with orange soda as his end reward. He refused more conventional payoffs like money or certain privileges to have a supply of carbonated orange drink. This is reminiscent of the classic pickaninny's unexplainable preference for and symbolic attachment to watermelon, and the more contemporary stereotypical association of Blacks with red Kool-Aid.

Keenan and Kel do not appear docile, yet, given their scripted Black bodies, if they were to genuflect, it would not be surprising. Keenan is an overweight Black male actor who often dons an Afro or some semblance of one, while Kel is a thin Black male actor with a close fade haircut who acts as Keenan's sidekick. They appear as coons without blackface and it is a shame to see them scripted this way. Unlike early minstrel show actors like Stepin Fetchit, who was a pathbreaker and a pioneer, although considered one of the most apparent culturally disloyal "sell-outs" of his time, they seem to have no excuse for their damaging caricatures recapitulating the 1900s pickaninny. I am not sure they are aware of this scripted correlation, but I can only hope they are ignorant of how deleterious this cartoon can be to young viewers whose popular cultural images of themselves are diverse, but still limited. I am inclined to agree with hooks, who declares, "Any African American who watches television for more than a few hours a week is daily ingesting toxic representations and poisonous pedagogy. Yet the ingestion of constant propaganda that teaches Black people self-hate has become so much the norm that it is rarely questioned" (p. 221).

*Rastus as Coon.* Like all the other coon types, Rastus was a cipher. He first was shown in Sigmund "Pop" Lubin's short *How Rastus Got His Pork Chops* (1908). Later, this character emerged in silent films like *How Rastus Gets His Turkey* (1910), *Rastus and Chicken* (1911), *Chicken Thief* (1911), *Rastus in Zululand* (1910), and *Pickaninnies and Watermelon* (1912), all of which stereotyped him as a foolish gambler as well as a chicken and watermelon-loving delinquent. In *Rastus in Zululand* (1910), Rastus daydreams about being deserted in Zululand, Africa. As Nesteby (1982) explains, the storyline adopts the Pocahontas/John Smith myth, but instead the princess Pocahontas is portrayed by an obese "pre-mammy" figure (p. 21). The Pathé Company and Sigmund "Pop" Lubin released separate and competing Rastus series, which were thematically consistent with the shiftless, ignorant Sambo caricature that had become so familiar. He was perhaps only distinguished, among the coon types, by his occasional interaction with and filmic transplantation to Africa.

He was not the first character to go to Africa or portray an African. One of the earliest films depicting such a character was D. W. Griffith's *The Zulu's Heart* (1908), a film short, which involved an African who turns against his tribesmen to help and to exemplify loyalty toward a White man. Nesteby (1982) claims this was the first American film to use Zulus. Rastus, though, was used to make the point that it was not just Black slaves who were savage, intellectually inferior, violent, and sexual derelicts, but that this began before their entry in the New World when they were in their indigenous context of Africa—essentially suggesting a helplessly inherent inferiority.

This was the beginning of a whole racist genre of blackface comedies that would later be followed by jungle movies like the 1920s Tarzan series that began with *The Adventures of Tarzan* (Cripps, 1977) and extended into the late 1950s with movies like *Tarzan and the Planet of the Apes*. The genre persisted into the early 1990s, with the movie *The Air Up There*, which subjugated "underdeveloped" Africa to the industrialized and powerful Western nations by misdirecting the audience's attention to a White basketball coach's desperate attempt to find an ideal basketball player. Naturally, since Blacks are imagined to be inherently more skilled athletes, he goes directly to the source of their ancestral skills—Africa. This racist depiction is characteristic of and recapitulates early 1900s scripting of the Black body.

According to Means-Coleman (2000), another representation of Rastus that has extended into the twenty-first century was his role as Chef Rastus, a Black cook who used a barely intelligible dialect to narrate stories, in a 1930s children's show titled *The Cream of Wheat Menagerie*. It takes no stroke of genius to realize this filmic presentation led to the now-sanitized image of Uncle Remus on the Cream of Wheat boxes existing on grocery shelves even today.

*Stepin Fetchit as Coon.* Certainly the most popular of all coon characters and the most noted Black Hollywood actor of the period, Stepin Fetchit, a former film porter, debuted in 1927 in *Old Kentucky* and played in nearly thirty films before 1935, many of which were part of a contract with Fox Pictures—a rarity for Black actors in Hollywood at the time. Stepin Fetchit, born Theodore Monroe Andrew Perry, rehearsed blackface minstrelsy before he became an on-screen icon. Initially, he and a friend did a traveling plantation show routine that they billed as *Skeeter and Rastus: The two dancing crows from Dixie,* which they later changed to *Stepin Fetchit: The two dancing fools from Dixie*. Stepin Fetchit, the actor, became a broadway favorite who also played a role alongside Moms Mabley in the 1974 hit *Amazing Grace*. His stardom and millionaire status came with a hefty price—his dignity. Even when it became evident via protests that his character was condescending and not respective of true Black cultural expression, he was said to have defensively responded, "I was a 100% Black accomplishment" (Nesteby, 1982, p. 177). Stepin Fetchit has often been presented as a mumbling, one-dimensional character who wears mismatched colored britches and suits.

Mantan Moreland, one among several emulators of Stepin Fetchit, played the Stepin Fetchit role-type for over 40 years from the late 1920s to the early 1970s. He acted in more than 300 movies, becoming the most prolific actor of the twentieth century (Watkins, 1994). He was especially known for his ability to dilate his pupils widely, heightening his coon image. In several of these films, he was a servant, such as the chauffeur Birmingham Brown in a series of Charlie Chan movies beginning with *Charlie Chan in Egypt* (1935). He has been described as a highly energetic and prodigious actor who could improvise and develop his own lines very well. In fact, he became known for his self-created popular line, "Feets don't fail me now!" Incidentally, Mantan was the name of a protagonist in *Bamboozled*, Spike Lee's filmic satire of minstrelsy. The plot was driven by Mantan, who is hired off the streets for his dancing and blackface stage-acting abilities to appear in a brand new television series. Blacking up before each show, Mantan became a beloved caricature who boosted network television ratings. Later, he experienced an identity crisis, but the idea was that it took him a long time after making money "hand over fist" before he was able to notice that his identity was at stake. Director Spike Lee, known for making politically charged and contemplative movies, released this cinematic appeal for American citizens to acknowledge the ontological injustice inherent in scripting the Black body as a utility, a self-hating instrument for espousing racist ideology.

*Uncle Remus as Coon.* Uncle Remus was another white supremacist inscription on the Black body. According to Bogle (1996), Uncle Remus was Uncle Tom's first cousin. His character was said to evolve from Joel Chandler Harris's reworking of fables told to Aesop by a Black slave and published as a collection entitled *Uncle Remus: His Songs and Sayings* in 1881 (Spaulding, 1990). So he, like Uncle Tom, was initially introduced as a fictive literary character who was also a narrator, and 55 years later he appeared in cinematic form as a coon in movies like *The Green Pastures* (1936) and Walt Disney's *Song of the South* (1946). While his cousin Tom would come to be known as a consciously obedient character who was attempting to be Christlike in his merciful understanding and tolerance of his oppressor's condescending and malicious behaviors, Remus was docile simply for no other reason than it was what Whites expected. His character expressed disdain for the newly freed Blacks and noted that they were lazy, shiftless Negroes who deserved slavery. Essentially, he was angry at freedom and in love with captivity (Silk & Silk, 1990).

There are many ways to describe Uncle Remus. Both in literary and the-atrical form, he was a sometimes toothless, gray-haired, modestly dressed racon-teur who would, in Black dialect, tell many trickster tales involving the now-famous mythical characters Br'er Rabbit and Br'er Fox,[6] among other animals. The story, in all its variations, pitted weak animals like the terrapin and rabbit against bigger animals like the fox, bear, and wolf. The smaller animal would always outwit the larger animal, with the moral being that brains will always reign victorious over brawn, and that the seemingly less advantaged always have an opportunity to rise up and overcome any obstacles so that they, too, could live somewhat successfully. This message, narrated by Uncle Remus via many different folktales, was a discursive strategy inscribed on the Black body by Whites to convince themselves that their stolen privilege and corruptive colonialist power did not prevent Blacks from enjoying some measure of suc-cess if they were docile. This figurative inscription of the Black body as being needful of subdual was meant to stymie insurrections and instill a message fore-telling the possibilities of end rewards for those who remained honorably com-mitted to their servile roles. If Black slaves or ex-slaves could just remain help-less and loyal to whiteness, then they would be okay. White slave owners' less than exegetical interpretations of religious text, particularly the Bible, led them to rationalize the slaves' intractable obligation to serve (Spaulding, 1990).

*Summary of Coon Stock Types.* No matter whether one is referring to the youthful and unaware pickaninny, the irregular and displaced Rastus, the happy-go-lucky and artistically talented Stepin Fetchit, or the complacent sto-rytelling Uncle Remus, coons dominated early minstrel show business. They, more strongly than any other character type with the exception of mammy and Uncle Tom, were the most inexcusable, protested, and despised by Blacks because they arguably embodied the most overtly hurtful stereotypes of Blacks as innately inferior, lazy, shiftless, illiterate fools (Bogle, 1996; Cripps, 1977; Means-Coleman, 2001). These four stock coon types—the pickaninny, Ras-tus, Stepin Fetchit, and Uncle Remus—were well-known, perennially funny, and docile protagonists. The coon, in all manifestations, had a personality that was distinguished from, but closely related to, the remainder of the stock char-acters in the pantheon—Uncle Tom, mulatto, mammy, and buck.

## UNCLE TOMS

Uncle Tom was monotypic as an accommodating, loyal, and faithful servant, who wanted nothing more than to exhibit Christian brotherly love and mercy toward others. Bogle (1996) describes him as follows:

[Edwin] Porter's tom was the first in a long line of socially acceptable Good Negro characters. Always as toms are chased, harassed, hounded, flogged, enslaved, and insulted, they keep the faith, n'er turn against their White massas, and remain hearty, submissive, stoic, generous, selfless and oh-so-very-kind. Thus, they endear themselves to White audiences and emerge as heroes of sorts. (p. 6)

The Uncle Tom character was introduced cinematically first in *Uncle Tom's Cabin* (1903), a 12-minute short adapted from Harriett Beecher Stowe's 1852 book of the same title that now has been translated into 58 languages and dialects. Sole mention of Porter's motion picture adaptation is not to slight the more than 500 stage play productions that preceded the film's 1903 release (Euell, 1997). After Porter, there were four other motion picture versions of *Uncle Tom's Cabin* released in 1909, 1914, 1918, and 1927. Porter's version of the film was innovative for its time, but later technologically dwarfed by D. W. Griffith's much-protested blockbuster film *Birth of a Nation*, which lasted three hours, still with no sound, but with advanced lighting and use of title cards as scenic frontispieces. A White actor initially portrayed Uncle Tom, but the 1914 and 1927 versions of the film included Black actors Sam Lucas and James B. Lowe, respectively, as the title character. Uncle Tom was the first among several stock minstrel figures to be played by Blacks, although the term, even in contemporary parlance, carries very negative connotations.

"Uncle Tom" is used to refer to a culturally unconscious, submissive individual who does not identify with any Black community, but instead prefers to see himself as a White-identified, cultureless, raceless, independent American citizen who can achieve the American dream without attaching himself to a Black community as long as he has God. He gullibly presumes the goodness of everyone, even when they have proven otherwise. Although somewhat disputed, some of our conservative political servants as well as scholars such as Clarence Thomas, Armstrong Williams, Shelby Steele, and John McWhorter have been typified this way because of their resistance to seeking a type of liberation that permits everyday marginalized group citizens to protest injustice that stifles their sense of liberty, especially in cases involving clear racial implications. Typically, what one is saying when claiming someone is an Uncle Tom is that the person has forsaken any real sense of community, that he cares more about individual achievement than sociopolitical forces that limit collective progress. In this way, the Uncle Tom character is somewhat of an anomaly because he is not viewed merely as an entertainment-related derivative, but also as one related to public servants gone astray.

Wilson Moses's (1993) interpretation of the Uncle Tom character is quite different. He contends that Uncle Tom has been vastly misunderstood and mythologized. Uncle Tom, according to Moses, did identify with Blacks, but was first and foremost a "Christ-like martyr" (p. 50) who bravely resisted any sort of dehumanization, especially of his own fellow Blacks. Moses recounts a story from *Uncle Tom's Cabin* in which Uncle Tom refused to whip the "hapless Casey,"whom the master has ordered him to punish. He also "acknowledges Eliza's right to flee with little Harry and does not betray her trust" (p. 56). Uncle Tom is explained as a messianic individual who makes the difficult choice of humbling himself as Christ would. Nonetheless, as Moses (1993) recognizes, Black slaves and present-day Blacks have great con-tempt for any characterization of complacency and deferential servility. Moses's point is well taken; there is a complexity to the Uncle Tom charac-ter that seldom is explored. It could be argued that his faithfulness is mistaken for a tragically uninformed complacency and devitalized dissonance; his Christian spirit is dismissed as a brand of undignified passivity; and his unselfish loyalty is deemed a nearly masochistic self-torture.

On the other hand, it is critical that we remember the cinematic por-trayals of Uncle Tom that launched a broad-based indictment of Black male loyalists as servile and stupid. In retrospect, a blackfaced Uncle Tom charac-ter that accepted an inordinate amount of violent physical, psychological, and emotional abuse at the hands of his master can only incense Black audi-ences. Sometimes slaves were coaxed to accept this abuse as obedience to God, and the Bible would be used to support this (Baker-Fletcher, 1996). This accent on abuse rather than a loving disposition is much more a com-mentary of Edwin Porter's 1903 cinematic interpretation of Harriett Beecher Stowe's *Uncle Tom's Cabin* than anything else. Porter's film set the precedent for a series of motion pictures that would continue to miss the point Stowe may have been trying to convey—that Uncle Tom was a Christian, morally strengthened family man whose obedience was truly guided by God rather than White men's social conventions and rules (Turner, 2002).

TRAGIC MULATTOES

Not surprising was the fact that Blacks were experiencing identity crises (Bogle, 1996; Cripps, 1977; Means-Coleman, 2001). This was depicted most evidently as a concern of White filmmakers in the embodiment of a charac-ter known as the tragic mulatto, a light-skinned female character who was tragically caught between right and wrong, good and bad, and, most impor-tant, Black and White. A mulatto is a person of mixed parentage, particularly Black and White parents, and, therefore, usually light-skinned. The tragedy that overcomes her is her predicament as a person considered Black, yet often light-skinned enough to "pass" for White. The dilemma is whether she should accept her socially ascribed blackness or reject it in favor of a more privileged whiteness. Her identity is always held in mind, as she negotiates these two cosmologies, knowing she is not fully accepted in either world because of her skin color (Bell, 1999). Her skin color is its own body politic that referees what is essentially a tug of war between intimacy and distance, desire and control, myth and truth. These themes emerged in the films *The Debt* (1912) and Dion Boucicault's *The Octoroon* (1913),[7] in which a White man has a White wife and mulatto mistress, both of whom bear his children. The two children, George and Zoë, grow up apart from one another, later fall in love, and eventually discover they cannot get lawfully married because they are siblings and she is partly Black, which means she is considered property. When her blackness is exposed, she finds out she is no longer free. The plot thickens when it becomes clear that Zoë will have to be auctioned off with the rest of the property due to legal debts and tax liens owed by the White proprietor. She is dreadfully attached to the misery her skin color brings her. In the 1859 play, Zoë exclaims:

> Of the blood that feeds my heart, one drop in eight is Black—bright red as the rest may be that one drop poisons all the flood; those seven bright drops give me love like yours—hope like yours—ambition like yours . . . but the one drop gives me despair, for I'm an unclean thing—forbidden by the laws—I'm an Octoroon! (as quoted in Anderson, 1997, p. 51)

The scripted message is clear that her body is inexcusably marked with a despicable blackness, thus she can do nothing but live a damnable existence.

The tragic mulatto was introduced in the cinematic role of Chick, played by 17-year-old Nina Mae McKinney, in White director King Vidor's first-of-its-kind talking-pictures movie *Hallelujah* (1929), a film that featured an all-Black cast singing, dancing, and representing utopic Black life. Bogle (1996) calls McKinney's mulatto character, Chick, "the movies' first Black whore" (p. 31). Years later, there was some speculation that actresses, especially light-skinned ones, if they wanted to be employed, had to play these roles and were offered small parts because of the limited White public interest in seeing sassy Black women characters on stage. Regardless of the reason, the actress who portrayed the tragic mulatto helped to introduce a most interesting persona, one who was problematized by Black ancestry, yet was halfway salvageable because of her White ancestry. The White audience sympathized with her plight, but the mandates of their negative whiteness ideology necessitated that they see her as having contaminated her whiteness. The mulatto is almost always referred to as the *tragic* mulatto, because her skin color automatically presumes that her identity must be negotiated. She simply cannot be happy being who she is because there is no ontological space for folks who fall in the middle of a Black–White polarity.

Naturally, this has changed over the years; although as Spike Lee's 1980s movie *School Daze* illustrates, there is some emotional residue that remains among Blacks as it relates to skin color politics and privilege. For example, in *School Daze*, Spike Lee pits the "jigaboos" (dark-skinned Blacks) against the "wanna-bes" (light-skinned Blacks) and suggests that the jigaboos are those who feel the strongest connection to African ancestral roots or at least a strong Black cultural consciousness, while the wanna-bes just want to be White. Of course, this is a false dichotomy of personalities, but one that has been the catalyst for a lot of ingroup dissension among some Blacks. It does have some historical credence in places like Louisiana where some Creole and Cajun people still are divided along racial lines.[8] This residue is still implicated in ingroup discussions of race and racism among Blacks (Gaines, 2001; Russell, Wilson, & Hall, 1992).

Nonetheless, there have emerged, as Anderson (1997) explains, three types of mulattos: "one who is a divided soul character who desires a White lover/husband and suffers a tragic fate as a result; another [sic] is the unhappy passing mulattos who denies her race and dies; the [sic] third is the exotic, restless, and mysterious mulattoes, who is inherently a sexual character" (p. 53). These three types correspond to three character types I call the *prototypical mulatto*, *passing mulatto*, and the *jezebel*. We have already discussed the *prototypical mulatto* character Zoë in *The Octoroon*, so I will now explain the other two.

*Passing Mulatto.* One passing mulatto character was that of Fredi Washington, a gorgeous light-skinned actress from Savannah, Georgia, who was probably best remembered as Pecola in the 1934 version of *Imitation of Life*. In that role, she was a gender and race-coded female tragic mulatto who attempts to "pass" for White.[9] According to Orbe and Strother (1996), "passing [sic] refers to the process by which bi-ethnic people conceal their African heritage and assimilate totally into the European American community" (p. 119). The fascinating thing about the character development of Pecola—which is typical of the passing mulatto—is that as Anderson (1997) evinces, the audience is led to believe she is White until that climactic and shocking moment when her blackness is confirmed, then her deception and, hence, her ethos is seen as vile. Within one cinematic glance, she undergoes a metamorphosis from God-blessed aristocrat and good citizen to a morally enfeebled plebeian—indeed—an impostor who deserves nothing less than damnation or death. The inscribed messages are as follows: Pecola can never be White, so she might as well get used to being Black and a part of everything Black, which is to be deprived of any admirable human qualities. Furthermore, passing will not be tolerated or justifiable; it must be treated as a form of treason, a felonious crime, rather than a minor infraction that comes with a lightweight penalty. Anderson (1997) suggests the penalty for passing, throughout many films involving the mulatto character, is typically exile or death.

A contemporary example of the passing mulatto, besides Alex Haley's title character *Queen* (Orbe & Strother, 1996), is Jennifer Beals as Daphne Monet, a protagonist in director Carl Franklin's *Devil in a Blue Dress* (1995).

This film was adapted from Walter Mosley's novel of the same title and set in the mid- to late 1940s. Monet plays opposite undercover detective Ezekiel "Easy" Rawlins, a character portrayed by Denzel Washington. Throughout this film, she is a phantom-like character Easy has been trying to find. One of the downplayed, yet very significant constituent parts of the film is the discovery that Daphne Monet is not White; she is really a mulatto New Orleans native named Ruby Charles. When her wealthy fiancé and mayoral candidate Todd Carter finds out her race, there is havoc because now his political career is in shambles and her presumed rags-to-riches lifestyle is terminated. The only one able to rescue her, and get her out of town, is detective Easy Rawlins and his sidekick Raymond "Mouse" Alexander. Initially, it may appear that this film does not fit among *contemporary* depictions of the passing mulatto because it is set in the 1940s, but it was produced in the mid-1990s when skin color politics were still quite relevant, as they are now. In keeping with the chiasmic mulatto themes of power and privilege as well as race and gender, *Devil in a Blue Dress* consistently reminds us of Hollywood's seeming inability to efface the monolithic and pathologized representation of Black bodies. Although the passing mulatto is exemplary of this, it is never more evident than with the jezebel.

*The Jezebel.* First introduced in Bertram Bracken's *Jezebel's Daughter* (1918) [a.k.a. *The Moral Law*], the jezebel character did not become popular until the release of William Wyler's *Jezebel* (1938), a film that received eight academy-award nominations and for which White actress Bette Davis received an Oscar for Best Actress. In Davis's role as Miss Julie Marsden in *Jezebel*, she is a nonracialized jezebel who is a strong-willed southern belle. Her significance, among the mulattoes discussed here, is that the jezebel character later became associated with stubborn, manipulative, lascivious Black women (Snead, MacCabe, & West, 1994). Naturally, the jezebel's character profile is well-aligned with the mulatto's sexually charged and devious nature, and later films like Kwyn Bade's *Loving Jezebel* (1999), a depiction of a clearly racialized jezebel, would draw this connection just as critical theorists and feminists have been doing for years. In each on-screen portrayal of jezebel, she is always at fault for her sexual splurges. Bade's rendition is no different. As film critic Roger Ebert (2000) discovers,

> the title of "Loving Jezebel" puts the blame on the women: a jezebel, we learn from a definition on the screen, is a woman who fools around with lots of men. Either definition would set up a sex romp, I suppose, but this movie is not quite what you'd expect. Within its romantic comedy we find a character that is articulate and a little poignant, and we realize Theodurus doesn't so much seek out other men's women as have them, so to speak, thrust upon him. (http://www.suntimes.com/ebert/ebert_reviews/2000/10/102705.html)

The same basic storyline emerges in the film *Jezebel*, which is set in 1852 New Orleans. Julie Marsden is engaged, but, as the film opens, we find her ex-boyfriend in a bar talking to her fiancé's relative. The ex-boyfriend was quickly dumped near the beginning of her engagement, but still loves her, so much so that when someone else in the bar speaks ill of Julie a fight erupts.

Meanwhile, Miss Julie, as she is affectionately called, gets upset with her fiancé, Preston Dillard, and tries to retaliate by publicly humiliating him. Although unmarried women usually wear white gowns to formal affairs, she decides to attend the prestigious Olympus Ball wearing a red dress and stubbornly insists that Preston escort her, prodding his masculinity by telling him he is probably afraid he will have to duel to save her dignity if a man says something scornful to her. He shamefully agrees to be her escort and discovers she is the one embarrassed more than he, so he makes her suffer by dancing in the middle of the floor after the awe-stricken guests have cleared the dance floor. When the ball is over, to her shocking disbelief, he ends the engagement and asks her to leave. She slaps him and stomps off to her home. She is melancholy, but occupies her time as a nurse assisting patients during an outbreak of yellow fever.

Three years later, the already-married character Pres arrives at one of Julie's two grandiose plantation mansions equipped with Black servants (which automatically suggests she has passed as White), and asks her to nurse him to health because he has contracted yellow fever. She immediately apologizes for her stubbornness and tries to win him back, but, unbeknownst to her, he brought along his newlywed wife, New York native Amy Bradford. Julie begins to scheme how to reinvigorate his affection for her, despite knowing he is married. Under those conditions, she agrees to care for him. Meanwhile, under her breath, she says, "I've gotta think, to plan, to fight." The storyline develops and we find Julie has incited a duel between two other characters, Buck and Ted. Her evil, contemptuous nature accompanied by an often malicious and seductive instinct is her trademark throughout the film. Just as with all stereotypical mulattoes, she becomes the object of gendered tension as the storyline progresses.

Rebelliousness and being a "bad girl" are only part of the jezebel personality profile. Physically, the jezebel as an archetype shares the physical attributes of the passing mulatto. She usually has long, thin, straight Black hair, thin lips, and a light-skinned almost-White or identifiably White complexion as she did in the character of Miss Julie. The personality of the jezebel has been described as "destructive(ly) animalistic" (Anderson, 1997, p. 118), "sexually aggressive" (Collins, 1991, p. 77), and a seductress akin to the title character in *Carmen Jones*. Jasmine Guy in television's *A Different World*, the character Nola Darling in Spike Lee's film *She's Gotta Have It* (1984), and Lisa Rae in *Players Club* are each jezebels. None of them attempts to pass; they are just scripted as beautiful, sexy, wanton bodies audiences crave to see.

Meyers (2004) contends, "The Jezebels' lewd conduct links them to the bad behavior and moral laspses associated with Black women and poverty" (p. 112). The latter two characters are certainly more characteristic of the jezebel as sex object. Anderson (1997) deconstructs the character of Nola Darling and suggests that she is never given the chance to appear unsullied, but is quintessentially aggressive in bed. Nola narrates her story, as the audience is permitted access to her sex life. In placing aside her privacy, Nola becomes exposed as a lustful woman with an insatiable sexual appetite. She is not satisfied with one man, and sometimes not even one per day. As voyeur, the audience plays witness to her sexual fantasies and rationalizations of her relational choices. In this film, director Spike Lee updated the images of Chick and Zoë, and offered a level of consciousness and self-reflection virtually missing from earlier dramatic portrayals of jezebel. Yet, he allowed the odorous residue dormant in patriarchal, popular cultural representations of Black women to remain. She is still a sex-crazed creature, a jezebel who never escapes from this cell. In fact, when I first viewed the movie, I thought Lee was trying to show us via a documentary how sex-related psychosis develops and unfolds. The mulatto, like the coon, mammy, and buck, is an intricate character with varied manifestations. No matter whether she is presented as a prototypical mulatto, passing mulatto, or a jezebel, she is a pariah to the upper class, caught in an epic struggle for her identity.

## MAMMIES

The mammy is another figure in the pantheon that is confounded by a scripted identity matrix. Contrary to the popular image of a middle-aged, dark-skinned, overweight mammy, Turner (2002) maintains that "actual" mammies or house servants were typically young, light-skinned or mixed-race, thin women. In fact, according to Turner, "Household jobs were frequently assigned to mixed-race women. They were unlikely to be old because nineteenth century Black women just did not live very long; fewer than ten percent of Black women lived beyond their fiftieth birthday" (p. 44).

The mammies were introduced cinematically, opines Turner, as a way to lessen their appeal to White audiences and recreate nostalgia for the antebellum south. Unfortunately, many overweight Black women on television and in film have been and continue to play the role of a middle-aged, dark-skinned, overweight mammy (Collins, 1991; Dates & Barlow, 1993; Means-Coleman, 2000). So, according to early films, a mammy, by definition, was a heavy-set complacent Black woman servant, who often was a maid or cook in addition to a surrogate mother of a White family's kids. She usually wore an apron and a cotton dress that came down to her ankles, and her hair was always pulled back and tied. Present-day depictions of mammies continue the image of an overweight Black woman as a stay-at-home or working mother who cooks, cleans, and takes care of her own kids. In both instances, she is most noted for being an advisor, comforter, and primarily headstrong motherly figure who holds the household together. In the early days of filmmaking, her character could often be seen embracing next to her bosom a weeping individual who had expressed some tribulation (Bogle, 1989, 1996). One never got the sense the mammy had any problems of her own, but only ones inherited from others toward whom she was helplessly empathetic.

Two of the earliest depictions of the mammy, consonant with this description, included the roles of Gertrude Howard as Beulah in *I'm No Angel* (1933); the Beulah character eventually became the protagonist and title character of an ephemeral network television comedy called *Beulah*. The other popular mammy was Louise Beavers, as Aunt Delilah in *Imitation of Life* (1934), whose Aunt Jemima character seemingly desired nothing more than seeing her White boss create a lucrative enterprise from her secret recipe for pancakes. *Imitation of Life*, based on Fannie Hurst's novel of the same name, became the springboard for the establishment of Quaker Oats Company's Aunt Jemima pancake products and later, to a lesser extent, Aurora Foods' Mrs. Butterworth's syrup, both of which can still be bought at your local grocer. Certainly Aunt Jemima pancake products are much older, more popular, and more aligned with Black body politics, but even Mrs. Butterworth is presented as an overweight woman wearing an apron and a homely dress with her hair pulled back and bandana tied to hold her hair in place.

One of the most celebrated mammy characters was Hattie McDaniel (a nursemaid to Scarlet O'Hara) in Margaret Mitchell's *Gone with the Wind* (1939), a role for which McDaniel won an Oscar, for Best Supporting Actress, a feat not to be repeated next until Sidney Poitier's receipt of an Honorary Oscar for his role in *Lilies of the Field* (1963). McDaniel was scripted as the unattractive and asexualized mammy who was quite straightforward about her opinions on race, relationships, and her supposed inferiority (Cripps, 1993; Watkins, 1994). As the character named Mammy she portrayed in *Gone with the Wind*, she was more assertive than her character portrayal of Aunt Delilah in *Imitation of Life*. If asked her opinion, she would give it, in her own signifying way.

Personally, the earliest remembrance I have of the mammy was her role in cartoons like *Tom & Jerry*. While the animated cat and mouse were running and tearing up the house, the director took time occasionally to show an often-headless animated mammy cleaning up and apparently cooking, since she always wore a cooking apron and seemed to be exiting from the kitchen. The camera focused on her large bosom, overweight thighs and calves, and her apron. Every now and then, the camera would get a shot of her from behind so that the viewer could be assured it was a mammy, since she would be wearing the characteristic cloth covering her head and tied in the back. She rarely had any speaking parts, and, as I recall, if she did, she would talk under her breath to express her dismay or disbelief of their playful antics. It seems, given her extremely limited role, she could have been left out of the cartoon, so it is even more peculiar why the director chose to maintain her presence. She became a symbolic backdrop that signified the show's attachment to a patriarchal and hegemonic legacy. That show, in retrospect, may seem subtly bigoted at first glance, but it was clearly and conspicuously racist.

Later depictions of mammy figures became even more sophisticated and somewhat difficult to detect because they were sometimes not cooks and maids in White families' houses. For example, Nell Carter in *Gimme a Break* (1981) was a classic mammy character, while the title character in *Thea* (1980s), a prequel to *Moesha* that somehow has outlasted *Moesha*, and remains in syndication on UPN, is a more contemporary mammy figure and a hair stylist. Other shows featuring contemporary mammy figures were *What's Happening?*, *What's Happening Now?*, *Family Matters*, and *Amen*.

Carter's role as Nell in *Gimme a Break* (a situation comedy that began in 1981) was as a housekeeper and nurturer of a White household that included a widowed police chief and his three daughters. She vowed to her terminally ill friend that she would take care of her family if she died. It is suspected Nell cared for these children as she did her own, but we never saw her children, if she even had any. Turner (2002) reminds us Nell had a Black boyfriend and Black professional girlfriend who appeared in only a few episodes. She was not extremely deferential, given the impetus for her character, but she fit the mammy profile, even down to the loud, raspy, but in her case high-pitched voice. Audiences seemed willing to excuse the inherent negativity of her mammy role because her White employer behaved much more like her friend than a mean, nasty tyrant. He had a pleasant disposition and seemed to recognize her as another human being worthy of respect; after all, she was doing the family a favor and could leave at any time. Of course, the show was only a couple decades removed from a time when Black women's cinematic and televisual roles were sparse, so any activism would have had to demonstrate a conspicuous producer intentionality to present demeaning and racist images. For those who were aware of minstrelsy, the deprecatory images did not need to be explained. Incidentally, Nell Carter's role is the most discussed post-1970s mammy depiction in modern academic literature (Bogle, 2001; Cummings, 1988; Dates & Pease, 1997; Means-Coleman, 2001).

The mammy is perhaps the most obvious modern-day minstrel figure to identify, initially because of her overweight physique, but also because of how she is portrayed as a husbandless, strong-willed matriarch principally preoccupied with domestic responsibilities. A contemporary example of a mammy still on television in 2004 is the cathectic character named Mamie, the maid in *Young & the Restless*. She is a barely recognizable variation of the mammy discussed so far. She is not obese, and, admittedly, her character has been transformed since her initial appearance on the show. She was first introduced as a short, average-sized woman played by an actress with the last name of Rodriguez, apparently Latina. Rodriguez was not only a maid in the Abbot family household, but was also considered part of the family, a surrogate mother who offered advice when asked, and who essentially took care of the family. After the Abbot's divorce, she was reintroduced and played by a new actress, about the same size. She and Mr. Abbot begin, in one episode, a post-divorce romantic fling, but just as television's Ethel Waters's 1950s title character Beulah, Mamie could not get her beau to marry her. So, on the next episode, the viewing audience is told the affair must have been simply a figment of her imagination, a reverie. Somehow, she is paid a lump sum of money to leave the Abbott home, and her character is now a well-off independent woman who plays the aunt of two other Black female characters, but still keeps in touch with the Abbott family and is considered, even in her emancipated role, a member of the family.

The mammy figure, in almost all her cinematic and televisual manifestations, was somewhat complex in that she was scripted in accordance with the age-old racial body politic; she was generally considered to have a physically and sexually undesirable Black female body with highly desirable and comforting personality traits. She was a two-dimensional character who was an honest, yet humble and servile, friend whom Whites could confide in; she had "mother wit" that translated into sound advice; and she was a respectable matriarch who represented wholesome family values. The two major characteristics she was missing were agency to define her self as she pleased and a dignified life of her own, something separate from other people's issues.

## BUCKS

Another figure in Bogle's (1996) pantheon is the brute who was almost always a tall, dark-skinned muscular, athletically built character and often either bald or with a short haircut. The brute or buck's primary objective was raping White women. He, essentially, refused to even attempt to control his insatiable sexual desires and urges; hence, the Black body of the brute was scripted to be nothing less than an indiscreet, devious, irresponsible, and sexually pernicious beast. This character explicitly showcased two major fears or anxieties of White men: first, theft of *his* woman by a maniacal, heathenish, and inherently violent Black male body, and, second, the possibility that she might be masochistically excited by his sexual nature and accept him despite his flaws, which might lead eventually to miscegenated offspring, hence defying the code of White racial purity. Some go so far as to suggest that White men's real fear, in the United States, was racial annihilation, since the de facto one-drop rule (Davis, 1996) indicated that if a human being had one drop of Black blood, the person would be considered Black (Welsing, 1991). Despite the rationale, this character embodied and was the projected vision of both the brutality of Whites who barbarically enforced whiteness ideology during slavery and thereafter, and the brutality of a Black man forced to a point of retaliation; however, the storyline almost always suggests the Black man's natural proclivity to commit violent acts without provocation (Pinar, 2001).

One notable example of a brute was Gus in *Birth of a Nation* (1915), who is described as a "Black renegade rapist" (Turner, p. 22), although Bogle (1996) implies he was actually an "attempted rapist" who, before assaulting the White female character Cameron, watches her run from him, fall off a cliff, and plummet to her death. His penalty was served when an entourage of White Confederate army men, whose bodies were covered by white sheets, met him. This one segment evoked mayhem among activists and slaves alike. The whole imagery of a virgin White woman, an uncontrollable Black brute, and an otherwise civilized society points to the Black brute as society's only poison. Though ridden with sundry problems, it was also cathartic for Whites, since the brute's capture and punishment (only after a trial with evidence presented) represented a measure of true justice and alleviation of one of Whites greatest fears: that Black men would retaliate against White rapists of Black women by surreptitiously taking his God-given White female companion from him (Rocchio, 2000). Luckily, she came to her senses and sacrificed her life instead of debasing herself by sleeping with her property, which would be equivalent in their minds to bestiality.

Bogle believes *Birth of Nation* marked the beginning of the Ku Klux Klan; however, this was the second genesis of the KKK. The first one failed after its members realized the cause for which they were fighting—the Confederate casualties—was antiquated. Historian C. Eric Lincoln claims Confederate General Nathan B. Forrest initially organized the KKK in 1865 in Pulaski, Tennessee. Pinar (2001) agrees and argues that the KKK were not the majority of southerners, but this group of angry Civil War veterans were White men who sought revenge on Blacks for assisting the North in their defeat. Again, there were still a few Confederate states allowed to retain slaves for a couple years past the Emancipation Proclamation of 1863 until the Thirteenth Amendment to the Constitution was signed in 1865. Even after this, mobs of White men wreaked havoc on these newly freed individuals, letting them know they would not be accepted as the full American citizens they had become. From 1865 well into the early 1900s, thousands of ex-slaves were brutally punished at the hands of White men by maiming, castrating, shooting, raping, and killing their Black bodies. As many as 120 Black men and women were lynched between 1900 and 1901. *Birth of a Nation* (1915) gave Whites a new reason to fight—everything they held dear—their White supremacy and their families, and probably in that order.

Paul Robeson's role as Brutus Jones in Eugene O'Neill's *The Emperor Jones* (1933), a role repeated from Eugene O'Neill's stage play, was quite a twist from the denigrative images discussed so far. Though Brutus is still stereotypically a violent, murderous brute, as his name implies, he is depicted as a stalwart hero, a pre-Stagolee badman and ladies' man who has self-pride and is intolerant of foul treatment. An international concert artist, Robeson had a deep baritone voice commanding of respect. Indeed, his character can be interpreted as a far-from-capricious angry Black male, and rightfully so due to his endurance of harsh and servile conditions. His murderous proclivity is inexcusable, so, as viewers, we are forced to reject his unethical behavior, yet we cheer his courage and steadfastness. Of course, this need not be celebrated too quickly. We must be mindful of Robeson's role as Bosambo in Alexander Korda's 1935 British film *Sanders of the River*. He was reported to have been ashamed of the film on viewing it in toto, and asserted that his character was a "smirking and indolent" Black man whose obsequiousness was evidenced by his deferential singing of *Sandy the Strong, Sandy the Wise, Hater of Wrongs, Hater of Lies* and his constant reference to the title character as "Lord Sandy" in addition to his genuflecting and/or sitting at the mere presence of Lord Sandy (Cameron, 1990). The flip side of this description is that Bosambo was appointed to be a king within Africa by Lord Sandy at the end of the film. Many of Robeson's roles were counterhegemonic, and he has been hailed for a body of work that bespeaks resistance to negative scripting of the Black body (Cripps, 1977).

A more contemporary exemplar of the brute can be found in *Shaft* (Gordon Parks's 1971 original and John Singleton's 2000 remake). In both films, there is the subtext of sexuality and violence. Shaft, played first by Richard Roundtree and later by Samuel L. Jackson, was a macho-rigid Black detective who magnetized and mesmerized beautiful women by his evident strength, unquestionable fortitude, and role as hero and savior of the community. This brute role of Detective John Shaft is justified, not only by his state authority, but also by the kidnapping of his daughter, which would make any father very upset. It is a variation of the family-in-distress formula that worked well for Charles Bronson, Clint Eastwood, and other badmen in cinematic history. Let there be no mistake: *Shaft* was a blaxploitation film that only reinvented and rearticulated the misogynistic hypermasculine hero who absolutely must satisfy his sexual urges, thereby hierarchizing the representational gaze. Both versions of the movie did this with the second version's highly advertised trailer with Samuel L. Jackson coolly explaining to a sexually interested woman, "It's my duty to please that booty." The sexist cinematic representations of women in general, but specifically Black women in the present example, are often ignored while the audience is led to concentrate on more visible and heightened aspects of the protagonist Brute's bravery, courage, and heroism. Bates and Garner (2001) claim that Shaft is a paladin warrior known for his state-authorized, and therefore justifiable, violence and also for being a true champion of justice. Perhaps the most significant and resonating characteristic of the paladin warrior is his interest in always prioritizing the interests and safety of his community. His function is to secure his people from external harm. So, we come to admire him for this role. I am convinced this is why hip-hop music's discursive construction of the thug and ruffneck (discussed in chapter 4) is so compelling and well embraced. From the days of minstrelsy to the present, the brute or buck image is still intact. It has invaded public life so much that it has become ingrained in the social consciousness, psychologically imprinted as a vivid picture of the typical Black man in the United States (Blount & Cunningham, 1996).

## SUMMARY AND IMPLICATIONS

The reservoir of negative inscriptions of the Black body is very extensive. No one book can claim to catalogue all the examples of racially inscribed bodies. From early Black corporeal inscriptions established during slavery and minstrelsy to more contemporary inscriptions within cinema, television, and music, at least one aspect is common to all—Black bodies have been thingafied, socially rejected, and treated as foreign to the American ethos (Diawartha, 1993).

I never had much interest in minstrelsy prior to writing this book. I understood its fundamental importance and relevance to mass media and popular culture, but minstrelsy evoked hurtful emotions within me and symbolized a retrogressive body politic. So, I perceived even the conversation of it as toxic and stayed away from it. I imagined I would have to contend with those feelings as I wrote this chapter, and, shockingly, it was a revelatory and cleansing process. It reminded me just how much representations and gazes of Black bodies have progressed and just how far we have left to go. The argument I constructed in this chapter, using a critical-historical approach, is that slavery and early racial depictions of the Black body have directly influenced the coherent scripting of Black bodies in contemporary cinema and television, but, more important, they have had deleterious effects on the psyche of African Americans. Slavery, lynching, Jim Crowism, and minstrelsy were not communicative events isolated to the Confederate South. These same racial attitudes existed among northern Whites and are pervasive, though to a presumably lesser degree, throughout the United States. These systematically and epistemically violent transgressions were systematically linked and enacted on Black bodies and, hence, African American identities. The period subsequent to the holocaust of enslavement was an unhealthy one according to Asante (1999). Asante asks, and I paraphrase, how does one endure a psychologically, physically, and spiritually devastating tragedy and not come out unscathed? He reminds us that no one offered Blacks psychological treatment or reparations; instead, they were left to fend for themselves in a society that kept them from the resources (e.g., employment, education, etc.) to do so. In outlining the origins of Black body politics, we are introduced to ways in which Black bodies are represented, rendered invisible, commodified, and made a spectacle. We also become cognizant of the historical contexts for the politicization that accompanied inscriptions of Black bodies. One such context was enslavement.

Since the slave trade began in the New World in 1517 (Franklin & Moss, 1988), Black people have endured centuries of oppression. Even after they were free, they would spend the next 40 years undergoing major adjustments into the 1900s and beyond. Major epochs and movements such as the Niagara movement that led to the founding of the NAACP and other civil rights organizations, the Harlem Renaissance, Back-to-Africa movement, Civil Rights Movement, feminist movement, and Black Power movement all contributed to the advancement in civil rights we experience today. Yet, there is still much work to do. For example, Cameron (1990) offered a historically rooted critique of contemporary Black film beginning with *Birth of a Nation*. He observed less than fifteen years ago:

> *Birth of a Nation* set out the racial imagery of the first fifty years of movies. Blacks were to be mostly invisible; when seen, they would perform for Whites. If they made themselves visible, they would become immediately threatening, sexually so if they were male. They were then "primitives." God and the angels would come down on the side of whiteness. In such an agenda, an "acceptance of servility" became characteristic of the Black race as it was seen on film. (p. 283)

Even at the beginning of the twenty-first century, Blacks are still fighting against civil injustice on an almost daily basis, especially in film and other popular media, and for many of the same reasons stemming from the genealogical origins of the scripting of the Black body. As chapters 2 and 4 indicate, Black women are just as likely, if not more so, to be scripted as sexual, yet the fantasia implicit in many popular films still suggests "God and the angels would come down on the side of whiteness," and this is evidenced in part by the pervasiveness of positive White images on film and television, compared to the fairly small number of positive images and representations of Blacks and other non-Whites (Entman & Rojecki, 2000). Black independent filmmakers of the 1920s through 1940s, such as Oscar Micheaux, Bert Williams, Ebony Pictures, The Birth of a Race company, and even the White-owned Lincoln Motion Picture Company, launched an often reactive counterhegemonic set of films that Mercer (1988) suggested was reiterative of the same strategies and tools of Black corporeal representation and inscription used by White filmmakers initially, but their rhetorical resistance strategies were highly effective. They were revolutionary for their time if, for nothing else, as motion picture companies whose principal interest was in trying to present more positive Black themes and characters. Certainly, several of the more avant-garde contemporary filmmakers like Julie Dash (*Daughters of the Dust*) and Haile Guerima (*Sankofa*) have been successful in producing a more diverse, expressive, culturally conscious, and complex inscription of Black bodies, but then they have been beneficiaries of those earlier Black filmmakers who refused to quiesce. Even still, progress toward broad-based emancipatory filmmaking is slow.

I agree with Dates and Pease's (1997) assessment, even several years later in the twenty-first century, that we still have present-day imagery reminiscent and perpetuating of stock minstrel figures. They posited:

> Some African Americans, along with the White decision-makers who control the media industries, are making money—and a lot of it—in a widespread use of television and motion pictures that defines Black people in ways that are more destructive than ever seen. What we see in the media of the 1990s are modern-era minstrel shows (sitcoms), movie thrillers, rap music and music videos that celebrate misogyny and violence, and that communicate parodied images of Black men, shucking and jiving con artists who joke about pathological behaviors and criminality, while playing the role of Black "bucks" to a White America. In the end, such images and attitudes diminish Black and White Americans alike. (pp. 81–82)

These linkages between past and present portrayals are not drawn to erect a nihilistic prophecy that Black bodies are trapped irreversibly and deterministically in a web of ontological despair. I believe the point being made is much more sophisticated and interesting. I contend that Black bodies must be aware of their historical and contemporary habitat in order to understand how they actively participate in or resist scripting. I am aware that by saying Black bodies can participate in their own scripting that inscription is not just an external activity robbing Black bodies of their agency, but that Black bodies may also rob themselves of agency using patriarchal inscriptions as the platform for alienating or detaching themselves from their natural and beautiful indigenous identities. They once were coercively scripted by a White male patriarchy and now some of them, despite being descendants who can only vicariously experience the horrors of slavery and early minstrelsy, disturbingly continue to carry out negative and racist representations, to their own detriment.

For example, Chris Rock thought it was humorous to pose for the front cover of the August 1998 issue of the popular magazine *Vanity Fair* as a coon in blackface with white makeup around his eyes and mouth to exaggerate his facial features. Many of his Black fans were appalled, but reasoned that because he is known to do politically charged standup comedy, perhaps he was trying to make a political statement. Black audiences waited for Rock to cogently articulate a justifiable rationale and, to their chagrin, he never offered one. Nonetheless, somehow he remains one of the most respected comedic entertainers in the United States. Indeed, he was not posing in black-face to entertain Black audiences. Certainly, one could argue that this was nothing different from what Dave Chappelle does in his show—offensive antics done to make a point. I would maintain that this was not a "sketch" or sitcom episode, but instead a public display of retrogressive thinking clothed as brilliant comedy. It is precisely this kind of complicity with White patriarchal inscriptions that leads to the negotiation of the palimpsest Black body, which paradoxically pays dividends (as exemplified by the continued success of Rock's career) while paying debts, although the latter far outweigh the former. Some would suggest that his wildly successful hosting of the 2005 Academy Awards Ceremony offers some redemption or that his politically savvy commentary elsewhere redeems him. Nonetheless, this only sharpens the confusion about why he posed in blackface for *Vanity Fair*.

With few exceptions, twenty-first century American popular culture—its producers and audiences—has rarely presented a straight-no-chaser, non-stereotypical approach to difficult themes like race, class, gender, and sexuality. Neal (2002) reminds us of this in his description of unappreciative student responses to coon-like televisual images on situation comedies like *In Living Color*, *Martin*, *The Jamie Foxx Show*, and *The Wayans Brothers*, all of which are either completely cancelled or in syndication. Unfortunately in film, for example, we have come to rely on signifying parodies, satires, and comedies like Spike Lee's *Bamboozled* (2000) and Malcolm Lee's *Undercover Brother* (2002) to inform and demonstrate to us the ridiculous racial conundrum with which we find ourselves being preoccupied. It is absolutely amazing that a physically coded, socially ascribed, and psychologically devastating Black body politic originating in the 1600s can still be so vivid today within virtually every confine of American life, and we not only live with it, but we participate in promoting it in a bevy of every day mass-mediated and popular cultural practices. The ideologically driven and institutionally sanctioned minstrelsy pantheon composed of denigrated Black bodies is still alive and well, and it is our obligation to change the narratives or not support these structured discourses of negative representation to which we have all become subjected and debilitated. DuBois (1903) asked, "How does it feel to be a problem?" Sadly, the inscription of Black bodies as pathological preserves the query.

# TWO

# Scripting the Black Body in Popular Media

## *Exploring Process*

Identities are the names we give to different ways we are positioned by and position ourselves in, the narratives of the past.

—Stuart Hall, 1997

I am conscious of the world through the medium of my body.

—Charles Johnson, 1994

In the previous chapter, I presented a genealogical criticism of Black body politics in the United States, stemming both from enslavement as well as early minstrelsy and leading up to contemporary mass-mediated stereotypes that have become nothing less than imagistic imprints of Black bodies. In this chapter, I will explore Black corporeal inscriptions in various popular media with a particular emphasis on what the scripts signify about Black identities. The major assumption made in this chapter and throughout the book is that pejorative inscriptions of the Black body are far from defunct. Instead, they interface with our daily lives and facilitate negative proscriptions about Black people and even by Black people, constantly interrupting the possibilities of social cohesion among cultural groups that have been racialized and therefore polarized. This act of restructuring social cognitions about race has been labeled "racial coding," "mythification," and "marking" (Snead, MacCabe, & West, 1994). After all, what does one do with fictive corporeal representations that eventually become so fixed in the public imagination that they are no longer considered false? In fact, after constant inundation of such images, these glyptic caricatures become verifiably true portraits of Black bodies that require transcendence before they can even be considered false again (Watkins, 1998).

In this act of reconstitution, Black bodies almost completely vanish from their indigenous habitat, and become adjectival signifiers of an obliquely scripted and capitalist-driven whiteness ideology, with residual traces and remnants of Black corporeal selves still persevering. One stream of logic that is meant to explain the tenuous "now-true" inscriptions about Black bodies is Lacanian psychoanalytic notions of the self as elusive. In this ontological view, it is not that the self is so complex that it defies meaning, but that our lives are intersubjective and so any thinking about corporeal representation and concomitant identities necessitates the recognition that meanings do not stand in isolation. Rather, meanings are co-constructed by multiple subjectivities and the process of this construction suggests there is no essential subject. There is only a co-constructed subject, an amalgam of interpolated interpretations; hence, we lose sight of what is true—in fact, we have no access to the truth.

This anti-essentialist rendering of the self is impressive as an epistemological reordering of truth. It relies on the premise that the self must be refereed and validated by a social collective, but it also fails to account for any possibility of agency until it is reinterpreted. For example, some poststructuralist feminists would argue that women's bodies "are point[s] from which to rethink the opposition between the inside and the outside, the private and the public, the self and the other, and all the other binary pairs associated with the mind-body opposition" (Grosz, 1994, pp. 20–21).

When bodies are syntactically presented as parts of a continuum, as Grosz recommends, rather than bifurcated categories, invariably liberatory potential emerges. The question is, "How do we recognize freedom when we see it?" In other words, if we are so enwrapped in a hackneyed, universally inscribed ideology that we can no longer decipher truth from fiction, how do we know when truth is present and falsehood disappears? How do we rectify something that is no longer considered wrong? If, as Hall (1997) maintains, our identities are positioned vis-à-vis our personal and historical antecedents, then it is critical that we explore our positioning as an effect of prior collective experiences, and—I would also add—the dominant, capitalist, and materialist impulse and will to preserve hierarchies of subject and subjugated, haves and have-nots, Whites and non-Whites.

This chapter, and book, does not intend to function as a defense of maledictory Black behavior, nor is it an apologia. In a haste to articulate the ontological facets peculiar to Black people, many theorists attempt to rescue Blacks from intense scrutiny. I do not agree that this should be the goal, but I think it is necessary to provide a fair balance of theoretic perspectives and currencies. In the end, it is imperative that we are able to explain, under-stand, value, and gain insight into actual Black identities, as opposed to mis-guided, diluted, and reductionist pop-cultural imprints of Black communica-tive behaviors. In this chapter, I begin with a definition of the scripting process. After explaining an analog of scripting and pointing out its ideolog-ical bent, the remainder of this chapter explicates and fundamentally argues three primary points: (1) The Black body is the location of specular and sym-bolic lynching; (2) Black people participate in the politicization of the Black body by resisting and complying with stereotypical images; (3) Black male and female bodies are economized differently. The chapter concludes with implications of Black body politics in popular culture and recommendations for future research.

## SCRIPTING AND THE GAME OF CHARADES

As Stuart Hall suggests in his essay entitled, "What Is this 'Black' in Black Popular Culture," identities are inextricably linked to and shaped by both contemporary social positioning and self-constructed narratives. Positions and counterpositions are named and arranged as individuals negotiate their identities while in interaction with others. As a result, self-definitions are complicated by cultural registers and social coordinates, which over time become concretized and situated between the center and the periphery. That is, through a normalizing practice people's lives become narratives, which are either aligned with or counter to the grand narrative. So, in metaphori-cal terms, to be Black and to be American is to be forced to participate in a public game of charades in which all interactants are subjected to sublimi-nal vagaries of the mind. As you well know, in a typical game of charades, a word is represented in riddling verse or by picture, tableau, or dramatic action. The contest is usually spontaneous, and requires that individuals guess what the actor is representing. There are always sundry guesses and only one correct answer. Perhaps the most attractive, alluring feature of the game is the bodily performance itself, its ambiguous meanings, and the elicited responses. But again, although there are many appropriate responses, there is *only* one correct answer for each performance episode. To truly con-sider the game as a metaphor for social activity, it is necessary to deconstruct the paradox created when the performance of the bodily text intends to mean one thing and is interpreted by the observers to mean another.

American popular culture is fascinated with the game of charades so much that it has produced its own complex White solipsistic versions, one of which centers around the varied iterations of the racialized *body* (Jhally & Lewis, 1992). The word "body" at the end of the previous sentence deserves further clarification. I use this term to mean two things, the composite body and the individualized body. The composite body is used to describe a given community or collective. Often when people speak in overgeneralizations or choose to racially stereotype, they are referring to the composite body. The individualized body widely varies, but has powerful implications. The physiognomic features and phylogenic differences are "markers" of the individualized body. These visual markers, I interchangeably call the corporeal zones. For example, some Black people's corporeal zones include nappy hair texture, wide noses, thick lips, and darker-than-white skin complexion, all of which come into play when an individual is interacting with a cultural "Other." There is no such thing as not seeing someone's corporeal zones; one's skin complexion or other markers may not result in unfair treatment by the Other, but they are certainly optic markers (Baker-Fletcher, 1996; Wiegman, 1990).

For example, communication scholar Regina Spellers (2003) discusses the interposition of body politics, looking relations, and cosmological screens. Spellers explains results from her qualitative examination of African American hair politics and remarks that nappy Black hair is undervalued in American popular culture to the extent that many Black women feel the need to fix, press, extend, or cover their nappy hair because they have been convinced it is not naturally beautiful. In fact, nappy hair is punctuated by what she calls the "kink factor," which represents a bodily discourse concerning heritage and identity, but, perhaps most of all, if maintained and exposed, self-love. Although the exhibition of women's hair does not approximate the sexual innuendo suggested by women's exposed and flaunted buttocks and breasts, hair is a very significant part of the body that can be and often is aestheticized and politicized. It is a marker of class, community, personal expression, and identity.

The inferences gained from the "markers," which emerge within communicative episodes, are particularly important to the study of human communication, where the analysis of preverbal communication (i.e., corporeal zones) goes virtually unexamined. Before the talk even begins, there are systemic pressures, personal experiences, and historical antecedents that are cued by the visible corporeal zones and have tremendous influence on the possibilities of popular cultural image development, longevity, fragmentation, and/or repair. These factors add to the gravity and severity of popular cultural images, especially in this age of cultural globalism and progressive technology where spectatorial images are omnipresent. As implied in chapter 1, when this game is played in popular culture, it tends to produce anxieties, insecurities, and fears for all parties involved, even when the scripted roles are reversed as in stage plays like *The Colored Museum* and *Confessions of Stepin Fetchit*, albums like rapper Rah Diggah's *Dirty Harriett*, or films like *Undercover Brother*. This calls to question the regulative function of inscribed subjectivities. Henley (1977) noticed that nonverbal enactments of the body were often read as cultural, political, and gendered, but did not thoroughly examine and articulate how the identity politics at work could potentially dismantle notions of seeing the self as agent. In the performative domain, mangled identities, as signified by newly inscribed bodies, may become disciplined scripts; hence popular cultural portrayals of Blacks, even by Blacks, discursively represent a speculum of whiteness ideology with myths of blackness being suspended in the public imaginary.

## WHAT DOES SCRIPTING AS SOCIAL ACTIVITY MEAN?

If we can accept dramaturgical scholar Erving Goffman's claim that human beings are all actors on a stage, then I have only two questions: who determines the scripts and when are they revised? Much of the body politics research involves reading the body as text via perspectival induction. Just as there is a difference between reading and writing, there is also a distinction between reading and scripting the body (Barthes, 1991). To read the body as text is to interpret its function, analyze its paraphernalia, and comment on its existence. Scripting is a completely different paradigm, which presumes that there are social vectors that determine how bodies are inscribed and how scripted roles for foreign bodies are enacted. So the fundamental question this chapter seeks to answer is, how do Black bodies get scripted in popular media?

In *reading* bodies as text, the discourse analyst does the interpreting of the written text with little to no regard for how and why the text was initially written; however, in analyses of scripting or inscribing bodies, the assessment turns inward so that the researcher becomes preoccupied with how the corporeal text is initially written and socially interpreted, or in a bit more sophisticated terms, how corporeal texts are disembodied and redistributed within social space. Essentially, the analysis of corporeal inscription involves an in-depth critical focus on both historical and contemporary manifestations of body politics. It is principally concerned with the intent as well as the underlying motivations for the inscription.

As with any theatrical script, the script is the text, and the act of scripting is the writing of the text. Therefore, to script someone else's body is to actively inscribe or figuratively place one's self, worldview, or ascriptions onto another projected text, which often requires dislocating the original text and redefining the newly affected or mirrored text as the counterpositional or oppositional Other. Of course, the I is never quite the same as the Other; in fact, in colonialist relations, inequality is well structured, and the privileged I is always at the center of the universe while the Other is usually on the periphery (Fanon, 1967; Giroux, 1992). As a result, we as media consumers unknowingly or subconsciously set up social cognitions that conform to specious mass-mediated stereotypes (Entman & Rojecki, 2000; Fisher, 1998). Through this process, we gradually come to know dialectically what it means to be Black by negating what it means to be quintessentially White; and we also come to know what it means to be female in relation to what it dialectically means to be male. Of course, this oversimplifies the nature of human behavior when we abide by such structured dialectics without questioning them in context or within their own range. The media rarely offers a complete composite of blackness or femaleness (hooks, 1994; 1995b; Kelley, 1997; Marable, 2001). Consequently, this act of negation is the linchpin of soured interracial and cross-gendered relations in the United States. Its functioning relies on social complicity with myths and stereotypes, which ultimately preserve social incohesion (Jackson, 2002; McPhail, 1994b).

In this study, scripting refers to the assignment of bodies, as understood by the scripter (e.g., the media), to certain locations of being, followed by a sociopolitical value-assessment of those bodies based on how well they match the script imposed on them. Though the intent of scripting is frequently to create harmony via homogeneity, the resultant effect in interracial scripting is often social polarization. This happens because the cultural norms, values, traditions, expectations, and behavioral codes of the newly introduced text are irrespective of those intrinsic textual properties that were already present.

The polarization occurs when the texts conflict and expectations are violated. Naturally, amending "deviant" behavior or preventing social penalty is impossible when the one being scripted cannot parry or preclude this activity. Edmund Husserl, the founder of phenomenological reductionism, speaks very fluently about the connection between consciousness and being. Perhaps the most insightful component of phenomenology is its recognition that all ontological "certainties" are subject to reexamination, deconstruction, or what phenomenologists call "disentanglement." By subjecting the life worlds of interactants to intense scrutiny while securing the intricate interplay of their differences, phenomenologists are able to comment on the lived experiences of individuals.

Likewise, social phenomenologists situate their analyses in public spheres, and demand a transformative examination of the social interior linking body with consciousness. In many ways, we all as human beings are amateur social phenomenologists seeking to make sense of the world around us, trying to connect what we see with what we have come to understand. Indeed, we are spectators, but we are also actors. Whether for social observation or not, it is clear that spectatorship is a psychical investiture, one that systematically orients and reorients the I–Other dialectical arrangements we have come to be familiar with via recapitulated social and discursive practices. One of those practices is scripting the Black body in popular media.

The scripting paradigm is partly nonunique in human communication studies; it is sometimes mistakenly understood to be solely self-fulfilling prophecy or what psychologists label as behavioral confirmation; however, it is complicated by an activity that may best be described as projection, a practice of encroachment involving the transposition of one's own negative "psychological baggage" from self to other. As with any projection, the major limitation of scripting is subjectivity—the scripter's autobiographical iterations that are left in the final construction. It is precisely this remnant that facilitates the tracing of whiteness ideology within popular cultural depictions of

Black bodies. I am not arguing that scripting as a discursive method is superior to reading. I am simply contending in this chapter that popular media agencies participate in designing bodies, particularly Black bodies, that are already constructed, and this subconscious and sometimes purposeful superimposition is a systematic endeavor to construct images of cultural Others that reflect the scripting agency's own xenophobic tendencies.

## SCRIPTING AS IDEOLOGICALLY DRIVEN

Scripting, as a discursive act, is ideologically driven. The peculiar arrangement of prescribed identities is, alone, an institution without which there would be no need to preserve the stifling disease of racism and the hierarchy that accompanies it. The Black body has become a text in which all behaviors are visual and discursive representations to be read as alien, unless those bodies are complicit in almost every sense with dominant cultural norms. The body and popular cultural discourse are inseparable, just as the behaviors that accompany the visual text are interdependent. In this way, the modern is fused with the postmodern in a manner that reveals significant commentary about ambivalence, social normality, cultural antagonisms, and the disproportionate shaping of mainstream discourse.

The primary objective of scripture as a process within current popular cultural media is to constitute the *utopic* American self in an effort to minimize the other, thus being consistent with what it means to be a centralized, rather than a marginalized being. I purposefully use the word "utopic," since the word as developed by Thomas More means "not a place"—a nonexistent locality. So, Black bodies that are defiant and decentralized, as in the case of some Black males, may be understood not necessarily as dystopic structures or delinquent nobodies, but marginalized identities seeking agency, affirmation, conjoinment, and recognition within an unfamiliar place. Often, these persons want to co-define and validate the centrality of their social positioning; they choose to act out their aggressions in public spheres to achieve these desired ends. This is a choice often deemed inappropriate because it does not comply with their assigned corporeal inscription, which is predicated on the premise that all rules and guidelines are to be defined by the dominant culture, and any violation of this agreement will be viewed as an intended infraction and subsequently penalized.

## THE BLACK BODY AS LOCATION
## OF SPECULAR AND SYMBOLIC LYNCHING

Lynching is a powerful word because of the way that it immediately conjures the intensity of public hangings. I utilize the metaphor of lynching in much the same way that American studies scholar, Robyn Wiegman presents it. She posits:

Lynching is about the law . . . the site of normativity and sanctioned desire, of prohibition and taboo. . . . Lynching figures its victims as the culturally abject. . . . Lynching provides a crucial locus for exploring the implications of this necessary end of "man" by drawing out the crises and contexts of racial hierarchies on the form and function of late-nineteenth-century patriarchal relations. In the turn toward lynching as a white supremacist activity in the post-emancipation years, we might recognize the symbolic force of the white mob's activity as a denial of the Black male's newly articulated right to citizenship. (Wiegman, 1995, pp. 81–83)

The analog of lynching connotes a disruption or interception of indigenous cultural activity. As Wiegman states, lynching is about "prohibition"— not allowing bodies to maintain their natural form. When racialized bodies are not in alignment with what it means to behave "normally," then the penalties that may take form are sociopolitical and prohibitive. The wordplay becomes important here, because the "popular" is contraindicated when the "normal" lapses. I think Mikhail Bakhtin (1981) says it well when he asserts that the popular and informal are the "vulgar" dimensions of everyday interaction, where ontological locale is called into question. Local differences are mapped out and deconstructed to mean backlash or rebellion, rather than defense or strength. Consequently, variance between and among persons is demonized and made spectacular. This sort of symbol-driven interplay creates a foundation for identity negotiation (Althusser, 1994). When offered the opportunity, as this analysis will reveal, Blacks may assimilate their perspectives and worldviews in order to attenuate the severity of the symbolic lynching process and ensure social survival.

## SYMBOLIC LYNCHING

The previously described form of symbolic lynching occurred in a recently televised toothpaste commercial. As I sat on my couch watching a cable television program, a commercial came on that was rather alarming. In this commercial, a white hand reaches down to pick up a toothbrush, the other hand is used to glide on the toothpaste in a swirl-like fashion. As the toothbrush with the white swirl toothpaste is lifted to the teeth, the camera gets a tight, close-up shot of a black-outlined medium-sized, bodiless (transparent) figure dancing all over the teeth. The white toothpaste is applied to the agitated teeth, and as the black-outlined figure is being dissolved, the voiceover script reads, in a most frantic tone, "Oh no, we have to get rid of the evil plaque man." The commercial closes. No face is ever shown.

This advertisement has several implications. First, from a critical perspective, I understood the black-outlined figure to represent Black people, and, after the script was spoken by the voiceover, it became clear that this figure, which appeared to be without body or gender, was actually a man. Cognitive psychologists have proven again and again that repetition of signs and signifiers eventually becomes an integral part of an individual's automatic and heuristic processing (Schacter, 1992). That is, if you show an image, symbol, motif, or action enough to a group or person, then after a while that group or person will associate even implicit representations of that image, symbol, motif, or action. In this case, the dancing motif works hand-in-hand with the "plaque man" identifier so that it becomes easy to discern that the "plaque man" is really a "Black man." Hence, no matter how much the viewer wanted to believe that the black outline meant nothing, the commercial implicitly suggests via both the symbolic black outline and the voiceover that the figure is Black. Silverman (1992) explains psychoanalyst Jacques Lacan's theory of the subject and the way in which it addresses the nature of signifying symbols. Silverman contends that "for Lacan, the definitive criterion of a signifier is that it abandon all relation to the real, and take up residence within the closed field of meaning. . . . Indeed, since signification constitutes the matrix within which the subject resides after its entry into the symbolic order, nothing escapes cultural value" (p. 346). This explanation of Lacanian signification facilitates understanding of the toothpaste commercial in that it permits us to rethink the direct and explicit objective of the commercial, which is to advertise toothpaste. Beyond that, we find that the commercial signifies, within a closed field of meaning, the subject of blackness. This subject is accompanied by all of its popular and cultural meanings. According to Silverman, "with the subject's entry into the symbolic order it is reduced to the status of a signifier in the field of the Other." That is, the commercial itself is reduced to a value-driven signifier of blackness. If we can accept that this commercial is symbolic and a signifier of social meaning, then the question is "What symbols and/or social meaning is being signified?" The following examples support the idea that the Black outline is more than simply an outline.

The erasure of the Black body in this commercial is profound. He is deemed not only insignificant, but a protest masculinity in motion, which must be dealt with before true health and balance can be restored. If you say the concluding line enough times, you'll notice how your tongue is inclined to replace "plaque" with "Black." Some may dismiss this interpretation as mere paranoia, but I contend it is beyond coincidence that the other mechanics of the commercial work hand-in-hand with this analysis. Second, I wondered why the Black man was bodiless. His transparency can be interpreted as invisibility or disembodiment. Ralph Ellison's *Invisible Man* captures the essence of corporeal elision nicely (i.e., omitting the body) when he states, " I am an invisible man. . . . I am invisible understand, simply because people refuse to see me" (p. 3). With Ellison's understanding of invisibility, it could be implied that the commercial is signifying that marginalized groups,

Blacks in particular, agitate normality and lack any real distinctive and ame-liorative form and function in our social world. Third, the figure is dancing, which is a popular cultural theme in commercial advertising, and frequently the dancers or entertainers are Black. This is consistent with my earlier analysis (in chapter 1) of the mammy, buffoon, coon, and Uncle Tom images as entertainment utilities in popular culture. The suggestion is that the worth of Blacks lies in their ability to entertain via sports, dance, comedy, drama, and so on. Perhaps the greatest assault this commercial launches is the ulti-mate dissolution of the Black body by the faceless and nameless universal White body. Because one cannot train the Black figure to behave appropri-ately, the only solution is to lynch or eliminate him from the equation.

Historically, the symbolic lynching of racialized Others is rooted in slav-ery, minstrelsy, and also naturalistic science. Yehudi Webster (1992), in his comprehensive overview of racial theory, clearly states that there has been more than one attempt to specify the origin of the term *race*; however, this issue has yet to be resolved. Nonetheless, most scholars do agree that natu-ralists, zoologists, anthropologists, and biologists are the progenitors of early racial theory. Cornel West (1993) reveals that the term *race* is derived from the French doctor Francois Bernier, who in 1684, devised it as a nomencla-ture for classifying human bodies primarily according to skin color.

In *Systema Naturae*, Carl von Linnaeus taxonomizes six human races according to skin color, geographical location, and civilization. The homo-Europeus was identified as being especially gifted with superior intellectual abilities. This was typical commentary among eighteenth-century natural scientists, and should be recognized as an initial contribution toward racial division as well as scientific analysis of human subjects. These classifica-tions created the foundation for modern presentations of African Ameri-cans throughout the disciplines. The formation of this body places the "white race at the center of history" (p. 34), with a conscious exclusion of other races' contributions (Webster, 1992). Stephen Gould (1981) provides further evidence of this by discussing the ideas of Georges Cuvier, a preem-inent scientist whose ideas were well respected after having founded the scientific disciplines of geology, paleontology, and comparative astronomy. Cuvier denounced the human potential of African natives by declaring them "the most degraded of human races, whose form approaches that of a beast and whose intelligence is nowhere great enough to arrive at regular government" (p. 36).

The research of polygenist Samuel George Morton is mentioned by Stephen Gould (1981), who reports that Morton collected 800 crania from various parts of the world, measured their respective volumes, and discovered a link between cranial weight and capacity for intelligence. European descen-dants had an average cranial capacity of 96 cubic inches, while Negro skulls weighed an average capacity of 83 cubic inches, thus giving evidence of superiority. Gould maintains that this was clearly the result of a deliberate distortion of the data. The skulls were packed with sand and it is suggested that the European skull was shaken, which allowed some sand to settle, while additional sand could be packed into the skull. The same process was not repeated for the "Negro" skull, thereby increasing the volume for the European skull while leaving Negro skull at its initial volume. This kind of manipulation was common among eugenicists who were most concerned with the purity of the White or European breed (Gould, 1981). The overall area of study became known as craniometry.

Anatomical differences and racial causation were the frontispiece of racial theoretical currencies. Charles Darwin's (1859) evolutionist thinkpiece *Origin of the Species* was one of the first works under the rubric of racial theory to reimagine the genesis of civilization outside of Africa, which we now know is the birthplace of humankind (Diop, 1991). For Darwin and many other eugenicists, Africa was a location from which many slaves were shipped to Bahia, Brazil, auctioned, and carried to the New World (Franklin & Moss, 1988), and since their opinions of slaves were unfavorable, they could not fathom Africa as the point of origin. This is not to mention that such an admission would counter the mythic social logic that Blacks were inferior (Jackson, 1999).

By the latter part of the eighteenth century, the Great Chain of Being was very popular, commonly referred to as *the chain*, "the scale of beings," or "one's rank in creation" (Lovejoy, 1960, p. 13). The chain is said to date back to the days of Aristotle, but was later developed by seventeenth-century philosopher Gottfried Wilhelm von Liebniz. The historiographical substance of this research as it relates to the present composite of body politics literature is invaluable. It provides an insightful commentary on the damaging associations and primitivity of early race pseudotheorizing and subsequent extrapolations in the areas of comparative science and, most important to this analysis, popular cultural media studies.

If for no other reason, this genealogy proves that racist hypotheses are deeply ingrained in science and education and easily spilled over into early films. While participating in the established dialogic I–Other formation, countless volumes have proven that Blacks had to see themselves as Other; they had to negotiate their identities to survive whether through armed or silent protest, or psychological struggle. In doing so, the risk was, and still is, that Blacks as the social Other found it difficult if not impossible to return to seeing themselves as the I (Gray, 1997; Hall, 1997; Johnson, 1994; Madhubuti, 1990).

Tzvetan Todorov (1984) names this principle, which evolved from Mikhail Bakhtin, exotopy, the externalization of the self as the spectatorial object. The television viewer's watching of the toothpaste commercial as a spectator located in the private confines of his or her own home distances the viewer emotionally and physically. The average viewer is conditioned to watch television without indagating the message, so the commercial and the producers' enclosed racialized message remains innocuous to the viewer. As a result, strategically implanted colonialist ideologies in popular cultural texts need to be strategically deconstructed, lest it remains axiomatic that the "subaltern subject cannot speak" (Spivak, 1988, p, 271).

## BLACK PARTICIPATION IN
## STEREOTYPICAL POPULAR CULTURAL IMAGES

Both Wallace Thurmon and Claude McKay persistently asked that they not be identified as great Black poets, but just great poets. Essentially, they were requesting that their bodies be omitted from the criteria used to determine their effectiveness. By taking agency in defining the self, Blacks regulate how they are scripted. Omitting the body or what I call corporeal elision is only one strategy Blacks use in popular media (i.e., music, film, and television) in order to reinvent themselves. For example, film director F. Gary Gray purposefully does films with multiple protagonists, one of whom is always Black. This was the case in both of his blockbuster films *The Negotiator* and *The Italian Job*. He is not grouped with Spike Lee, John Singleton, or the Hughes Brothers when people think of Black film directors. He is much more likely to be mentioned when people think of the hottest movies of the year and their directors. Essentially, he is performing corporeal elision. Unless we see a "behind-the-scenes" cable television special about the movie or hear about him from a friend, we may never know he is Black. He could easily have an all-Black cast, which would almost automatically cue the average moviegoer that he is probably Black. The strategic inscription and/or proscription of the Black body is an activity that either sustains or resists assumptions regarding how blackness as an optic and political marker is represented by Blacks and others.

The Michael Jordan commercial for Hanes underwear is a good example of how this works in reverse. That is, there are also multiple media moments when a superstar is featured without respect to race, but the medium implicitly codifies the subject with racial implications. This commercial is part of a series of ads for Hanes underwear that juxtapose White and Black sports figures. The commercial opens with two White ladies sitting on a bench in what looks to be a wooded area, perhaps near a park. They appear to be guessing whether men are wearing boxers or briefs. A White gentleman walks by them, and they turn their heads and look, seemingly pleased with his clothed physique. The assumption is that he is wearing Hanes briefs. It is unclear what gives them this impression. Then, to the right of the screen, basketball superstar Michael Jordan emerges, and walks by slowly with his suit jacket thrown over his shoulder and held by two fingers. The ladies look astonished and very pleased to see him. He turns to them and says, "Don't even ask; they're Hanes."

The commercial is laced with multiple implicit themes, none of which are immediately evident. Yet, when applying a critical lens, one becomes most evident to me. There is the popular theme of White and Black male phallic comparison. The commercial does not focus on the crotch, but it is evident that boxers and briefs are worn to cover the genital region. This somewhat destroys the commercial's innocence. The commercial could have easily had all men in it, but two out of three Hanes commercials shown during the same general time period featured men and women, with the women checking out the men and making remarks about the men wearing Hanes, which does strike curiosity in their interest about men's underwear. Is it the hope of Hanes that women will inspire men to wear Hanes because men want to impress their women? That is possible, though I would think not likely.

Additionally, both Hanes men's underwear commercials I have seen have one Black and one White male in them. The Black male is in both cases the more popular of the two, so viewers get the sense that he is preferred. There seems to me to be no other logic that Hanes has chosen the model of Black men wearing Hanes, but it is peculiar that there is a Black–White dialectic present, especially when we consider the age-old myth about White and Black male phallic comparison. This myth suggests that Black men have larger penises than White men and are therefore more virile.

In the Jordan commercial, the actual Hanes underwear is not shown, so the myth is kept intact. The answer to the myth about genital size is unsurrendered.

Lehman (2001) explains the subversive politics of phallic representation:

> The penis in our culture either is hidden from sight, or its representation is carefully regulated for specific ideological purposes. Centering the penis may seem the ultimate patriarchal tyranny, but it is no coincidence that the most traditional men have been comfortable with the silence surrounding the penis and its absence or careful regulation within representation. Silence about and invisibility of the penis contribute to a phallic mystique. The penis is and will remain hidden until such time as we turn the critical spotlight on it; paradoxically, we have to center the penis so that eventually it may be decentered. (p. 494)

It seems odd "to center the penis" as Lehman (2001) explains, primarily because it is always hidden in North American culture. The mystique, when implicitly revealed, is sometimes difficult to detect. As a viewer watching the Hanes commercial, it almost seems to me that the commercial is not about underwear at all. I am no more convinced to purchase Hanes underwear after watching the commercial than I was before viewing it. The commercial, like the toothpaste commercial mentioned earlier, signifies something other than advertisement of a product. It implicitly comments on race and sexuality.

Sexuality is filled with complex signs. One of the obvious extensions is desire. In this case, the most preferred choice is clearly the athlete extraordinaire and beloved stud Michael Jordan over the no-name White character, but his superstar status was downplayed as though it had nothing to do with their demonstrated preference for him as they stared at his clothed body. The fantasy the commercial develops is fueled by the fact that the White women are impressed with Jordan's choice to wear Hanes because they suit him well. The Hanes underwear, however, were never revealed, which teases the sexual desire even more and leaves the question of penis size or sexual interest unresolved. According to film director Isaac Julien, "Desire is always the axis along which different forms of cultural policing take place." The Michael Jordan Hanes underwear commercial is a prime example of how desire registers cultural policing.

The myths and stereotypes that popular media present often go unchecked and unrefereed. There are instances in which the images are portrayed by, for, and about Black people. According to Stuart Hall, the body has been historically used for both, "cultural capital" and "canvases of representation." The willing participation of Blacks to surrender their bodies for cultural capital or for the verification of stereotypes is what I call complying with the illusion. This complicity is described in greater depth in chapter 4. These myths and stereotypes are illusions, not because they are completely false, but that they are literally figments of the American or more accurately, popular cultural producers' imaginations. *In Living Color, Martin,* and *Homeboys in Outer Space* are three sitcoms that have bathed in this reverie. When these fairly recent shows were on the air, it was sometimes hard to tell whether the skits were supposed to be ironical or truthful. While it appeared to be an open forfeit of mass-mediated identities, it could be argued that this form of mockery was pure trickery, suggesting that it was complicit with the stereotypes when it was really a form of resistance. I find this strategy to be more frequent than necessary. For example, in the movie *Great White Hype,* comedian Jamie Foxx turns to one of the lead characters who apparently is trying to intimidate him by standing in his face and, in a half-retaliatory tone, says, "You ain't my father, are you?" Excerpts like this one comply by scripting the Black body as fragmented and unaware. There are numerous snippets like this one that reveal an amazing web of ignorance about Black people and an even greater malicious urge to cast Black bodies pejoratively.

Within any discussion of Black popular culture, it is imperative that scholars, at some point, comment on the "popular," for the popular presupposes public display and consumption as well as public performance. The popular, according to Bakhtin (1981), is not only vulgar, but "carnivalesque." In other words, popular media images, complicit with negative stereotypes, are represented from radio, television, film, and print to gallery art, graphic design, architecture, and the worldwide web, and these negative images are designed to be expansive, entertaining, playful, amusing, and masquerading. Yet, the effects can be extremely deleterious, even when produced by Blacks for Blacks.

## BLACK MALE AND FEMALE BODIES
## ARE ECONOMIZED DIFFERENTLY

Black male and female bodies are often negatively implicated as visible economies even in some Black director's own depictions of Black experiences. Scripts of Black bodies include a dialogue of multiple discourses or utterances, two of which are race and gender. Mikhail Bakhtin's (1981) literary interpretation of dialogia is appropriate when discussing visible economies, since it refers to the interchanges between two "utterances" on the same text. In this instance, there are two very prevalent textual identities, both of which are optic markers, operating within the same text—that of gender and race. I approach this area of concern with special care and probity, because too often Black women's blackness has been the synecdoche for all gender realities. When this happens, the adjectival signifier "Black" often supersedes the identity prefix "woman" (hooks, 1994). Neither gender nor race is an unquestionable and essential category. Each elicits conversations of authenticity, purity, and exclusion. Strategically, these discursive formations designate spaces or locales in which people are meant to live. But, as structures, they are ambiguous and constraining, and surely destined for eventual collapse. While Black signifies what is natural and immovable, the study of Black as a race adjective facilitates porous rationalizations of genetic and biological positioning, primarily because race is a patriarchal, exclusionary concept. Consequently, although I cannot change who I am as a Black person, social categories are in place that privilege some skin tones over others. So, being Black is not as easily manipulated as how I see being Black. This lends itself well to an ambiguous interpretation of Black.

Black male bodies are not just commodities; they are also racially encoded targets. As indicated earlier, Black bodies, as are all bodies, are preverbal texts with corporeal zones that cue personal, relational, and sociohistorical antecedents that are then used to make judgments about how we social interactants will behave toward one another. When considering skin color, hair texture, and weight as corporeal zones, it makes sense that a heavyset, dark-skinned Black male with unkempt hair will cue different reactions than a thin, lightly complected Black male who is well groomed. Our discussion of the muscular minstrel brute and the typically ectomorphic Uncle Tom mirrors this in the same way that the overweight dark-skinned mammy image elicits different responses from the lightly complected, sexy Jezebel. Contemporarily, when we add the variable of personal history or vicarious experience with Blacks via stereotypical mass-mediated images, then we have a formula for racial anxiety as well as sociopsychological and epistemic violence.

Racial anxiety and preverbal surveillance are but two of the seeds of racial profiling. Too seldom do scholarly texts explore the ways in which racial profiling unfolds via these racialized bodily inscriptions. For example, racial profiling has been discussed extensively in the popular media via books, news, films, and so on, but not often scholarly venues. Though we can point to special issues like that of the *Journal of Intergroup Relations* for discussions of this, what is clear is that racial profiling is a nontangential phenomenon that is hidden until revealed via some heinous act of misdirected policing in contexts varying as widely as traffic arrests and taxicab drivers ignoring potential Black male customers to shopping, banking, housing, and academics (Davis, 2001; Kincheloe, Steinberg, & Gresson, 1997; MacDonald, 2003; Meeks, 2000). The perspectives differ as widely as the contexts.

For example, journalist Heather MacDonald (2003) asserts that anti-profiling measures like tabulating the race of drivers pulled over during routine traffic stops have been thwarted to exacerbate a problem that has been concocted by those who have demonized police officers. In her investigation of police officers' perspectives of racial profiling, she unsurprisingly discovered that they feel vilified when all they purport to do is protect and serve. In her mind, MacDonald sees racial profiling as a "collective fairytale." However, after reading books by Davis (2001) and Meeks (2000), it is clear that "driving while Black" is not an invisible issue or one without substance. Davis (2001) presents countless statistics across the nation and Meeks (2000) shares multiple narratives testifying to the existence of racial profiling and the subsequent excessive police force so typical of racial-profiling cases.

One of the most recent tragedies witnessed in the news is that of Cincinnati native Nathaniel Jones, a 350–pound forty-one-year-old dark-skinned Black male who we later discovered had traces of PCP in his blood. According to the *Cincinnati Post* (2003),

> Firefighters trained as emergency medical technicians were called to the scene of the North Avondale White Castle on Mitchell Avenue [in Cincinnati, Ohio] where Jones was dancing and acting oddly inside the restaurant. They called police when Jones didn't cooperate with them. Video from cameras inside Cincinnati police cruisers show the police arriving, then there is a 97-second gap followed by the resumption of the video. The tape clearly shows the massive Jones launching a roundhouse punch at one of the officers. In the next few minutes, police yelled at Jones 16 times, demanding he place his arms behind his back to be handcuffed as they repeatedly struck his torso and legs with their nightsticks. (http://www.cincypost.com/2003/12/04/cfam120403.html)

He was the eighteenth Black male to die during a routine police stop since 1995. In December 2003, there were 16 cases pending in Cincinnati alone, with 14 being racial-profiling cases and 2 wrongful-death suits.

What is hardly understood is that these cases are not about police making arrests; they are about people's humanity being seized. Although privileged White citizens like MacDonald (2003) would like to believe that cases like that of Amadou Diallo are few and far between, marginalized group members marked by class, race, and gender have everyday experiences that tell a different story. Although some would like to believe that racial profiling is disconnected from an analysis of Black male bodies in the media, it is critical to note that racial profiling is merely the xenophobic result of a media-induced racial anxiety. It is essentially an outgrowth of a rather arcane set of bodily inscriptions already transmitted via every type of mass media from radio and print to film, television, and music. This anxiety has led to a parasitic relationship between media and community relations both feeding off of one another for semiotic and symbol-driven information about what is real. Naturally, this relationship has become a catalyst for the development of visible economies of race and gender.

Since the gendered body is almost always associated with flesh, which cues the American obsession with sex, then the male or female body is often scripted in popular media as a sexual instrument used for fulfilling pleasure and satiating desires (Bordo, 1989; Borisoff & Hahn, 1993; Grosz, 1994). One example of this is the SuperBowl XXXVIII halftime show when Justin Timberlake snatched the right side of Janet Jackson's blouse while performing. Despite Timberlake's retrospective contrition, he said immediately after the performance, "That was fun. It was quick, slick, to the point. We love giving y'all something to talk about" (http://www.drudgereport.com/mattjj.htm).

Yet, the male body is economized differently from the female body (Butler, 1990; Collins, 1990; Houston & Davis, 2001; Stecopoulos & Uebel, 1997). Men are valorized in popular media much more than women. This is evident when we consider the recent scarcity of female heroes with which popular audiences have become acquainted. The few who we were introduced to were respected for their "masculine" traits such as "Buffy the Vampire Slayer," the character Storm in X-Men, the character Niobe in Matrix Reloaded, and the character Lara Croft in Tomb Raider, to name a few. Yet, as of late, new female characters have been introduced in The Matrix and X-Men who have been more effeminate, though certainly sexualized.

The antique conversation regarding sex roles, from Sandra Bem's (1993) model to the more recent comparative anatomy paradigms informs the intellectual community that masculine behaviors are those that are forceful, assertive, competitive, dominating, intrusive, and achievement-oriented. Feminine behaviors are those that are nurturing, deferential, polite, sensitive, courteous, alluring, and compassionate (Houston & Davis, 2001). The definition of the American hero is based on a patriarchal model, so naturally, until that standard completely shifts, the majority of those who qualify for hero status must be men or masculine. In a very aggressive marketplace, this forces women to occupy two conceptual bodies in order to succeed—that of a man and a woman. The notion of double bodiness or dual corporeality is without question the greatest obstacle to the development of successful and healthy interpersonal relationships. On the one hand, the female body is expected to be delicate, soft, and nurturing, but these traits limit the woman's overall success.

Director Paris Barclay's comic spoof entitled *Don't Be a Menace to South Central While Drinking Your Juice in the Hood* (1996), written by Shawn Wayans, Marlon Wayans, and Phil Beauman, boldly confronts the demeaning and misogynistic apparatus of pop-cultural filmmaking. In a scene when Tray[1] (Marlon Wayans) is preparing to go stay with his father, his mother (played by Vivica Fox) turns to him and says, "I'm going to miss you, baby." Tray responds by asking his mother if she will come visit him, call him, or just keep in touch. She snaps back, " Now, Tray, you know there ain't no good Black female role models in these movies." The entire movie is a postmodern parody, which incisively comments upon negative popular cultural images.

There are many more films that are much less instructive than *Don't Be a Menace*. In fact, the majority of past and present movies choose to comply with the illusion that women are dispensable bodies to be acquired and spent. According to Farley (2002),

> Nudity is one of the quickest ways to get on top in Hollywood, and one of the quickest ways to be relegated to the bottom. . . . But then again, Hollywood actresses discover time and time again, that when an actress drops her bra or her panties, the sound echoes around Tinseltown. Sharon Stone had been knocking around Hollywood for years in B-minus films. . . . But after she posed for *Playboy* in 1990 and flashed her nether regions in *Basic Instinct* (1992), suddenly she was Hollywood's most prized female thespian. (p. 187)

Even more frequently, Black women function as signposts of lust and desire within popular culture generally, and Black popular culture in particular; this can readily be seen in movies like director Spike Lee's *She's Gotta Have It* when the main character Nola Darling indiscriminantly makes bedfellows out of three different men. Spike Lee spends an enormous amount of time portraying Nola's sexual appetite and exhibiting the three males' techniques in engaging her eroticism. Naturally, this cinematic motif conjures the construction of the Black women's sexual mystique. It is interesting, as West (1993) points out, that "Americans are obsessed with sex and fearful of Black sexuality. The obsession has to do with a search for stimulation and meaning in a fast-paced, market-driven culture; the fear is rooted in visceral feelings about black bodies and fueled by sexual myths about black women and men" (p. 119).

This motif is prevalent among White and non-White filmmakers, such as in the case of the recent Black male-directed blockbusters—*Waiting to*

*Exhale, Soul Food*—and the Black male-produced Oscar-winning *Monster's Ball*. In each of these films, there is at least one woman who incidentally wears the sexiest, most revealing clothing and becomes the primary object of lust. This same woman is ironically scripted to be at least one of the most desirable female characters, yet she is always the least intelligent and the poorest choice-maker.

In Black director Forrest Whitaker's *Waiting to Exhale*, Robin (Lela Rochon) is a very attractive advertising executive. She is not scripted as being unintelligent, but she is the film's poorest choice-maker. She associates with and dates a variety of men, but the ones with whom she falls in love are highly incompatible and irresponsible. One boyfriend is always drunk, high on drugs, or planning some conniving scheme. The other is married, but allows her to be his mistress on occasional evenings, and emphatically informs her that she is not to have an attitude about his laggardly progress in ending his marriage. At the end of the film, she is pregnant, and the father is a guy who is too immature to be a parent and/or a man.

In her examination of the movie, Harris (1999) suggests that the Terry McMillan, the author of the book *Waiting to Exhale* on which the movie is based, was simply trying to convey her personal reflections on the struggles and idiosyncrasies of relational development and companion searching. Harris does concede, however, that the movie can be and has been interpreted as Black "male-bashing," but was meant to be an emotionally cleansing venue for women who have undergone trauma in past relationships. Even as I consider her arguments, I am also cognizant of the economizing of Black bodies in this film, particularly the way in which sexiness is tied to incompetence and ignorance.

In Black writer-director George Tillman Jr.'s *Soul Food* (1997), there are a number of poor choice-makers, but the most obvious is the stray cousin Faith (Gina Ravera), who has no job, and is known by the family to be perpetually in limbo. She stays with the older sister Terri (Vanessa Williams) and her husband Miles (Michael Beach). Kenny is a recording artist and Faith is an aspiring actress and dancer. She is already an exotic dancer and has appeared in exotic videos (certainly aligned with the stereotype of the sex-driven Black women minstrel figure). She is just waiting for the next opportunity to become a star. Eventually, she and Kenny, the husband whose marriage was already on the decline, have a sexual rendezvous in his recording studio on the roof of the house. His wife, Maxine, catches them in the act. It could be said that the husband made the poorest choice, but the cousin was scripted to be the one with the most frequent and severe poor choices. The movie reveals very little about her past, except to say that she is a perennial thorn in the family's side. She is known in the family as the mischievous and irresponsible one who never seems to bring a project to completion. She is the only one introduced to viewers as primarily unethical and she is the only one viewers see partially naked. So, she lures viewers in with her spontaneity and holds their attention with her sexual perversity.

In Black producer Lee Daniels and White director Marc Foster's academy award-winning *Monster's Ball* (2001), Leticia Musgrove (Halle Berry) becomes the object of lust that entices the audience. Despite pre-release attempts to downplay the much-anticipated sex scene with Halle Berry and Billy Bob Thornton, audiences were entranced with the idea of seeing fashion model and beauty Halle Berry in the nude. Virtually every entertainment venue discussed the movie and tried to interview the director and/or lead actors Thornton and Berry. In several published interviews, Berry indicated she almost did not get the part because she was considered too beautiful. She worked feverishly to obtain this part and prove she could play a role that was scripted for a low-income, unattractive single mother and widow. Leticia Musgrove is a grieving, poverty-stricken woman whose husband is on death row and whose son was killed only minutes into the film. Hank Grotowski, a prison guard with a racist upbringing, is depicted as her guilt-ridden savior. He is portrayed as guilty because he was the guard responsible for executing her husband, but as he develops a relationship with her, he never reveals his role in her husband's final moments in the execution chamber. Seeing her impoverished condition, he expresses kindness toward her. He extends an invitation to give her a ride to work at a diner where she is a waitress and he has his morning coffee, and graciously offers to transport her back home from the diner.

Eventually, he fixes up and gives her a truck he had sitting around at his house. He also shows his willingness to listen to her stories about her husband, son, and life. She is grateful for his kindness and friendship. Suddenly, the movie takes an abrupt turn with the critical sex scene in the movie. Hank and Leticia are sitting down talking in Leticia's living room and, unexpectedly, she grabs Hank and begs him to "fuck me." He is stunned at first. Then, she moans and groans, exposes her breasts, and takes his hands and places them over her breasts. She drops to the floor and begins caressing his genitalia. By this point, he is almost fully undressed, and the viewer is led to believe he vaginally penetrates her from behind. In an attempt to make a raunchy scene seem partially romantic, voyeuristic, or at least aesthetically sanitized, the camera is situated low to the ground and behind a table, so that the audience's view of what is going on is partially blocked by the legs of the table and other furniture. After about a minute or two of this commotion, the scene fades.

The point of the scene other than to sell movie tickets to anticipatory audiences waiting to see Halle Berry's naked body is unclear. The scene does not fit well in the sequence of events up to that point and is very disturbing. One of the fascinating and somewhat disturbing tidbits of information about the movie that emerged is that producer Lee Daniels "had it written into

Halle's and Thornton's contracts that if they didn't like the sex scene, if they weren't comfortable with it, the film couldn't be released" (Farley, 2002, pp. 202–203). After receiving some encouragement from her then-husband Eric Benet, Halle approved the scene for release. The scene took her and Thornton five hours to shoot. Apparently Eric Benet was convinced that the scene would be cathartic for Halle who had not heretofore really shown her uninhibited and exotic side. Farley (2002) suggested that Halle and Eric saw this as an artistic challenge and not a moment when her body would be presented in a deprecating manner. Many Blacks responded with outrage and saw her body being exploited (Farley, 2002). It has been falsely rumored that she has been compensated close to a million dollars in exchange for her nudity. Halle Berry's biographer Christopher John Farley (2002) debunks this rumor and writes, "Halle was paid $100,000 for her part. After all her expenses, she would say later, she cleared about $5,000" for doing the movie. The movie was hugely successful on several counts. For one, it was shot for $3.5 million and grossed $31 million at the box office. Even more important, Berry was awarded an Oscar for her performance in *Monster's Ball*, becoming only the third Black woman (next to Whoopi Goldberg in 1990 and Hattie McDaniel in 1939) to have done so in the history of U.S. film. Halle Berry is the only Black woman to get an Oscar for a *lead role* rather than a *supporting role*, as in the case of Hattie and Whoopi. Although many of her fans are elated that she won, it is very disappointing that it was for portraying a character who only complied with the stereotype that Black women are lascivious and sexually charged. She is the only Black woman of interest in the film and, of the few women shown in the movie, she was clearly the poorest choice-maker.

In each of these films, the Black female characters are scripted as relatively strong Black women trying to hold together their lives. However, while they inhabit the counterposition of strength, their weaknesses become paramount. The characters' limitations overshadow the positive in many cases, but they are strong again in the end. The sex motif is recurrent in these films, and many others (with lead Black female actors), that have been released within the past ten years. If it is true that the physical body represents a community of the self, then it must also be true that the degree to which the body is exposed is a political statement about how the self is defined and understood. Sexiness has a scripted definition, which leads the viewing audience to believe that the female character's sexiness is based on her physical beauty, whereas the male character's sexiness is based on his personality, including his intelligence, heroicism, bravery, and aggressiveness. The female's sexiness is determined by the degree to which she reveals her body. That is, a woman who is scripted as sexy is thought to be so due to the amount and kind of clothing she wears (e.g., lingerie versus a jogging suit) coupled with the length and style of her hair. Certainly, other factors emerge, but these are the dominant variables, which contribute to eroticism within popular media.

Black males are economized differently from Black women, usually as heroes, thugs, studs, servants, agents of the law, and a surplus of other images. The one iteration that stands out most in recent films is the stud, pimp, player, and mac daddy images. These films litter the popular cultural genre of film with movies like *Boomerang*, *How to be a Player*, *Thin Line Between Love and Hate*, and *Booty Call*. This short list of films speaks volumes about the valorization of female conquest in a patriarchal society. In *Boomerang*, comedian John Witherspoon is invited to a dinner. He plays the father of David Alan Grier in the film. As he makes a feeble attempt to give advice to his son in the presence of his son's dinner date, he remarks, "See, you can't get pussy-whipped. You got to whip that pussy." This comment coincides with bell hooks's (1995a) contention that much of popular cultural images in the media are "hypermasculine penis-as-weapon assertions." The manipulation of the penis as an abusive instrument is consistent with misogynistic perspectives, which are reified through scripted bodily texts that parade all over the silver screen.

Of the recent blockbuster films targeted for the African American audience sector, *Love Jones*, *The Best Man*, *Brothers*, *John Q*, *Best Man*, *Barbershop*, and *Soul Food* are the only ones that come to mind that give credence to the fact that there are "good" Black men and women who are alive, sober, unmarried, heterosexual, employed, educated, without criminal record, and capable of healthy loving within a monogamous relationship. Some of the latest films, songs, news clips, and books would have you to believe that it is virtually impossible to have all of these characteristics in one Black man or woman. Black female and male bodies are economized differently, but in popular media their worth is practically the same. Black men have the ability to be oppressor and oppressed, so the value of their bodies is often argued to be greater at times. The double-bodiness, involving race and gender, of Black women requires extra work to meet social expectations. I would contend that the resistance to positive representations of Black women in the American popular media is very intense, especially, when one considers that there are still very few female heroes (or sheroes). The efforts of cultural workers are much needed in this venture.

## IMPLICATIONS FOR BODY POLITICS RESEARCH

Future body politics research must critically and carefully examine the production of popular cultural media. Dramaturgical scholars use the term "script" to mean a variety of things. The interpretation of scripting within this book as a refereed analysis of popular cultural production is needed to provide a balanced perspective of textualized bodies. Embracing new paradigms almost always enhances the nature and scope of scientific inquiry. Gender has been a focal point of critical communication inquiry for over a decade. Increasingly, communication scholars have imported the works of anthropologists, psychologists, sociologists, historians, and literary experts to encase our own gender commentaries. Frequently, communication theories have also been exported to define and describe cultural nuances within workplace organizations—and elsewhere. However, gender, like race, poses complex and often avoided questions and disturbs the guilty consciences of traditionalists. And, it's sad that they can be labeled "traditionalists," because the term implies a loyal attachment to a certain historical legacy. In this case, the legacy has failed to inscribe the cultural heritages of marginalized global communities. The nature of this exclusionary canon formation and perpetuation is the impetus for the introduction of Black body politics research. Led by bell hooks, Patricia Hill-Collins, Audre Lorde, and Michele Wallace, the Black feminist efforts within this brand of theorizing have heightened its presence within contemporary gender scholarship since the late 1980s to hundreds of books and articles addressing the topic today.

Extant gender research examines the communicative, sociological, and psychological dimensions of mediated behavior. That should continue, and it should be culturally specific. As with all gender scholarship, Black body politics theory must explore the following: the causes/influences and motivations for behavioral tendencies; the history of injustice to marginalized groups; the identity issues that constrict or expand self-knowledge and relationships with others; and proposed solutions for the restoration of balance among males and females.

Because of the ongoing process of scripting in popular cultural media, it is particularly important how Blacks deal with overt expressions of Black resistance to scripting. Furthermore, how do they extinguish negative meanings about blackness? A few answers to these questions will be presented in chapters 3 and 4. The challenge is to critically assess scripted hegemonic discourses, which only enhance intercultural anxieties, fears, and insecurities within daily interactions. The goal should be to offer a viable set of paradigms, which produce refreshing and revealing discourse about the efficacy of communicated identities.

# THREE

# Black Masculine Scripts

The Body, as the text of signs written by experience and recorded as marks of character, is a mnemonic medium in which are inscribed the principles of the content of culture.

—Hawes, 1998

"Race," as the progenitor of racism, occupies a peculiar position in the lives of African Americans, for truly, we are the reason why racism as a social disease still has utility in the United States of America. It is not because we have created it, but that we are the primary canvas upon which the racist's insecurities, fears and anxieties get projected.

—Jackson, 2000

Sociologist Manning Marable (1995) asks, "What is a Black man in an institutionally racist society, in the social system of modern capitalist America?" (p. 26). He answers his own query by contending that the discursive labels placed on Black male reality characterizes him as a social contaminant. This is an ascription that serves to pejoratively encapsulate his existence, forcing him to respond. Cornel West (1993) would perhaps reply that the Black body is treated as cultural capital and commodified in the popular marketplace. The materialistic dividends gained from exploiting Black bodies are lucrative, while the nonmarket values of love, hope, and collective sharing are dismissed. It is not that capitalism is immoral; it is amoral—it has no regard for morality, only concern for achievement of monetary ends. If one surrenders capitalism, one must also concede the exploitation of Black bodies and the negative projections that drive this exploitation. Instead, Black bodies continue being commodified in a number of ways throughout everyday American life, and this practice is mirrored in popular culture.

As Leonard Hawes notes in the opening epigraph, the body is a text, a medium through which individuals come to familiarize themselves with other human beings. Most important, however, the body has a mnemonic function; it becomes part of our spectatorial memory. So, as people come to know Blacks, they also come to know Black bodies and the degree to which these bodies are portrayed in their varied manifestations.

In chapter 1, I identified and traced the history of Black body politics during slavery and early minstrelsy, and in chapter 2, I defined and explained the process of scripting or inscribing Black bodies in popular media. Now, in this chapter, I intend to hone the discussion to Black men in particular. I do acknowledge that women can also be masculine; however, I want to concentrate on men. Rather than keeping the discussion broad and all-encompassing of the total composite Black community, I feel it is necessary to move from an extensive examination of Black males as they correlate with Black women to an intensive examination of Black masculinity and its interpretations. In doing so, I will look at several highly popular and evident inscriptions of Black masculine bodies in popular culture.

By now it should be clear that the corporeal text is ineludibly complicated by signs and symbols of various realities and experiences. One of the most immediately visible "scripts" or figurative markings that may be found on the body is that of race. Several studies have explored the politics of the body via an analytic technique known as "reading" the body as text. These deconstructive critiques are simplistic in nature, though sophisticated in process. Reading presupposes that there is an already scripted body that can be read by an independent observer from an objective stance. In contrast to reading, scripting is described in terms of writing, so the body is theorized as a canvas, which is written on or scripted by another. The term "scripting" is used to signify that human beings discursively assign meaning to their perceptions of others in an effort to structure their observations and reflections concerning difference. A scripter is usually an institution or individual in a decision-making position who has the authority to develop and mass-distribute images. This may occur via television media, for example, in which case the network executives and/or writers make critical decisions about racial, cultural, class-based, gendered, or homosexual representations on a daily basis.

Scripting never indicates a social condition or discursive act that is irreversibly predetermined, predestined, or inevitable. Otherwise, there would be no possibility for liberation or rescripting. The scholar's objective in analyzing scripting is to decipher what the author of the script intended to suggest when she or he inscribed or assigned meaning to the bodily text. It is critical that scholars understand that the specularities that emerge as a result of the human gaze are nothing more than reproductions of the self, which is engaged by the visual text.

As with all performed scripts, racial scripts are recreations, reinventions, or alterations of the self in motion. Susan Bordo (1989) asserts, "the body is . . . a medium of culture." That is, the body is a direct translation of a cultural negotiation between ourselves and others. When the body is inscribed, a palimpsest script emerges based on several considerations such as how we see ourselves, how others see us, and how others' perceptions influence how we define ourselves. If others' perceptions are their own fantasies and projections, do we respond by acting out those fantasies and behaviorally confirming those projections? Since the body is a discursive text whose meaning is concretized through communicative practices, fantasies that are behaviorally confirmed are treated as powerfully real, and often result in real fears, anxieties, and insecurities. However, what happens when the original text is dismissed, erased, and replaced by a projected or imagined text? What happens when those unmatched projections become social expectations or scripts assigned to others to perform?

Unfortunately, not all scripts are written to celebrate human and cultural differences; some are meticulously crafted to classify, remanufacture, and fragment them as in the case of racial scripts (Gardiner, 2002). The rearrangements and representations of cultural realities promote singular interpretations of racialized bodies. Robyn Wiegman (1995) labels this "corporeal enslavement," "bodies as narrative commodities," and theorizes this discursive disfigurement as an illusion:

> This illusion is predicated on the ascendancy of a visual regime in which the very framework of "black" and "white" designates authentic, natural races. . . . This is a primary figuration of the processes of subjection we now live within, visible economies that too often feature integration without equality, representation without power, presence without the confirming possibility of emancipation. (Wiegman, 1995, p. 41)

Racial scripts coupled with gender scripts produce a rather interesting pastiche such as with the Black male body. The public narratives pertaining to Black men's lives comply with several racialized projections about the Black masculine body as: (1) exotic and strange, (2) violent, (3) incompetent and uneducated, (4) sexual, (5) exploitable, and (6) innately incapacitated (Jackson & Dangerfield, 2002). According to the *Random House Collegiate Dictionary*, "projection is the act of ascribing to someone else one's own attitudes, beliefs, etc." In other words, it is an I–Other dialectic constructed to transfer one's own "baggage" to the Other so that one does not have to deal with it. It is the structured dismissal and displacement of one inscribed body while superimposing another and all the values that accompany the newly inscribed or placed body. Consequently, if the Black masculine body is Otherized and labeled violent, then that would logically suggest that the "I" gets labeled "nonviolent." Within this chapter, we will discuss each of these projections/scripts followed by an analysis of M. Night Shya-malan's film *Unbreakable*, which is presented as an extended example of the "Black masculine body as innately incapacitated" script. The chapter will end with a discussion concerning the present and future implications of organic social scientific research.

## BLACK MASCULINE BODY AS EXOTIC/STRANGE

As Maya Angelou has said in public presentations time and time again, "All knowledge is spendable currency depending on the market." The epistemic violence that accompanies Black male corporeal inscriptions is indicative of a market that chooses to represent Black male bodies as foreign, exotic, and strange. We need only revisit Robert Mapplethorpe's photography exhibits to be assured of this interpretation. In his analysis of Mapplethorpe's artistry, Kobena Mercer (1999) correctly asserts,

> Each of the camera's points of view lead to a unitary vanishing point: an erotic/aesthetic objectification of Black male bodies into the idealized form of a homogenous type thoroughly saturated with a totality of sexual predi-cates. . . . The fetishistic logic of mimetic representation which makes pre-sent for the subject what is absent in the real, can thus be characterized in terms of a masculine fantasy of mastery and control over the "objects" depicted and represented in the visual field, the fantasy of an omnipotent eye/I who sees but who is never seen. (pp. 436–437)

The unclothed Black masculine body is exoticized; his black skin is accented with the right angles of light positioned to direct the gaze to his muscularity and complexion. As Mercer suggests later in his essay, in varying photos, the camera also places the Black male's phallus or buttocks at the center of the visual field. The inscribed narrative parasitically feeds off of the mythological and historical presuppositions of the phallic imago. The Black male's sculpted body is on display, not with the same inscription as Sarah Bartmann's objec-tified Black body in the 1810 Hottentot Venus exhibit. In that exhibit, she was placed in a cage in England to publicly display her apparently unusually oversized buttocks. Later, her extricated genitalia (Chase-Riboud, 2003) were placed on display. Again, the Black male in Mapplethorpe's exhibit was not presented in nearly the same savage way as the Venus Hottentot exhibit. Instead, his naked body appears as an athletic specimen, an iconographic spectacle, an idealized Other aesthetically codifying the hegemonic subcon-scious proclivity to see the Black body as exotic or strange.

Although seemingly tangential, I think it is critical to note here that this preoccupation with seeing the body as strange is the hallmark of the xeno-phobia introduced in early race films like *Birth of a Nation*. As described ear-lier in chapter 1, films like this sought to position the Black body in a space inferior to White bodies. As countless studies of race films have already indicated, the darkening of the skin prior to minstrel shows was designed to psychologically affect the way audiences saw Blacks. The correlation between heinous criminal behavior and dark skin complexion was made clear. There was hardly any positive attributes to be observed in the entire cast of minstrel characters. This intentional sabotage was important because the characters were not supposed to be likeable unless they maintained their "place" as servile, genteel, ignorant, gibberish-talking, lazy, and shiftless utilities. It was also important for early filmmakers to show audiences that Black minstrel characters like the coon could never resemble Whites because, as their skin color symbolically indicates, they were so distantly Black, but the more they act in accordance with proper White-accepted norms of behavior, the more social rewards they might enjoy. To illustrate this, film producers had to depict what life would be like if Blacks did not comply with these stereotypes. This imagery sustained hatred and anxiety toward Blacks to the extent that Blacks were considered, if not despicable, then strange at best. This is precisely why there was such a public outcry about *Time* magazine's digitally darkened front cover portrait of an unshaven O. J. Simpson in 1994 while covering his criminal trial. Incidentally, *Newsweek* ran the same cover without the digital makeover and Simpson's face reflected his true light-skinned complexion. *Time* magazine's antics were perceived as a sensational act of criminalizing or vilifying him before the jury deliberated. The specular representation of Black male bodies, whether in journalistic venues or in the Mapplethorpe exhibit, can be understood as representative of a rather visible historical residue indicative of racial inscription.

Although Robert Mapplethorpe admitted his admiration of the Black male body and saw it as beautiful, it is hard not to notice his visual isolation of sexualized body parts and, within this historiographical practice, what he must have anticipated would be museumgoers' immediate emplacement of the masculinized Black body as an accoutered symbol of perhaps their own detached sexual fantasies, the body's perceived virility, and, in contrast, loathed Black skin (Looby, 1997). The Black male body, at times, is obliterated and fragmented. In some images, his buttocks and thighs are shown so he is represented as a headless, motionless, heartless assemblage. In other images, the penis is the accented image.

With Mapplethorpe's visual imagery, we are confronted with a crucible of interiority, turning our gaze inward and grappling with unmediated emotions. Simultaneously, for some, beneath the sheen of Mapplethorpe's photography, the visual field may conjure the Mandingo image, which is one counterpart to the Hottentot Venus corpus. Mandingo was an African warrior, prideful, strong, and muscular. He is most associated with being a protector of family and community. Unlike Mapplethorpe's *Black Males* (1986), Mandingo was not initially sexualized; hence, the Mandingo image is not riddled with scopophilic undertones preoccupied with flesh. Instead, he is a mythological hero, a proponent of justice. There is nothing strange about that, and somehow that makes him uninteresting.

Unlike the act of being eroticized or sexualized, the exoticized Black male body in Mapplethorpe's work is a penetrating sign, which unveils private anxieties about sexuality and also social fragmentation, for the Black body would not be as strange or exotic if it was placed in the field of normalcy. The Black body is presented as spectacle and specimen. This visual exercise only serves to remind us of Bordo's (1994) contention that "the Black man has been forced to carry the shadow of instinct, of unconscious urge, of the body itself— and hence of the penis-as-animal, powerful and exciting by virtue of brute strength and size, but devoid of phallic will and conscious control, therefore undeserving of worship or even respect" (pp. 270–271). Unfortunately, even in the most seemingly innocent and objective depictions of erotogenic Black male bodies, the corporeal inscription represents a social fixity that makes the act of looking seem perverse. Stares and glares at the glossy photographs of naked Black male bodies incite intrigue and stimulation, and contrarily reminiscence of the social designations and foul patriarchal inscriptions attached to it. Taught to see Black skin as sinister and despicable, onlookers and audiences do not know what to do with a photograph that supposedly can be interpreted in any given manner. At the moment of the gaze and the initial interpretation of resultant feelings, the looker is faced with the responsibility of his or her decipherment. As opposed to images purely evolved from the artist's creative imagination, the photograph replicates the image of a real person, which reifies the interface and facilitates recognition of the common boundaries that preserve the I–Other dialectic and its concomitant discursive formations. The xenophobe, in truncated distance from the objectified Black body, is then confronted with all of his or her fears about both the image and the persons that inhabit these bodies.

## BLACK MASCULINE BODY AS SEXUAL

Numerous writers have participated in lengthy discussions about the perceived nature of Black masculine bodies as sexual (Belton, 1996; Boyd & Allen, 1996; Connor, 1995; Majors & Billson, 1992). As Elizabeth Grosz (1994) suggests about the social body in general, corporeal scripts of this sort can be very dangerous and tend to function "to represent, to symbolize social and collective fantasies and obsessions: its orifices and surfaces can represent the sites of cultural marginality, places of social entry and exit, confrontation or compromise" (p. 193). Thus far, with the "Black masculine body as exotic/strange" inscription, I have explored some of the sexual underpinnings of the Black male body; yet, more in-depth attention must be given to sexuality in particular.

Like the minstrel brute who is sexually perverse and thuggish, contemporary representations of Black males are socially constructed to comply with the stereotype of the sex-crazed Black male.

Earl Ofari Hutchinson (1994) recalls that when some Whites see that he does not conform to the projections they have constructed or learned, then he is told that he is not like the rest of them [Black males]. Marable (1995) claims that there were three major social constructions or conditioned beliefs held by White men during slavery about Black males: Black males are intellectually inferior; Black males are a political threat; and Black males "symbolize a lusty sexual potency that threatened White women" (p. 27). Marable further posited that it was common practice in the colonial era in Virginia, New Jersey, and Pennsylvania to castrate Black males who tried to flirt with White women, learn to read or write, or hit a White man. According to Marable, in many cases, the Black male was sexually mutilated prior to execution. Although this practice is now illegal, one conduit through which this activity is maintained is via symbolic and specular lynching of the Black body (e.g., racial profiling), which is practiced so much that the physiognomy of the Black male has become a marker that continues to cue a very real sense of threat and anxiety.

Notwithstanding the myths of Black sexual prowess and phallus size, there is historical significance to the "Black Masculine Body as Sexual" stereotype. As explicated in chapter 1, historically, when white slave owners wanted to penalize the Black male for acts of ferocity, aggression, or disobedience, they would perform one of two activities: emasculation or murder/lynching. Emasculation refers to cutting off the penis. This removal of the phallus symbolized the denial of black masculinity. Essentially, this would prevent the black male's body from performing its normal sexual reproductive function and eliminate the threat of miscegenation. This also was a primary form of lynching. Another form was murder, although antiseptically explained as preserving eugenicism or maintaining the purity of the White breed. For example, Cunningham (1996) recounts that Emmett Till, a 14-year-old black boy, was hunted down and killed by a mob of White men in Ku Klux Klan robes in Mississippi for whistling at a White girl. Till's death became a signpost of Black racial misery throughout the South.

These acts of aggression against Blacks signified prohibition and assimilation. The slave master's narrative suggested that Black male bodies were lynched when they did not comply. The truth is that the slave's body was at once an object of disgust and admiration—hence, his body was seen as a threat (Best, 1996). His body was used as an object of labor, and, in the process, his body became very muscular. This was especially threatening as it potentially attracted white women, who were forbidden from contact with Blacks except as it related to manual labor.

Author of *American Body Politics*, Felipe Smith (1998) argues that Black male castration protected against the unspeakable rape of the White woman "in the White imaginary" (p. 162). Smith retells the story of William Lee Howard, a Baltimore doctor, who claimed that the "gigantism" of the Black male penis is biologically predetermined to complement the demanding "peculiarity" of the Black female genitalia. Howard further commented that White women were only interested in sexual relations with the Black male because of his immense size and the enduring act of copulation. The assumption is that the Black male will retaliate against White males, who raped Black female slaves, by raping White women. This horrific ontological fantasy and projection about Black men that combines power, race, desire, and symbolic capture is a common theme in fiction literary works. It is manifested in popular culture (e.g., music, dance, theater, etc.) as much more than an impulse. Rather, it is mythically portrayed as a pathological way of being, a fundamental sexual question that gets spontaneous and reflexive responses on an almost daily basis.

## BLACK MASCULINE BODY AS VIOLENT
## (OR WHITE MASCULINE BODY AS NONVIOLENT)

Throughout his many writings, Foucault has spoken fervently about power/knowledge domains in which bodies are disciplined objects. One way to maintain dominion over bodies is to police them and treat them as separate; to determine patterns of behavior, then assess penalties that only apply to certain populations that exhibit that *most severe violative* behavior. Consequently, those populations will eventually succumb to authority. Their bodies, if masculine, will be treated as masculinities in protest rather than *normal*. They are rendered powerless, though the popular discourse still scripts them as violent derelicts that must be tamed.

In the case of Black masculine bodies that have been scripted this way, the primacy of their weltanschauung (worldview) has been interrupted and their cultural self-knowledge has simultaneously been subjugated. After all, once deemed criminal, who wants to hear a narrative that attempts to justify their indespicable humanity? At that point, they are treated as "throwaways"; they are bodies contained in the name of justice. By apprehending power via policing and legitimate authority, and by controlling public perceptions about these bodies, negative discursive representations of them become paramount. These inscriptions are so pervasive that, unlike the uncontaminated White body, even when a Black body has not been criminalized, he is suspect (Dixon & Linz, 2000; Entman & Rojecki, 2000; Hutchinson, 1994). The fascinating dimension of this inscription process is the conspicuousness of this vile discursive and material practice in, for example, the news media, especially when the criminal inscription is supposed to be written on a White male body instead of a Black male body (Campbell, 1995). Let us examine the Columbine school shooting as an example.

On Tuesday, April 20, 1999, "two young men" entered Columbine High School in Littleton, Colorado (a suburb of Denver) wearing black trenchcoats, armed with sawed-off shotguns, a semiautomatic rifle, a pistol, and 32 home-made bombs stuffed with nails and shotgun shells. One of these bombs was a 20–pound propane tank with nails and BBs taped to it so that, when it exploded, it would send projectiles flying into the air. When this day-long tragedy came to an end, the two "gentlemen" had killed 12 students, one teacher, and them-selves. The public discourse about this tragedy was very intriguing. As critical observers of the media, we have noticed that when the media reports crimes per-petrated by Black males, negative projections are revealed in the language of the report. Terms like "juvenile" and "delinquent" are common referents to young Black male assailants. The race of the criminal is always clarified at the begin-ning of the broadcast or article. In contrast, media reports of White male crim-inals are neutral to positive in their use of language. For example, on the night of the Littleton, Colorado killings, I listened attentively to the news broadcasts. *Larry King Live*, CNN, *20/20*, and *60 Minutes* were all very neutral in reference to the assailants. First, there was never any mention of the race of the killers. They were identified as "students," "young men," "gentlemen," "suspects," and "gunmen." Later, it was confirmed that the assailants were two White male members of a school gang called "the Trenchcoat Mafia"; they were Eric Harris and Dylan Kleibold, ages 18 and 17, respectively.

In a series of televised news reports and newspaper articles, several com-ments were made about the nature of the attack. One seemingly middle-class White female resident stated on CNN, "This is the kind of thing you expect to happen in the inner city among those with lower socioeconomic stan-dards." Another gentleman remarked, "You just don't expect this in the sub-urbs." Every major newspaper and television news program in the country assigned priority to this "mass murder" story and none of them even made mention of either the fact that there were 12 other school shootings initiated by young White males or that the self-labeled "trenchcoat mafia" was an organized gang. Somehow, after multiple shootings, it is still surprising that "this sort of thing happens in the suburbs."

This is evidence of an internalized sense of superiority possessed by "mainstream" media outlets. Ministers and crisis intervention specialists were dispatched, and President Clinton held a news conference and later announced that he would "free up" approximately $1.5 million to donate to the families of the victims. Both of the previously mentioned comments cou-pled with the president's gesture were rather disturbing, since they implicitly confirmed the projection that predominantly White neighborhoods don't have crime, but mostly minority neighborhoods do. In addition, Clinton's donation sent a resounding message that some lives are valued over others, especially since the president has not offered to financially support the count-less families of victims slain by senseless killers in America's inner cities.

The link between discourse, ideology, and power is indissociable and is often manifested in our conversational discourses, as in the case of the previously mentioned interviewees. In his discussion of conversation as performance, Leonard Hawes (1998) claims that "as discursive practices, conversation articulates the experience of subjects' consciousness with the meaning of sociohistorical conditions." He further adds:

> Insofar as ideology consists in the ways and means by which meaning and signification serve to sustain relations and structures of domination, conversing articulates meaning with experience, which produces consciousness as embodied subjects at the same time it produces history and reproduces sociocicultural formations. (p. 290)

The personal testimonies and media reports were confirmations of the projections around class and race with respect to Black and White masculine bodies. They also are direct commentaries on how citizens internalize the assessments related to the sociohistorical conditions that confine the Black body. The Black body is consistently scripted as an inherently violent, irresponsible, and angry street urchin, while the White male body is scripted as a young, innocent, and immature individual. "They were just kids who wanted attention," one White female criminologist explained on Geraldo Riviera's evening news special broadcast about the Littleton, Colorado, killings. These "kids" meticulously planned this devastating day of destruction and massacre, but were typified as "suburban kids who somehow went wrong." Psychologist Amos Wilson (1990) vividly portrays the criminalization of the Black male as juxtaposed by the purified perceptions of the White male:

> In the eyes of White America, an exaggeratedly large segment of Black America is criminally suspect. This is especially true relative to the Black male. In the fevered mind of White America, he is cosmically guilty. His guilt is existential. For him to be alive is to be suspected, to be stereotypically accused, convicted and condemned for criminal conspiracy and intent. On the streets, in the subways, elevators, parks, in the "wrong" neighborhood. (p. 37)

For example, about five years ago, Susan Smith, a mother of two young children, took her kids for a drive. She buckled their seat belts and put them in the back seat. Then, she drove down to a local embankment, placed the car in gear, and jumped out. As she watched the car drown in the water, with her two kids inside, she contemplated her next move. She went straight to the police and frantically cried as she told them that a Black male carjacked her and kidnapped her children. The police put out an all-points bulletin in search of this fictitious Black male assailant. Her story was immediately believable, perhaps because it verified the social stereotypes constructed about the Black male. As Wilson suggests, "he [the Black male] is cosmically guilty. His guilt is existential."

Since the introduction of the early minstrel brute character Gus in *Birth of a Nation*, the media have helped to portray the Black man as a violent, harum-scarum bogeyman who often becomes ensconced in a life of crime. Nightly newscasts parade a number of criminal offenders, the likes of which appear to represent a disproportionate number of non-White offenders (Oliver, Jackson, Moses, & Dangerfield, 2004). According to Entman and Rojecki (2000),

> The FBI estimated that 41% of those arrested for violent crimes in 1997 were Black (and 57% were White); 32% of those arrested for property crimes were Black. . . . Public [mass-mediated] perceptions exaggerate the actual racial disproportion. . . . By a 1.5:1 (241 to 160) ratio, White victims outnumber Blacks in news reports. . . . The average story featuring Black victims was a 106 seconds long; those featuring white victims, 185 seconds long. (pp. 79–81)

These authors have illustrated that the public portrayals of Blacks as violent are often misguided and unjustly framed. Several studies have confirmed that the media tend to reinforce racial stereotypes, social deviancy, and delinquency of Black males (Dixon & Linz, 2000; Entman, 1992; Entman and Rojecki, 2000; Gray, 1997; Heider, 2000). For example, Dixon and Linz (2000) analyzed local television news programming in Los Angeles to uncover whether Blacks, Latinos, and Whites were equally represented as lawbreakers. Their results indicated that televised crime stories presented on Los Angeles news stations were biased in their coverage. Blacks were found to be almost two and half times more likely to be portrayed as felons than Whites. Also, with an actual arrest rate of 21% in Orange County, California, the televised coverage showed Blacks as perpetrators of crime 37% of the time. Dixon and Linz argue that biased coverage of this sort solidifies the perception that Black males are habitual lawbreakers, much more so than Whites or any other cultural group. The reality, in Los Angeles and Orange County, was that Blacks were arrested less frequently than Whites and Latinos.

Another study illustrating the social cognitions that have been deeply entrenched in the subconscious of media consumers is one concerning "the face of crime" (Oliver, Jackson, Moses, & Dangerfield, 2004). In this study, the researchers were interested in the extent to which individuals' memories of photographs in news stories reflect a feature-stereotype association or prototype of the "typical criminal" that exaggerates Afrocentric features. In other words, the central investigative concern was whether participants would link "Afrocentric features" (i.e., fuller lips, wider nose, skin tone, etc.) to stereotypes of aggression, criminality, and violence. The results indicated that when given a memory task related to a set of print news stories just read (some positive and some negative), participants misidentified Blacks who had "Afrocentric" features with more violent crimes. The researchers found that when participants were allowed to use facial reconstruction software to select facial features, they would more often than not exaggerate the photo to accommodate a stereotypical perception that those with Afrocentric features are aggressive, criminal, and violent, despite photos that would present some Blacks with Afrocentric features who were prize winners or who had received promotions.

Clearly, this stereotypical portrayal of Blacks as criminals has political implications. Evidence of this politic of representation can be uncovered in African American film director John Singleton's release *Baby Boy*. This film sensationalizes African American violence, treating it as normal and indicative of African American masculine behavior. This ghettocentric imagery is quite consistent with what Lott (1999) euphemistically labels a "culture-of-poverty thesis" in which "the Black urban poor are conceived of as an isolated group of individuals whose behavior is aberrant and dominated by pathological cultural values" (p. 111). Singleton has been heard discussing the movie during various televised pre-release interviews and he has pridefully touted the film as the most ghetto film ever. It wins that award hands down as it depicts murders, group beatings, and pervasive Black-on-Black violence. Even the male–female relationships were pathologized and characterized as violent love–hate companionships dependent on sexual gratification as a means of psychological release from relational stress. Threats of domestic abuse were frequent throughout the film. A boyfriend slaps one female protagonist and the audience is made to believe she deserved the slap. In fact, what Singleton shows the audience is that women are poor choice-makers who are sexually driven, and, although independent, also need to be controlled by a man. This misogynistic film effectively demonstrates patriarchal hegemony and the politics of racial and sexual representation in the mass media. It, like so many other mediated agencies, commodifies Black lives and colludes with the notion that Black families, Black girls, and Black boys are being reared by incompetent, barely educated, barely employed, ghettoized, and deviant Black male and female parents who know nothing of love and so much of violence. The film and its director ask us to view the film in context as one realistic portrait of African American life in South Central Los Angeles, which, by industry standards, is the most violent and incidentally one of few U.S. cities so heavily populated by Blacks. The movie is set in a Los Angeles neighborhood that visually looks pleasant and peaceful. The homes are nice and accented by beautiful palm trees in the front yards. It looks like a great place to live, until we see Black males shooting at other Black males as they sit on a porch or are driving down the street and we are left to contemplate the old fear-filled adage, "there goes the neighborhood."

The politics of race and black masculine identity have produced a peculiar anxiety in the United States. Mass-mediated imagery and cultural production are sedating us further so that we are unsure whether this is "art" or reality. This is also evidenced in the perception of the Black masculine body as a sexual object.

## BLACK MASCULINE BODY AS INCOMPETENT/UNEDUCATED/IRRESPONSIBLE

There have been several deficit/deficiency models of black masculinity, which have proposed a pathologized version of these identities. Oliver (1989) contends that "Blacks are disproportionately represented among Americans experiencing academic failure, teenage pregnancy, female-headed families, chronic unemployment, poverty, alcoholism, drug addiction, and criminal victimization" (p. 15). These social problems, presumably due primarily to Black males, have led to perceptions of Black masculine incompetence and inferiorization. The early representations of Black males as coons suggested total incompetence and, although this imagery was conspicuously controlled by the film producer, some of this fatalism spilled over into the lives of Blacks living in despondent slave conditions. In the present day, it is not that some Black males intrinsically sense that they cannot achieve, but rather the social conditions and mass media reinforcement of stereotypes remind and convince the Black male population that they will experience struggle that is inevitable. Hence, there is still reinforcement of media-induced stereotypes in everyday encounters with Blacks. This leads to a stifled sense of progress. For example, Entman and Rojecki (2000) assert,

> More generally, television's visuals construct poverty as nearly synonymous with "Black," and surveys show Whites typically accept this picture, even though poverty is not the lot of most Black people and more Whites are poor than Black. . . . In this sense news images encourage the sense of the prototypical Black as poor and the prototypical poor person as Black. (p. 102)

The media link Black poverty with Black crime, incompetence, and poor education. These false media images seem almost insurmountable. Eventually, images of this sort will affect anyone's worldview. This is not to suggest that Black male delinquency or deviancy is excusable, but that not all Blacks or Black males are delinquent. Sociologist Manning Marable (2001) asks,

> What is a Black man in an institutionally racist society, in the social system of modern capitalist America? The essential tragedy of being Black and male is our inability, as men and as people of African descent, to define ourselves without the stereotypes the larger society imposes upon us, and through various institutional means perpetuates and permeates within our entire culture. (p. 17)

These social conditions and stereotypes coupled with cultural expectations for Black males can become overwhelming. Besides the social idea of Black macho rigidity (or the tough guy image), cultural mandates on Black masculinity have historically been centered around being a good provider. As a result, a Black male who cannot take care of his family almost immediately loses his "rights to manhood" or is viewed as not being a man. If the stereotypes of Black male incompetence and/or uneducability were true, Black manhood would be easily surrendered. Adaptive and protective behaviors are often employed to counter these stereotypes and have created a dual sensibility with respect to how Black masculinity is defined in Black versus White communities.

So far, the three stereotypes discussed are powerful statements that have a tremendous influence on how Blacks define and negotiate their masculinities. As I will discuss in chapter 5, masculinities are perceptual categories in flux. That is, anyone can be masculine, but perceptions of masculinity in the United States are often made synonymous with bravado and macho rigidity. A negotiation of masculinity ensues when perceptions of an individual's masculinity prompt that individual to reconsider the meanings attached to his masculinity or else maintain and defend his existing perception. This negotiation of identity within varying contexts produces the "in flux" nature of Black masculine identities. This vacillated consciousness is characteristic of the communicative process of negotiating identities. Identity negotiation refers to the win, loss, or exchange of one's ability to maintain one's own cultural worldview. Frequently it is, by nature, an act of resilience to outside pressures to constrict or narrow self-definitions with an adverse effect being a constricted or narrowed sense of self-efficacy. As Marable (2001) suggests, Black masculine identity development is impossible without acknowledging and countering the stereotypes that threaten the survival of Black masculinity.

Scripting the Black masculine body as incompetent often involves several implications related to not being able to love or maintain steady employment (Madhubuti, 1990). After Terry McMillan's long-awaited book *Waiting to Exhale* hit the newsstands and bookstores, many women couldn't wait to buy a copy. It especially became the anthem for single Black women. When the same-titled movie debuted, controversy ensued. Black males mildly protested saying that the book and movie did not represent them and that Black films and artistry must be more responsible with the images placed in the mass media, since there are already enough false representations of Blacks. Terry McMillan's response was that this was her life, her story, and her prerogative to tell it. She admitted that she could not and did not intend to speak for every faction of the Black community. The movie negatively portrayed every Black male in the film with the possible exception of Gregory Hines. Arguably, Hines's role was neutral, although he seemed to be the only unemployed person in the film. We can only assume he was retired, since he was an older gentleman living in a nice house and was in no rush to find a job. After having watched the film several times, I can see how some would regard Wesley Snipes's character as positive as well. He is a businessman who just finishes attending a convention in the hotel where he meets Angela Bassett's character. Snipes's character has a drink or two with her, and, after a getting-to-know-you conversation, they head upstairs to Bassett's room. The movie does not portray them having sex, but the book on which the film script was written does include a lovemaking scene. If we base our analysis strictly on the book, Snipes's character has some redeeming values despite sleeping next to a newly acquainted woman in her room while his dying wife is at home waiting for him to return from a business trip. He did speak of his wife often and shared with Basset's character how much he loved his wife and even admitted he has never cheated on his wife because he loves her so dearly. It sounded genuine enough in the way he communicated it to her. Nonetheless, as a married man, I would not want my wife sleeping next to and intimately holding another man in his hotel room, whether or not they had sex. That is why I have included Snipes's character among the set of Black males in the film who were not positive representations.

One of the largest motifs was that all the Black males were scripted as being incapable of loving or relating responsibly (with the exception of Gregory Hines's and perhaps Wesley Snipes's character). Literary works are replete with examples of incompetent, unemployed, and irresponsible Black males who cannot properly care for their families or lovers. From Elliott Liebow's *Tally's Corner* to McMillan's second novel *Disappearing Acts* to Richard Wright's *Native Son* and beyond, these negative images bombard the literature. In film, the popular characterizations of the Black male are as studs, pimps, players, and criminals and these images are packaged as ghetto culture distributed for mass consumption. Consequently, "the ghetto action film cycle was extremely successful at the box office, producing substantive profits in only a few weeks of theatrical release" (Watkins, 1998, p. 193). This is clearly presented in films from the blaxploitation era such as *Superfly*, *The Mack*, *Shaft*, and *Sweet Sweetback's Baadasssss Song* to more contemporary filmic narratives such as *Colors*, *Pimps Up, Hos Down*, *Player's Club*, *Booty Call*, *A Thin Line*, *Life*, *The Wood*, *Best Man*, and *Brothers*.

## BLACK MASCULINE BODY AS EXPLOITABLE

Frequently, Black masculinity is also politically treated as a site of frustration, pleasure, and exploitation (Boyd, 1997; Boyd & Allen, 1996). It is widely known that approximately one out of every three Black males in America is involved at some level in the criminal justice system. African Americans constitute close to 50% of those incarcerated in U.S. federal prisons, yet they are only 13% of the U.S. population (Pinar, 2001; Smelser et al., 2001; Wilson, 1990). When hearing these figures, we might ask: who is responsible? Certainly, Black males cannot be vindicated for the crimes they have committed, and a racist criminal justice system also cannot be held fully liable for influencing rebellious behavior. However, some Marxist and cultural critics would contend that in a post-industrial marketplace, racialized bodies are commodities exchanged for social capital (Madhubuti, 1990; West, 1993; Wilson, 1990).

The incarceration of criminals satisfies political agendas by building new prisons, which in turn creates new jobs, exploits inmates through cheap labor, maintains social order, and reinforces legal penalties for deviant behavior (Booker, 2000). Countless volumes have been written about the prison industrial complex, so I will not reiterate that massive literature here. I refer to it because of the way in which it has facilitated the politicization of the body and belabored it as a textuary designed to constitute difference (Shilling, 1993). The commodification of Black male bodies translates into direct and indirect policing of those bodies, despite the fact that Blacks, overall, use fewer drugs than Whites (Miller, Alberts, Hecht, Trost, & Krizek, 2000). For example, a few years ago, Congress decided to pass a law that convicts violators with a 5-year prison term for either possession of 5 grams of crack cocaine or 500 grams of powder cocaine. Equating 5 grams of crack with one-half of a "kilo" of powder cocaine was unfair, inequitable, and suspiciously administered to disadvantage Blacks, who were the primary users of crack while Whites primarily used the powder version. The likelihood of a Black person carrying 500 grams of powder cocaine is minimal; however, someone being apprehended carrying 5 grams of crack is a much more likely scenario. Naturally, this biased law contributes to the maintenance of the "one out of three" statistic mentioned earlier and preserves the stereotype that Black males are criminally prone and nothing more than protest masculinities.

George Lipsitz agrees with this perspective and points out another disparaging statistic: "Black Americans make up only 12 percent of the nation's drug users, but account for 43 percent of felony offenders convicted for drug offenses." Essentially, this is one among many ways in which Black males are being exploited as participants in a cyclical, politically constrained public event that perpetually labels them as criminals.

A powerful illustration of this reality and its concomitant inscription of Black masculine bodies being exploited is found in a new board game by Underground Games, Inc., a Black-owned game company, entitled, "Life as a BlackMan: The Game." The irony is that the game itself could be considered a means of exploiting Black males' ontological experiences, though I prefer to see it as an instructive device that purports to guide its players through the various lifeworlds of young Black males. It is heralded by CEO Chuck Sawyer as "the first and only board game to depict life from the perspective of a minority" and "the party game for the next millennium" (http://www.blackmangame.com/text/game.htm). Here is how it is described:

You're an 18-year-old black male high school graduate entering society. Where will you begin the game? Glamourwood, Black University, Military or Ghetto? What type of person, or shall I say Character Type will you be? Creative, Intellectual, Athletic? Do you know good from evil? Will it be Church or Crime? Crime equals Police and Prison. Do you have enough money for the Dream Team Attorney? If not the Public Defender is free of charge. What kind of car will you drive? SUV, Used Car, Bucket, or No Car at all? But remember you need a car to get around in Downtown. There's plenty of Action in the Cards, 360 in all, and it takes for 15–45 minutes to complete an entire game. There's only one goal in Life As A BlackMan the Game? and that's FREEDOM. No more going around in endless circles. (http://www.blackmangame.com/text/game.htm)

So, upfront, you are told that you are the embodiment of an educated high school graduate who is an 18-year-old Black male. You also roll the six-sided die to determine whether you are creative, intellectual, or athletic. Up to six players may participate and all players operate at the behest of the government. By obeying the legitimated state authority that also controls the purse strings, players have the greatest chance of not only survival, but also eventual freedom, which is the absolute objective of the game. As a first-time player, the assumption may be that you, as an 18-year-old Black male, have endless possibilities, just as any other high school graduate throughout the country. However, the instructions quickly yank you back into reality only to find you are given four options/destinations determined by the roll of the four-sided die: military, university, ghetto, or Glamourwood. All of them except the ghetto sound promising, but, even in the ghetto, one may become a "successful street pharmacist" who is never caught or convicted, or one may become a star athlete who overcomes and escapes the ghetto conditions. No matter what the route, decided by chance, there is always the likelihood that the player will land on one of the many squares throughout the board labeled "Police" or "Racism," both of which frequently signify negative behaviors enacted against the player. Players may also find themselves visiting other districts of the game board such as Corporate America, Church, or Prison. Even if all goes well, there may still be family issues like a relative moving in that may lead to debt or the ghetto if the debt is not properly and punctually handled.

Without calculating the odds of being successful, it is clear that the game's creator is trying to convey the intricacies of being a racially and culturally marginalized group member. The game is essentially a translation of Black masculine young-adult corporeal inscriptions. Assuming the game is true to life (and from what I can tell, I can only speculate that it is) and there are six players participating, then it would stand to reason based on past studies that one-third of the players would be in poverty or chronically unemployed, two players would not receive a college degree, at least one of the players would have a fairly short life span and/or be imprisoned at some point during the game, and at least three players would have a low per capita net worth (Blank, 2001; Chideya, 1995; Hecht, Jackson, & Ribeau, 2003). There is a certain coping that accompanies these statistical outcomes, yet, as stated earlier, the point of the game and the concept of "Black masculine bodies as exploitable" stereotype is that Black masculinity is constantly represented as a site of frustration, pleasure, and exploitation.

Admittedly, the game only has so much illustrative potential, since it is constrained by rules, instructions, and guided alternatives. Unlike real life, players have their lives predestined by a mere chance roll of a die, but the game's players must start somewhere and the fact is, at birth, we have no control over the conditions in which we are reared or the parental influences that will help to shape our lives. Although players may still be disturbed that they have no control over their fate; one must remember it is a game, an entertaining representation of Black male life, and every game has these limitations including the age-old family favorite *Monopoly*, which has recently been bastardized in the form of a game, invented by David T. Chang of St. Marys, Pennsylvania, named *Ghettopoly: The stolen property fencing game*. The press release reads:

> Ghettopoly, the new stolen property fencing game from Ghettopoy.com, has thousands of playas in hysterics. The creative, compelling and hilarious board game sends playas round 'n round the ghetto trying to buy stolen property and acquire the most money. But watch out! The banker is a Loan Shark. You cuz may rob yo' wheels. And you may end up in the 'mergency room with bills to pay. (www.ghettopoly.com/sections/news.asp)

The game description is similar, but a bit more vulgar: "Buying stolen properties, pimpin hoes, building crack houses and projects, paying protection fees and getting car jacked are some of the elements of the game. Not dope enough? . . . If you don't have the money that you owe to the loan shark you might just land yourself in da Emergency Room" (www.ghettopoly.com/catalog/displayitem.asp?product=1). The game is equipped with 40 crack houses, 17 projects as well as ghetto stash and hustle cards, and the game pieces are as follows: A Pimp, Hoe, 40 oz. Machine Gun, Marijuana Leaf, Basket Ball, and Crack. So, here we have an interesting dialectic between a game called "Life as a Black Man" created by a Black man to explore the lived experiences of Black men from an insider's perspective and a game designed by an Asian man to explore a fantasy world of Black people who are socially, economically, and morally deprived, poverty-stricken, helpless, and destitute. Arguably, each game may be considered an exploitation of Black lives and experiences. Yet, Chang's game is blatantly racist and so obviously an outsider's stereotypical and morally bankrupt representation of a community about which he knows so very little. Although Chang's game received plenty of news coverage for its carnivalesque images and representations, it is apparently selling very well. Perhaps this is due to our natural voyeuristic impulse as consumers, but I am more inclined to believe that it is also our learned proclivity for accepting stereotypes as entertaining.

There is a sense of Otherness inherent in exploiting Black masculine bodies for monetary profit or cultural capital. The exploitation of Black male bodies continues with rappers and hip-hop artists who conform to the brute images via pronouncement of a thug life and thug mentality. The gangsta rap genre of hip-hop music has become so ensnared by this brute image that artists have begun to lay claim to an authentic blackness and vie for the ultimate thug persona. As you will read in the next chapter, this has become nothing less than an industry-sanctioned spectacle designed to package, sell, and distribute inscribed Black bodies as commodities in the public marketplace, and these Black artists have complied with this act of misguided consumerism (Watts, 1997).

So far, I have explained five projections of Black masculine bodies as strange, sexual, violent, irresponsible, and exploitable. The final projection discussed here is the Black masculine body as innately incapacitated. What follows is an in-depth discussion of the movie *Unbreakable* as an exemplar of this projection.

## BLACK MASCULINE BODY AS INNATELY INCAPACITATED

An indisputable and tragic social reality is that Black men's lives have been pathologized and labeled as innately incapacitated, violent/criminal, exotic/strange, and constantly seeking external validation (Boyd & Allen, 1996; Jackson, 1997; Orbe, 1998). Black men are all too often vilified because of the color of their skin. Racialized images of Black men presented by the media are synonymous with poverty, crime, and a number of other social ills. While it can be argued that huge strides have been made to counter these images, the constant images shown via the media serve as daily reminders that negative depictions of Black masculinity still prevail. It seems unreal that, even at the dawn of a new millennium, the images of Black men continue to be ones of utter disdain. Yet, this is the reality of how black men are presented to the world. These portrayals are vivid and distinct throughout everyday life, especially in popular culture. It is this prevalent set of stereotypical depictions of Black masculinity as a stigmatized condition or of Black males as an endangering and "endangered species" that becomes elucidated in films like *Unbreakable* by M. Night Shyamalan. *Unbreakable* has been rumored as part of a planned trilogy to be distributed by Touchstone Pictures.

Though the images of black masculinity are receiving increased attention, these images are also becoming more complicitous with the negative projections about Black masculinity (McPhail, 1996). In exploring the meaning of projections, it is necessary to recognize the intrapsychic challenge to accept or reject the oppressor-oppressed dialectic. When projecting an image onto a text, it is presumed that you first own the image, which is then projected onto another screen using some instrument or device. In popular culture, writers and directors who show audiences certain character portrayals or scripts, and then leave the audience to interpret, embrace, or critique them own these images. Racialized projections present stereotypical racial portrayals, which represent the fears and anxieties of those controlling the images and commenting on the social contexts in which the film is audited.

Nowhere is this process of racial projection clearer than in the 2000 movie, *Unbreakable*. The movie stars two acting heavyweights—Samuel L. Jackson as Elijah Price, whose moniker is "Mr. Glass," labeled as such because of his fragile bones, and Bruce Willis as David Dunn, film director Shyamalan's self-professed "Everyman."

Every movie is unique in that it presents to the world the vision of the writer and the director (Giroux, 2001). Thus, at least considering the viewpoints of these people becomes critical to understanding the plot of the film, as well as the final product. For *Unbreakable*, the writer and the director are one and the same—M. Night Shyamalan. According to the official website for the movie, the concept from the movie stems from Shyamalan's questions about his own identity. He comments, "That is what this movie is really about—discovering your destiny and asking yourself questions like 'what am I supposed to be doing with my life'—and the pieces of your life somehow seem to fall into place and make sense when you find the answer" (video.go.com/unbreakable/html/making/production.html). I will return to the significance of that statement in a moment.

Of particular note is the development of Shyamalan's characters, as well as the actors chosen to fill the role of these characters. While there are five main characters in the movie, Samuel L. Jackson and Bruce Willis's are the most important to the movie and to this analysis of the images that are projected. Commenting about the development of Jackson's character, Shyamalan states: "I tailor-made this role to his kind of sarcasm, his drilling eyes that glare at you and that kind of staccato when he talks. I literally watched and listened to what words would sound good coming out of his mouth and tried to write the kind of spitfire knowledge that he can do so well into the script" (http://video.go.com/unbreakable/html/making/production.html).

Shyamalan also states that the character of David Dunn was written specifically for Bruce Willis, and that Willis was asked to play the part even before the script was completed. The producer of the movie commented that Willis's "Everyman" image is part of the reason that he is so adored by fans (see http://video.go.com/unbreakable/html/making/production.html). It becomes clear that even in the conceptualization of the film, the writer/director had specific images in mind when creating these characters. The images associated with Jackson and Willis were pivotal in the development of their characters.

## DESCRIPTION OF THE PROTAGONISTS' SCRIPTED IMAGES

Director Shyamalan describes Elijah as "mysterious and haunting." Elijah is a bogeyman with dark skin, thick lips, wide nose, and a hairdo that can only be described as a crooked Afro. He dons black gloves all of the time and is generally well dressed. His glass cane accents his outfit. His pupils are usually dilated, and bluish, although the eye color may be a symptom of his bone disease. In general, he appears weird, strange, and indeed exotic and this is coupled by the fact that he is shown as a child living with his mother in a high-rise apartment building in the ghetto, a euphemism for the projects. Elijah is the ultimate "Other," contrasted by David's appearance as a White male with blue eyes, thin lips, narrow nose, and dark neatly groomed blond hair living in a big house in a middle-class neighborhood.

Although Elijah appears most financially successful as a business owner, he is not shown having property, but David, who lives off of meager university security guard wages, somehow was able to invest enough to own an upper middle-class home. Of course, David does have his wife to assist with paying bills—she is a physical therapist. Another contrast between the two, which emphasizes Elijah's estrangement from the "Everyman" status is family composition. David's background is never revealed, but we do know that although his marriage has its problems, the two parents live together and are raising their child. Elijah's father is never shown. His father is not pictured in the scene of the delivery room at birth nor is he shown at any other point throughout Elijah's life. So, again Elijah offers a full contrast to the life of David. In fact, Elijah can no longer be seen as an exaggerated caricature whose wig is lopsided and whose principles are disproportioned.

Elijah is the popularly scripted portrait of "Every Blackman." As his character profile unfolds, we find that he is a struggling, eccentric, evil-minded, enangered foreign Black body whose pronounced features make him a most feared bogeyman. His disposition is one of perpetual emotional disturbance, driven by his need to see the world as being against him. He is poisoned by this nihilistic attitude, which forces him to have nothing but disdain for a superimposed divine system that has relegated him to a position of incapacity. As Shyamalan stated, Elijah speaks in an intimidating staccato tone with deliberate gestures and piercing eyes, which restate his volatility. He is shown to us as principally "ethnic," a word that derives from the Latin *ethnica*, meaning heathen and the Greek *ethnikos*, meaning foreigner or stranger. His racial appearance almost forecasts his nefarious personality because of how society manufactures race as a product of Black and White, evil and good, impure and pure. *Unbreakable* demonstrates complicity with this artificial racial construction

## UNBREAKABLE SCRIPTS OF
## BLACK MASCULINITY IN *UNBREAKABLE*

The premise of the movie is that a train crashes and kills all the passengers except David Dunn. He not only survives, but also emerges completely unscathed. Then, he meets a comic book dealer named Elijah Price who strongly believes Dunn is a superhero with supernatural powers because of his miraculous escape. After convincing Dunn, a stadium security guard, that his predestined role in life is to protect humanity, Dunn begins practicing his supernatural powers, which are only weakened by his "poison," his fear of breathing underwater. We know based on the director's remarks that Dunn is an ordinary citizen who is scripted to look and act like an average person in any city throughout North America, and, of course, racialized body politics suggest that normalcy looks a whole lot like White (male) bodies. Set in Philadelphia, this film takes the viewer into the lives of these two characters and unfolds a story about destiny, life purpose, and the epic struggle of good and evil.

Jackson's character, Elijah Price, is a presumably well-educated comic book connoisseur who has a disease known as osteogenesis imperfecta, which results in abnormally fragile bones, early hearing loss, and whites of the eyes that appear bluish. As signified by the suffix "genesis," the disease typically begins at birth, as it has with the character of Elijah Price. Elijah, as a young child, is embarrassed by this disease and becomes a social recluse. Elijah's mother serves as his protector and inspiration throughout his entire life. In an effort to help Elijah overcome his mounting childhood depression about his illness, she buys him comic books in exchange for his promise to periodically leave the house, intermingle, and do things that others do. That becomes the only reward toward which Elijah will attempt to work, and it also seems to become his savior from depression. Incidentally, we later learn two things: he takes comic books very seriously and he considers them instructive indicators of real life.

Midway through the film, Elijah confides in David (Bruce Willis's character) that he has spent one-third of his life on a hospital bed reading books, particularly myths as narrated by comic book authors. His mind is enwrapped in fantasia, preoccupied with a make-believe universe in which the scales of justice are weighed by the good and evil committed by persons who are dialectically defined by one another. That is, human beings come to know themselves by seeking out a source of opposition on whom they may juxtapose and justify their own existences. This is explicitly noted in the film when Elijah says, "If there is someone like me in the world and I am at one end of the spectrum, couldn't there be someone else opposite me at the other end? Someone who doesn't get sick, who doesn't get hurt like the rest of us? And, he probably doesn't even know it, the kind of person these stories are about, a person put here to protect the rest of us, to guard us." After having said this, Elijah asks David about why he thought he took the job as a security guard. He gradually convinces David that David's purpose is to protect. David becomes the subject or the "I" and Elijah takes on the role as object or the "Other."

As with any grammatically arranged sentence, the subject or predicate nominative has agency to control the action. The verb directly relates to the subject and is enacted by the subject on an object. The object becomes the canvas on which the action is projected. The principal function of the object or the "Other" is to be acted on by the subject. The object needs the subject in order to be whole. Without the subject, the object makes no sense and has no purpose, so it cannot afford to be passive. It must actively seek out the subject for self-completion. However, the subject only needs the verb to be complete the sentence. This sentential dialectic is crucial for explaining the hero–villain, good–evil, and White–Black dialectics in the film. Each of these pairs is exemplary of the subject–object and I–Other dualities. They become parasitic on one another as they mature. As stated earlier, a villain is nothing without a hero, just as the object is nothing without the subject who carries the action. But, the hero, David, never has to be self-aware. He has no need to discover his supernatural powers in isolation. The villain, Elijah, produces that awareness and that strong desire to discover David's extraordinary powers because Elijah has a vested interest in doing so.

This vested interest is revealed as the movie jumps some twenty or so years later during which time Elijah opens a fine art gallery, which only showcases framed sequential comic book art. He becomes consumed by this placebo, immersing himself in comic books, which seems to alleviate some of his pain by temporarily diverting his interests. Besides Elijah's persistence in pursuing conversation with Dunn and insisting on Dunn's innate superiority, this is all moviegoers know about Elijah until the last ten minutes of the film, during which Elijah's innocent, yet mysterious curiosity unfolds and his real purpose and role as an evil nemesis is revealed. It is rather interesting how this occurs.

After David's heroic and physical powers become self-evident, he contacts Elijah to tell him he is correct about his suspicions concerning his extraordinary capabilities. David asks Elijah what he should do next. Elijah instructs David to "go where people are" and that he would know what to do. That night, in order to save a woman from being killed by a burglar, David strangles an intruder.

The next day David attends a showing at Elijah's art gallery. They go in a back room, and Elijah asks whether the sadness and incompleteness David previously felt had subsided now that he had saved a woman and become an anonymous hero. David admitted he felt great. Elijah reaches out his hand and says, "I think this is where we shake." When David reaches out his hand to shake Elijah's hand, an electrifying shockwave is sent up David's arm and he is suddenly able to see images of all the deaths Elijah caused. This is the last sequence of events before the final dialogue.

The final soliloquy as an act of racial signification is very informative. Elijah apparently is caught in an existential crisis. He is not sure who he is, so he petitions the help of David. The Black–White dialectic is evoked and their standpoints are interrogated. We are assured that Elijah is incognizant of his ontological "location" and purpose in the world. Though he has money and success, he is deprived of the capacity to make a difference. Since he felt he was missing his "mirror" or dialectical reflection, he sought out his missing counterpart in the I–Other dialectical arrangement. The counterpart to his nefarious and heathenish Black male body was a genteel and normal White male body. Once the representational gaze at Elijah's innocence is corrected, we discover Elijah's ontological position. Elijah says to David, "We are alike, we both drown when we get water in our lungs. We are connected!" David stares in disbelief. Then, in the concluding lines of the movie, Elijah divulges his secret intentions when he calmly states,

> Do you know what the scariest thing is? To not know your place in this world. To not know why you're here. That's, that's just an awful feeling. I almost gave up hope. There were so many times I questioned myself, but I found you . . . so many sacrifices just to find you. Now that we know who you are, I know who I am. I'm not a mistake. It all makes sense. In comics, do you know how you can tell who the archvillain is going to be? He's the exact opposite of the hero!

This monologue ends the film, as David is awestruck by the morally debased Elijah.

It is no mistake that David is White and Elijah is Black. The relationships established in this film are intricately woven but simply structured, fixed on the representational and specular dialectic between normal and abnormal, good and evil, Black and White. The director M. Night Shyamalan grants David superhuman strength. Although he is supposedly a common "Everyman," he is scripted as a White man. One of the other fascinating subtextual commentaries is of class. David is a working-class White male sentinel whose job it is to be a guard, or should I say guardian, of people at the stadium where he works. He makes an honest living doing nothing fancy, but he takes care of his son and his cohabitating, yet estranged spouse. He is a father and provider who helps his family live comfortably in their middle-class home. His character is admirable. He represents the American ideal. As the story develops, we find he is able to detect evil in would-be criminal perpetrators, but somehow the evil and cunning nature of Elijah escapes him, maybe because he trusts Elijah as he would a friend.

Just to show the contrast, it is important to reiterate that Elijah is a sequential comic book art dealer and sole proprietor of a plush store located in a thriving Philadelphia shopping district. David is shown wearing ball caps, jeans, and T-shirts; on the other hand, Elijah, with his crooked Afro, dark skin, and bulging eyes, is seen with a leather trench coat and a glass cane. For the most part, although Elijah arguably wears long coats to cover his broken bones and perhaps other imperfections, he is generally stylish. It is easy to get the sense he is at least middle class; yet Shyamalan is quick to show us at the beginning of the film that Elijah is from humble beginnings, having been reared in what appears to be a high-rise apartment building akin to the projects. Interestingly, as the storyline progresses, one of the subtextual inscriptions seems to be that although he is successful and physically removed from the projects, he has only moved from suspected societal menace as a Black male to a very real nemesis and mass murderer.

"Mr. Glass" is born fragile and incapacitated. His childhood disease is no excuse for his fragile morality; that is just the way he was built. What is most intriguing and relevant to this analysis is his racially inscribed body. He is one of our worst nightmares: a success by all American capitalist standards, and just when we began to put aside our reservations about his blackness, we come to find he is actually what the public imagination has inscribed him to be—a vicious bogeyman cosmologically trapped in a Black body.

The final monologue discloses the interest of the film in complying with the illusions about race in the United States. One can plug in almost any social issue that has been correlated with race and it makes sense—poverty, crime, welfare, affirmative action, and many other issues. As sociologist John McWhorter (2000) posits in his book *Losing the Race*, there is a social perception that Blacks have accepted entry into a "cult of victimhood." He argues that Blacks have agreed to a social positioning that paralyzes them and prevents them from achieving success; hence, they do not know their place in the world. They have given up hope and only find reprieve in displacing their aggression toward their own personal incapacities on Whites, asking Whites to serve as their dialectical scapegoat. Essentially, McWhorter is contending, like so many others, that Blacks are constantly seeking external validation to feel complete and whole.

This sort of logic sanitizes racist hegemony, offering an antiseptic ointment that can be easily applied to marginalized group inadequacies and feelings of institutionalized exclusion. Although it sounds reasonable on the surface, it presents a flimsy set of propositions that encourage marginalized group members to comply with negative stereotypes, social positioning, and dismissal of their identities in favor of an altercast that homogenizes Americans from diverse backgrounds and causes them to assimilate.

Movies like *Unbreakable* offer no outlet. They maintain rigid categories of racial polarity while espousing a doublespeak, which appears progressive until penetrated beneath the surface. Elijah is the archvillain, bereft of the capacity to be humane. He is barbaric. He is what we imagined him to be— innately incapacitated.

## COMPLICITY THEORY AND SOCIAL CONSTRUCTIVISM

By using the notion of complicity to analyze the film *Unbreakable*, the idea that "the Other" is somehow *necessary* is emphasized. McPhail (1991) defines complicity as "an agreement to disagree" (p. 2). Complicity centers on the idea that people tend to comply with the classifications and identities that are placed on them; they may do so even as they confront the traditionally accepted norms, labels, or actions. In fact, this may be the case, even though the thing that is being complied with may be inaccurate or downright unacceptable. Complicity then becomes pivotal in understanding how society comes to accept the images that are presented by the media. Fanon (1967) highlights the importance of the I/Other dialectic as a component of this notion of complicity in his landmark text *Black Skin, White Masks* when he suggests that the "I" exists for the Other. McPhail (1991) adds to the discussion the following sentiment: "The other illustrates the problem of language in Western culture in its most extreme form, as a figure made flesh that reifies the existence of an essential reality, a reality 'out there,' separate and distinct from the human agents that interact within it" (p. 1).

Thus, while the act of complicity is essential in reaching an understanding of how movies such as *Unbreakable* work to influence society's beliefs about Black masculinity, one must also consider how complicity is linked to social constructivism. Identity is a socially generated construct. Hecht, Jackson, and Ribeau (2003) note that "identity is defined by the individual and co-created as people come into contact with one another and the environment. As people align themselves with various groups, this co-creation process is negotiated and boundaries, symbols, meanings and norms are developed and modified" (p. 41).

In other words, the self is only created by contact with the other; there must be an "other" in order for there to be an "I." This is where the relationship between complicity and social constructivism becomes clear. If someone blindly accepts the reading of self that is projected by the "Other," then that person is complicitous—accepting the identity placed on him or her by the Other. Likewise, blind acceptance of the images projected in *Unbreakable* signals an acceptance of the socially constructed images of Black masculinity.

The basic philosophical tenet of the complicity paradigm is that all successful human interaction requires balanced and harmonious energy. It is only when two or more energies are incongruent that imbalance and disorder is introduced (McPhail, 1991, 1994). While balance is the goal in most inter-actions, maintenance of balance is a leading indicator of complicitous behav-ior, as is the case with Elijah Price and David Dunn in *Unbreakable*. Price asks Dunn to comply with the belief that he is a walking hero. The finale of the movie demonstrates that Price actually conforms to his role as the Other or the villain. This is clearly demonstrated in the closing lines of the movie when Elijah announces, "Now that we know who you are, I know who I am." Both Elijah and David's identities were socially constructed by others, but more important is the complicity that is demonstrated by these characters.

## IMPLICATIONS OF BLACK MASCULINE SCRIPTS

Implicit in all the projections and corporeal inscriptions discussed in this chapter is the idea that the Black masculine body is viewed as a threat much like the minstrel brute discussed in chapter 1. The brute is considered a derelict who is dangerous not because he did anything, but because his black-ness is a signifier of abnormality. This is ever so clear in Staples's (1994) nar-rative about his experiences as a student living in a neighborhood adjacent to the University of Chicago. He recounts an episode that occurred in late fall one year. He habitually walked the lakefront during nice weather, and one evening, at sundown, as he was returning from his walk, he noticed a woman walking alone. The woman noticed him and began walking quicker. In order to relieve her anxieties, he took an alternative route. This recurrence became obvious to him. He recalls:

> I'd been a fool. I'd been walking the streets grinning good evening to peo-ple who were frightened to death of me. I did violence to them by just being. How had I missed this? I kept walking at night, but from then on I paid attention. I became an expert in the language of fear. Couples locked arms or reached for each other's hands when they saw me. Some crossed to the other side of the street. People who were carrying on conversations went mute and stared straight ahead, as though avoiding my eyes would save them . . . I tried to be innocuous, but didn't know how. The more I thought about how I moved, the less my body belonged to me. I became a false char-acter riding along side it. (p. 202)

Staples is vividly describing the inscriptions placed on his Black masculine body. Before being given a chance, people accessed information they might have heard about Black masculine bodies as strange, violent, irresponsible, exploited, and incapacitated with pent-up aggression. Staples remembered these people were frightened of his presence, that his mere existence, no mat-ter how innocent, "did violence to them." Their preconceived perceptions of him were fixed in a representational gaze that vilified his body to the extent that he felt disembodied or dispossessed of his own body. They read his body as foreign, and, in doing so, began to impose a negative script on him. His body became, for them, an inscribed object with which even Staples was unfamiliar. Their fantasies and projections about his body as a demonic hob-goblin and a horrifying preverbal discursive text were being engaged. His cor-poreal zones—Black skin and nappy hair texture—were of immediate signif-icance to the encounter, indeed his body had been encumbered by their inscriptions, their corporeal politic.

Foucault (1977) notes: "One would be concerned with the 'body politic,' as a set of material elements and techniques that serve as weapons, relays, communication routes and supports for the power and knowledge relations that invest human bodies and subjugate them by turning them into objects of knowledge" (p. 28). When applying this idea to Black masculine bodies, these corporeal inscriptions are politicized, and, in popular media, they are diacritically represented as a set of "weapons, relays, communication routes and supports for the power and knowledge relations." These identities are deployed and negotiated with struggle at the center of the exchange; that struggle is the result of inscribed social predicates. Difference as a pillar of identity is constituted, grounded in representational gazes and hegemonic inscriptions of Blacks' everyday experiences and aspects of being. These expe-riences and personal histories are numerous, and must be explored in order to better understand the formation and maturation of not only corporeal inscriptions, but also self-definitions.

Scripting, like stereotyping, often has deleterious effects. Imagine the child who has internalized the assumptions about his or her existence and has begun to formulate a sense of self by retaliating against misguided projections. This child is already contemplating achievement possibilities. Now, consider how empowered that child will be if he or she can come to understand that the possibilities are limitless, the range of potential is without boundaries. That is the gift that every majority group member has at birth; they do not have to think about difference (McIntosh, 1994). Their scripts are designed to promote growth, stability, and oneness with self. It is peculiar to these per-sons why minorities are so preoccupied with difference. It is because their vis-ible differences are sometimes used as social apparatus for withholding or maintaining privilege at their own discretion (Crenshaw, 1988).

Paul Gilroy (1992) recommends rethinking the I–Other dialectic as flows rather than fixities. That is, rather than concentrate on cultural ances-try and heritage, cultural citizens should allow their selves to reside in the moment, in the location most relevant to now. By doing so, he argues, there will be less historical strain, and our inquisitions will be newer, fresher, and less bound by historical baggage. His offering is enchanting—titillating, actu-ally. As we escape into this Gilroy utopia, it seems liberating to think of our-selves of co-authors of all history henceforth, not just the most immediate history that is signified by a fleeting set of moments with which we did nothing really productive. At the same time, this utopic instant seems anachronistic, as if we have visited this temporal space previously, but have no historical reference point, conjunctural protocol, or discursive strategies for managing the social crises in which we find ourselves. The point is that, by erasing history and its consequences, we simultaneously affect the outcomes, the now. Even if we purge ourselves of the emotional baggage that sometimes promotes nihilism, we still are left with the contemptuous objectifications, scripted irregularities, and materialist practices that inhabit our capitalist milieu. The solution must be more profound than a prescribed historical amnesia. Many cultural critics and popular writers are addicted to quick fixes and half-baked solutions. They are also bound together in this conceptual mode of forgetting, which frees up psychic space to reconsider ontological options, but leaves us devoid and in a space that only remanufactures the current social conditions. Instead, solutions must include remembering: we must remember the past perils so they can later be avoided; we must remember that when we unravel privilege, we have a colonialist subject standing there; we must remember that epistemic violence is attached to a power/knowledge matrix, which includes its own body politic; we must remember that forgetting is ignoring symptoms of a disease that is deteriorating our social bodies.

# FOUR

# "If It Feels This Good Gettin' Used"

## Exploring the Hypertext of Black Sexuality in Hip-Hop Music and Pimp Movies

For the most part, Black sexuality was cloaked in White fantasy and fear. Black women were thought to be hot and ready to be bothered. Black men were believed to have big sexual desires and even bigger organs to realize their lust. White men became obsessed with containing the sexual threat posed by Black men. During slavery and after emancipation, Blacks both resisted and drank in sick White beliefs about Black sexuality. Some Blacks sought to fulfill the myth of unquenchable Black lust. The logic isn't hard to figure out: if White folk think I'm a sexual outlaw, some Blacks perhaps thought, I'll prove it. Other Blacks behaved in exactly the opposite fashion. They rigidly disciplined their sexual urges to erase stereotypes of excessive Black sexuality. . . . They interrupted White pleasure and profit one body at a time.

—Dyson, 2001

Much of the assault on the soulfulness of African-American people has come from a White patriarchal, capitalist-dominated music industry, which essentially uses, with their consent and collusion, Black bodies and voices to be messengers of doom and death. Gangsta rap lets us know Black life is worth nothing, that love does not exist among us, that no education for critical consciousness can save us if we are marked for death, that women's bodies are objects, to be used and discarded. The tragedy is not that this music exists, that it makes a lot of money, but that there is no countercultural message that is equally powerful, that can capture the hearts and imaginations of young Black folks who want to live, and live soulfully.

—hooks, 2003

Feminist film critics maintain that the dominant look in cinema is, historically, a gendered gaze. More precisely, this viewpoint argues that the dominant visual and narrative conventions of filmmaking generally fix "women as image" and "men as bearer of the image." I would like to suggest that Hollywood cinema also frames a highly particularized *racial* gaze—that is, a representational system that positions Blacks as image and Whites as bearer of the image.

—Watkins, 1998

Thus far, we have discussed the origins and history of Black body politics in the United States, the definition and process of scripting in U.S. popular media, and common stereotypical inscriptions of Black masculine bodies. This chapter will examine how Blacks comply with stereotypical inscriptions within the culture industry and why. Naturally, the title foretells the consumerist impulse to support images with which the public is familiar *and* the producer's inclination to feed the public's imagination about what Ross and Rose (1994) coin "postindustrial urban America(n)" (p. 71) Black bodies. The producers' distribution of these images occurs while being attentive to the general lure—the hypertext of sexuality.

Often when researchers discuss sex and the body in popular culture or everyday human activity, they rightfully make reference to feminist and other culturally progressive writings, for they have been the most perspicuous commentators on this subject (Butler, 1990; Foster-Dixon, 1993; Grosz, 1994; Hamera, 1994; Smythe, 1995). In alignment with these scholars, I am convinced, just as Watkins (1998), that there are also numerous other corporeal inscriptions enmeshed with gender and the hypertext of sexuality, including but not limited to race. It is also clear to me that most of the mass media research concerning Black popular culture seems forcibly divided into either audience or producer analyses with not nearly enough examination of how these are entwined. Their inextricable linkage is taken for granted in the following discussion in which I will concentrate on the elaborate sexual inscriptions on Black bodies within hip-hop music and the resurgent production of pimp movies. This chapter might otherwise be titled, "Pimps, Hos, Bitches, Thugs, and Thug Misses: Exploring the Hypertext of Black Sexuality." Although it is about the aggrandizement of sexual dysfunction in Black popular culture, I feel compelled to advise the reader upfront that I am neither claiming nor insinuating that Black popular culture invented, has a monopoly over, or is the sole proprietor of sexual perversion—only that it is a vehicle through which brilliant hip-hop and pimp film artists have further impoverished the conditions in which Black bodies are already negatively scripted.

As I explore the hypertext of sexuality in Black popular culture, specifically Black film and hip-hop music, I am reminded of Bill Withers's song "Use Me," a classic with a refrain that says, "If it feels this good gettin' used, then use me up." Withers describes an ordinary, yet tragic situation in which he dutifully remains in a relationship although he is being treated as a relational utility. His rationale for doing so is that he feels he is enjoying some modicum of pleasure from this parasitic arrangement. One gets the sense his companion is sexually exciting and that he enjoys being used because he enjoys being gratified by her. In this chapter, I maintain that many Black popular cultural icons, namely hip-hop artists and some Black film producers, have developed such a relationship with the music and film industries. That is, although these artists are aware that these industries have ghettoized blackness, then turned it into a commodity and packaged it for mass consumption, they have been complicit with this stereotype. In fact, it is clear they have facilitated this imagery for profit, fame, and material gain (Watkins, 1998).

Withers's song is only one point in a stream of popular cultural commentaries concerning sex and sexuality as an element of a deviant and ghettoized blackness. One musical genre that centralizes these themes is rap music.[1] Rap artists consider themselves street raconteurs. Many of these contemporary hip-hop lyricists regard their role as aural bridges between the gang, thug, and pimp-related elements of the inner city's underbelly and the more diverse and well-to-do petit bourgeois and affluent segments of society. By mimicking sexual freedom, narrating ghetto life, exposing hypermasculine anxieties, and elucidating criminally strategic behaviors, gangsta and thug rappers, whether male or female, vie for an authentic and panoptic blackness designed to expose the essence of Black existence (Wiegman, 1995). This implicit competition within the hip-hop discourse community and in many Black films is signaled by the urban call to "keep it real," which suggests that being down to earth is synonymous with being able to claim and navigate ghetto life despite one's real origins (Hecht, Jackson, & Ribeau, 2003). In fact, if one has grown up in any place other than the projects, very little respect is granted within this discourse community. This automatically allows Black ghetto dwellers composed of otherwise incarcerated voices to be set free to poetically articulate, dispute, and rhetorically reimagine an urban battleground in which dwellers are proud, strong, and most fit to survive.

Nonetheless, while caught up in a digital war to technologically determine who has the top rhythmically impressive billboard hit, most "crunk"[2] booty-shaking video, or most lucid film portrayal of indigent Black life that "keeps it real" while not worrying about getting "props" from music award foundations, artists have become entangled in a moral and ontological crisis (Toop, 1984). This crisis is with regards to the direction and influence of a

public consciousness tainted by industry-driven racial and gendered differences throughout popular culture that have been essentialized. This is the
case especially in the interrelated entertainment genres of music and film
where exposing ghetto life is the most lucrative kind of Black cultural and
corporeal expression.

For example, in a Black Entertainment Television (BET) interview with
filmmaker John Singleton after the release of *Baby Boy* (2001), he claimed
his movie about a dependent twenty-something adult Black male who lives
at home with his mother in a bad neighborhood in Los Angeles surrounded
by violence, drugs, and criminal mischief was not sensationalizing ghetto life,
but merely presenting one story about the truth of ghetto living. He claimed
this is the way he grew up in South Central Los Angeles; this was merely a
snapshot of his life. Later in a series of interviews about the movie, he bragged
this was the most potent, true-to-form ghetto movie he has ever seen. In an
effort to produce, direct, and depict the ultimate ghetto movie, artists like
Singleton comply with the controlling gaze and ominous ideological inscriptions of the Black body as a menace, an act that distances blackness from
everything conventional and morally familiar so that everyday American citizens are assigned to the position of spectator when observing blackness.
They cannot relate to it because it is not a part of their real world. It appears
manufactured. While it represents a real part of someone's life, it is presented
as a universal depiction of what it means to be Black. It is carnivalesque in
function and, hence, remains a rough, tattered, and vulgar dimension of common public American life (Boyd, 1997; MacCabe, 1999; Rose, 1994;
Watkins, 1998). Stuart Hall (1992) explains this detachment as a spectator.
He points out that since it is not of the elite or high culture but rather "popular" culture, it is merely an escape, though spectators gaze at it to remind
themselves of their own comfort. Even still, this distancing conditions audience psyches to associate blackness with civil disobedience, criminal habi-
tats, psychosexual dysfunction, dependency, as well as the ghettoized underclass and to be alarmed when these "malignant" Black bodies are performing
in alignment with "normal" White bodies. The enormous complexity of this
phenomenon is daunting. As Trend (1994) laments:

> Not surprisingly, media villains and political scapegoats are often indistin-
> guishable, whether it is in the implied ethnic criminality of [John Single-
> ton's] *Boyz n the Hood* (1991) and *Bugsy* or the foreign menace of *Shining
> Through* and *The Hunt for Red October* (1990). On one level, it is argued that
> such films help to coalesce an audience around the fear of a common demon
> that throws national parochialism into relief. But this analysis fails to
> account for the complex economies of attraction and desire that also char-
> acterize constructions of difference. As Ernesto Laclau has suggested, any
> entity is both defined and limited by objects of alterity (Laclau, 1991).

> Because the externalized Other is simultaneously a figure of antagonism and radical possibility, it constitutes a part of the self that the self both wants and fears. (p. 231)

So, within a public sphere where market relational values like love, civility, and morality are discursively bound, the symbolic fixity of unruly Black bodies fuels the economy of race relations while satiating audiences' consumptive impulses to be entertained, absorbed, and fascinated by this arcane set of racial differences. This happens in much the same way as the lynching scenario, discussed in chapter 1, during which members of the lynch mobs pulled out Kodak cameras to preserve the memories of the event. In both cases, the I–Other dialectic is engaged with audience members both co-producing and validating the lynching while remaining its spectators.

Curiously entangled in this dialectic are Black bodies that have come to access themselves via the discursive inscriptions promulgated by popular media (Wiegman, 1990). Moreover, they have come to see themselves as victims desiring what appears to be a far-fetched indeterminacy and sense of agency to define and create their own realities (Smith, 1998). Consequently, estranged Black bodies in popular culture too rarely transcend the surfaces of their imposed inscriptions and thus are forced to cohabitate and become complicit with a manufactured ontological double. If they are not exoticized through popular motifs like singing, dancing, playing sports, or being criminalized, then Black bodies are sexualized (Dyson, 1994; George, 1992; Tate, 1992; Watkins, 1998).

Popular culture, particularly film and music, is littered with intoxicating hedonistic images, patriarchal imprints, and occasionally aesthetically sanitized inscriptions of Black bodies (Watkins, 1998). In fact, Gray (1989) and Gilroy (1990) remind us that film and music are powerful conduits through which individuals are introduced to localized conceptions of attenuated blackness. These institutionally sanctioned conceptions parade as authentic notions of a Black self. Within this chapter, I will explore notions of Black authenticity, a theory of complicity, and Black bodies as sites of sexual eroticism, exoticism, and objectification in Black popular culture.

## BLACK AUTHENTICITY AND ESSENTIALISM

In the popular phrases, "I'm representin," "keepin' it real," or "stay Black," the predicates describing who one is representing, how real is defined, or what Black means are omitted. This begs the question of authenticity, of what is true, what is real, verifiable, and constitutive of blackness that makes it automatically so. The presumption is that we need not explicate or interrogate issues of representation, the realness, or blackness—they are terms already reduced to their immediately interpretable meanings. However, the omission becomes even more conspicuous when we begin discussion of Black cultural *expression*, or *the* Black *experience*. The glaring fact that there is singularity inherent in each of these constructions, when they both should be rightfully pluralized, is what is meant by essentialism. In defining the immutable essence of a thing, by Western standards, it can be put to a valid test of systematic observation, which will prove its accuracy and veracity. If it does not meet these tests, then it is considered untrue and inauthentic. Certainly, it is clear that blackness among Blacks is most well understood within its cultural and cosmological parameters. The primary concern, however, is how Black corporeal inscriptions produced by Blacks sometimes parade as authoritative reflections of *true* blackness when they only represent a fractional set of what Black means. Examples of this are ghettocentric representations of blackness promoted as being indicative of "real" Black life (Boyd, 1997; Costello & Wallace, 1990; Krims, 2000). For instance, thug rapper Trick Daddy (2001) raps about his representation of thuggery during a song entitled "I'm a Thug" on his album *Thugs Are Us*. He explains how his clothing and sported gold teeth are only minor indicators of his thuggery. Instead he is a thug because of how he grew up.

English and Africana Studies Professor Mark Anthony Neal (2002) discusses his exploratory in-class focus group of student perceptions concerning hip-hop and indicates, "Many students feel that if you don't have an attitude, if you don't act a certain way, if you aren't from the ghetto, the perception is that you are not Black" (p. 188). He further comments,

> Some of those who embrace [rapper] DMX include relatively well-off middle-class Black young people who may be bound for professional careers, but crave acceptance by their Black peers and have also based their perceptions of blackness on hip-hop video and the 'ghettocentric noir' cinema. As a result, whatever its salutary impulses, there is a cost to this ghettocentric romance, as if Black urban youth somehow define the essence of the Black experience. (p. 188)

Neal's (2002) reflections concerning the opinions of his students, whom he calls post-soul babies, are insightful. While trying not to appear didactic or effusive with regards to what authenticity means, I think it is important to be mindful of encoded commentaries concerning authenticity before framing the following discussion with complicity theory.

In an attempt to decipher and explain what is real in the imaginary, metacommunicative universe of popular culture, Black hip-hop artists and Black filmmakers have frequently drawn boundaries between the authentic and inauthentic (Dyson, 1996). These arbitrary demarcations are well justified in their minds, since ghetto perpetrators are frustratingly discomfiting to these artists, because *true* thugs are making money telling their own true stories while *impostors* lie about ghetto experiences and make ghetto life experiences seem surreal. For example, while asserting their ownership of an authentic thug experience, thug hip-hop artists Jay-Z, Ja-Rule, and Earl "DMX" Simmons discuss their disconcertion with thug imposters in their song entitled, "Murdergram." They explain that "squares" would never understand their thug lifestyle, because they have never had to struggle in a climate where despondency and nihilism are the norm. This comment is also in response to the ever-increasing presence of Black crossover artists who allegedly have "sold out" the Black community and began writing and performing for a broader market including White audiences. The criticism is concerning the supposedly profligate and indignifying nature of crossover artistry, how it taints the artistic elements of hip-hop production by forfeiting and diluting the essence of blackness. In order to thoroughly understand this indictment, one would have to be acquainted with the humble beginnings of rap music when rappers would sell their homemade rap music cassette tapes out of their trunks (Cummings & Roy, 2002; Perkins, 1996). They desired larger distribution, but many of them were not willing to seek this distribution at the cost of their allegiance to maintaining their own voice and "keepin' it real."

Now that rap and hip-hop music have gained prominence for their straight-no-chaser, hardcore approach to narrating urban life, there are impersonators who want to appear "ghetto" or claim their attachment to ghetto life when in fact they have never lived in the ghetto and have only walked through it, at most (Kitwana, 2002). So, Black authenticity in this regard calls into question discursive points of disarticulation and implies that this mimicry bastardizes blackness. By compromising notions of physical and ontological space and place, impersonating artists jeopardize the authenticity, the realness, of Black ghetto life as depicted by *true* thug-centered rap and cinema. The question is: Who will tell the true ghetto life stories? The controversial and interrogatory reply is, "Does it make them less Black because they tell a different story? Moreover, how do we know what is true and why does it matter who tells the story?"

Authenticity and essentialism issues are neither new in hip-hop music, nor in Black popular culture. Scholars like Michael Eric Dyson (1994), Cornel West (1993), and Paul Gilroy (1990), among others, have addressed this extensively throughout the years. What is new is how authenticity claims emerge not only in hip-hop music, but also in Black pimp films, both of which seek to expose Black male sexual domination over Black females and therefore remain complicit with early White hegemonic inscriptions of Black bodies.

## A BRIEF NOTE ON COMPLICITY THEORY

According to its progenitor Mark McPhail (1991), the idea of complicity "manifests itself in terms of an adherence to the problematical ideological assumptions of position and privilege inherent in critical discourse" (p. 5). As discussed in the earlier example about *Unbreakable*, Blacks become complicit with negative inscriptions of their bodies when they uncritically adopt structures designed to demean or essentialize blackness.

Toward their recovery from this inscriptive damage, McPhail (1998) recommends "coherent integration of similarity and difference" (p. 115), which will result in a more sophisticated, holistic, and revelatory understanding of cosmological nuances. This demands that individuals situate notations of self and other on a continuum of thinking about racialized bodies but does not privilege one cosmic glance over another. McPhail argues that this is especially necessary of popular culture. When examining sexuality in hip-hop music and film, it is axiomatic to decipher representations of subject and object, elite and subaltern, but also the internal contradictions attendant to these inscriptions.

By using the notion of complicity to analyze thug personae and the pimp–whore complex, "the Other" is necessarily emphasized as both subject and object when speaking of marginalized group persons. McPhail (1991) adds to the discussion the following sentiment: "The other illustrates the problem of language in Western culture in its most extreme form, as a figure made flesh that reifies the existence of an essential reality, a reality 'out there,' separate and distinct from the human agents that interact within it" (p. 1). Reclamation of agency is not always liberatory however. Sometimes it can inspire the manufacturing of an equally debased and elitist subjectivity, which leads directly to multitudinous objectifications. Such is the case with the brutish personae of the thug, ruffneck, and pimp, each of whom attempts to retrieve agency only to become complicit with patriarchal inscriptions that deny others their dignity and respect.

## THUGS AND ROUGHNECKS AS
## CONTEMPORARY BRUTES AND
## SEXUAL SUPERINTENDENTS

The thug or ruffneck is a contemporary manifestation of the contumacious brute image, and the thug image is enjoying an epoch in which it is able to captivate audiences of rap fans throughout the world (Ogg & Upshall, 2001). Consequently, thug-related themes have become commonplace in rap and hip-hop music. It did not begin with present-day hip-hop music; it is the contemporary musical brainchild of militant 1960s poet pioneers such as Sonia Sanchez, Haki Madhubuti (nee Don Lee), Gil Scott Heron, and *The Last Poets*, as well as gangsta rap pioneers N.W.A. (Niggas wit Attitudes), who are said to be the first to use the term on their song "Gangsta, Gangsta" (George, 1998). Their obscene antics may be attributed to forerunner Luke "Sky-walker" Campbell, who was probably the first to appropriate and market sex-shock in rap music on a global scale with men and women having sex on stage at his concerts (DeCurtis, 1999). He was the archetypal rap artist-pimp publicly overseeing sexual coupling. This interloping was recast as simply obscene and became the subject of a high-profile First Amendment trial (Perkins, 1996). Regardless of the outcome, which tremendously slowed his multicity tour, almost bringing it to an end, Luke Campbell proved just how potent sexually charged rap music could and would become, and precociously introduced a new brand of "rump-shaking" that would continue to rise to different levels of aggressiveness with thug rap (Ogg & Upshall, 2001).

In fact, as Tricia Rose (1994) maintains, "hip-hop articulates a sense of entitlement and takes pleasure in aggressive insubordination" (p. 60). A spin-off of gangsta rap music, the thug role is a vivid manifestation of that "aggressive insubordination." Thugs perpetuate the myth of a socially sanctioned Black male warrior, who, by mere coincidence, is also sexually charged. As both Trend (1994) and Bates and Garner (2001) suggest, it is entirely too uncritical to assert that entertainment audiences are so engulfed by the venue and "irresistibly drawn to violence" (p. 138) and sexism that they become completely unaware of their consumption of these hegemonic images. Audiences' attraction to certain pedestrian images are not accidental. People make choices to engage their negative and arguably counterproductive specularity of race and gender. As a result, when we hear hip-hop music lyrics referring to the thug, ruffneck, O. G. or G. (i.e., original gangsta or gangsta, respectively), we should not be surprised that we simultaneously hear laudatory labels like "pimp," "mack,""playa," "big baller," and "dog,"[3] several of which refer mainly to his acquisition of cash, in addition to the male's sexual conquest of women and/or the whole mystique of his genital enormity (George, 1998). This is characteristic of popular rappers like Trick Daddy, Tupac, 50 Cent, Jay-Z, Snoop Doggy Dog, the Lox, Dr. Dre, Cash Money Millionaires, Treach from Naughty By Nature, Nas, Ludacris, and Nelly. Each of their scabrous public personae revolves around a ghettocentric personality that accents material wealth gained by previously struggling urban youth who have now superseded those despondent and uncertain conditions (Jones, 1991; Kelley, 1997). As their televised videos demonstrate, they are also lascivious pimps who without fail are surrounded by beautiful, often sculpted, scantily clad females. These females have four primary functions as they gyrate and genuflect throughout the video—to engage the audience's voyeuristic gaze, to embody the apparatus of sexual pleasure, to fuel the fantasies and imaginations about her innately lascivious nature, and to serve as instruments controlled by the thug. Ja Rule demonstrates this last point in his song, "Bitch Betta Have My Money," in which he likens himself to the infamous pimp Iceberg Slim, and suggests that his pimping of women is just part of the game. Ja Rule and Case explain the thug mentality in another song entitled "Thug Life." In this song, they forthrightly declare their awareness that thuggish behaviors and treatment of women are inappropriate, but they rationalize that resistence requires lawlessness. A thug, by nature, does not abide by the rules, and that is a work of pride, not disdain.

Thugs seek to reposition the Black male body as being in control of himself and *his* women. I purposefully wrote "women," to suggest that a thug never commits to one woman because then he would not be a "playa"; he would be weak or soft as sensitive, loving, nurturing, and monogamous, and it is contrary to the definition of the mack to be weak. One of the hallmark characteristics of a thug is his desensitization, his emotional paralysis. In other words, a thug does not feel, except when his territory (i.e., family, physical space, or physical person) is threatened. Thugs see themselves as being committed, not necessarily to the community in terms of enhancing its infrastructure, but to "keeping it real" by remembering the people, the dilapidated housing projects, and the "hard knocks" lifestyle and exemplifying this remembrance via their clothing, hair styles, walk, talk, improvisational discourse, dances, and virtually every conceivable dimension of their lives. With exceptions like rapper-turned-president/CEO of Def Jam Recordings Jay-Z who has continually returned to his New York community to "give something back," many contemporary rappers who identify with the thug profile somehow have convinced themselves they have taken agency in lifting up their communities by claiming their origins in the ghettoes, which supposedly ensures that they have not forgotten their Black heritage. To prove this, they make gallant attempts to define their realities and rescript their Black bodies; instead, however, they have only complied with the stereotypical illusions about Black male bodies as violent, irresponsible, and lewd. Even though the mostly oversized prison-inspired apparel, Timberland boots, and regionally defined accessories (i.e., bandanas, gold teeth, cornrows, etc.) accompany the thug image for some and immediately conjure negative images, they are merely the epicenter of a more arcane inscription— the essentialism of the Black male image and presentation of it in consonance with the archetypal minstrel brute belonging exclusively to the underclass.

Mark Anthony Neal (2002) tries to unravel the magnetism some segments of the general population who do not belong to the underclass have toward performances that glorify thug life:

> I have plenty of students who embrace DMX as a viable [role] model, and not all of them hail from the ghetto or live the less savory side of life that DMX and his lyrics embody. The natural question is, why would working- and middle-class Black college students embrace such a figure. It doesn't quite take away all the mystery to ask the parallel question: Why do so many White middle- and upper-middle class students embrace the Smashing Pumpkins, Aerosmith or Marilyn Manson? (p. 187)

The thug is compelling because of his ruggedness and his authentic ghetto-centrism. Rappers DMX & Dyme's song "Good Girls, Bad Guys" on DMX's . . . *and then there was* X album explains why some women are attracted to thugs.

Female rapper Dyme, whose name has become synonymous with a sexy and attractive non-ghetto "good girl," is in dialogue with DMX. In this exchange, Dyme expresses how DMX's thuggish, edgy, hardcore bad boy image lures her into being a rebel. Everything from his daredevil antics to how he sexes her body to even his thug uniform of Timberland boots and jeans excites her. He admonishes her to rethink her choices, which apparently are either being with a straight-laced, genteel, law-abiding citizen who probably will not be able to sexually satisfy her or with a fearless, sexually outrageous thug who can make her feel safe. Against all odds, she chooses the thug.

The thug is a modern brute, which is revered for his Stagoleean[4] disposition and feared for his out-of-control, haphazard, and volatile behavior. He is uncontrollable and that aspect of his personality becomes mysteriously attractive to some dymes. Perhaps it is impulsively connected to their internal desire to feel assured that they will always be protected and safe from external harm and, if properly guided by her, the thug or ruffneck can prove to be a strong and positive father, and strong husband to the dyme or "dyme-piece" as she is sometimes called. Although the sporadic behavior of the thug does not promise the regularity that childrearing requires, his bar-none attitude adds a sense of security that a non-thug may not be able to supply. This is his lure, but it comes at the price of his being noncommittal, which eventually contributes to the dissolution and incohesion of Black families. It also leads to the steadied perpetuation of negative Black masculine scripts.

## THUG MISSES

Unlike the weak character disposition of the dyme, thug misses are no domesticated armpieces to be sported by the thug, because they, too, are thugs. According to Dyson (1996) and Rose (1994), these female thugs are prophetic in their unrelenting resistance to the undercurrent of male dominance and female submission. In an effort to formulate and enact a subversive politic that disputes the pandemic paternalism of hip-hop's old boy's network, the most popular and rising cadre of female rappers and hip-hop artists have labeled themselves "gangsta bitches" (Shelton, 1997, p. 111). In much the same way Black power and civil rights activists and conscious musicians like James Brown repossessed the until-then negative term "Black," making it positive with the slogan "I'm Black and I'm Proud," or in the same way that Eve Ensler's *Vagina Monologues* rescues women's agency by purging, then claiming, initially invective epithets like cunt, bitch, and pussy, "gangsta bitches" have decided to take the derisive term "bitch" and used it to refer to women who are angered by some women's passive resistance strategies or simply acceptance of patriarchal abuse. They are boisterously and boldly exclaiming, "Yeah, I am that bitch you are talking about, so what's your point?" This is never so clear as it is in Lil Kim's (2000) song "Suck my Dick" on her album *The Notorious Kim*. She boldly asserts that people from the projects know that a rough exterior is the ultimate badge of dominance, and if men can do it, then why not women? She turns the patriarchal discourse topsy turvy and suggests she is the real mack.

Lil Kim is representative of a set of female hip-hop thug artists that I will call *thug misses*[5] and ruff ryders.[6] They have developed a trendy erotogenic persona of the no-nonsense "around-the-way" or ghettoized girl. The seemingly endless list of such artists includes popular hip-hop artists Lil Kim, Foxy Brown, Ciara, Da Brat, Khia, Eve, Gangsta Boo, Missy Misdemeanor Elliott, and the FlipMode Squad (including Rah Digga, Groove Armada, and Trina). The words "hard," "raw," and "sexy" best describe the perverse scripting of thug misses' Black bodies. They are reactive, young, Black "down-for-whatever" females who, like their thug and ruffneck counterparts, are inviolable ruffians supposedly ready for any kind of confrontation or challenge, physical or otherwise. As they "hit the chronic" and "grip the 40s," and do the things the male rappers do, they are using these gestures as an "alternative economy," perhaps even a "prop" (Shelton, p. 111), but, for them, it is part of the ensemble that constitutes the thug image. It comes along with the "black net cleavage, flawless skin, and coiffed hair" (Shelton, p. 113) that bespeaks a certain maturity one might expect of a male-scripted heroine; however, it is their creation. Essentially, they see themselves as warrior-princesses. The mythic Xena, princess warrior would be considered too soft for their tastes, but the idea resonates. Instead, thug misses are ghetto soldiers with an involutive split personality, both delicate and sexually pornographic as well as courageous and bold. They are not necessarily promiscuous, just defined by their raw, sexualized disposition.

Even more profound is the masochism inherent in this sumptuous interplay of difference and devaluation. The Black female rap artist has always functioned on the periphery of the rap music industry, so this re-produced image is meant to retrieve her agency and prove her worthiness while formulaically attracting consumers, because it is what consumers are used to viewing—Black women's bodies objectified and sexualized. Of the thug misses listed earlier, Rah Diggah, who perhaps is most like Xena, is the least likely to be scantily clad. She intentionally evacuates the site where her Black female body is seen as simply an object of male pleasure and attempts to teach her audience that thugging requires revolution and involves being in control. Self-perceived as one who will lead females away from their colonized location, their site of suffering, through being a thug, Rah Diggah calls herself "the Harriett Tubman of hip-hop" in her song "Do the Ladies Run This." Incidentally, even the title of the album signifies her interest in re-emplacing the anteriority or leadership of Black women in cultural production. In the vein of Homi Bhabha's (1992) postcolonial lines of thought, she, along with other thug misses, is attempting "to speak Outside the sentence or the sententious . . . to disturb the causality" (p. 56) and to mount a subaltern rebellion.

Rah Diggah was dubbed by *YRB* (Kandi, 2002) fanzine as the "Harriett Thugman" of hip-hop. She perceives herself as an insurrectionist, repossessing her Black body by taking control over her own lyrics and thug persona. In concert with this thug image, she also has developed a creative gangsta line of clothing called Rugged Apparel, combining cross-stitched jeans with chain-link chokers and sterling zippers and buttons topped off with a half-cocked brim.

On her debut album *Dirty Harriet*, she proclaims her own independence from male approval and asserts her own lyrical skill on being on par with anyone. By keeping her persona "gangsta," she ensures that audiences will see her as neither weak, tender, nor overly effeminate or one who is able to be overlooked. As an aside, the audiences she is directing her message at are mostly those that have come to be known as the "Black youth culture" despite the fact that non-Blacks represent the majority of gangsta music consumers (Harper, 1996; Watkins, 1998). As mentioned previously, Digga attempts to counter the sexualized image that often accompanies the thug miss persona, and simply asserts herself as hardcore and lyrically savvy. In this sense, as Pozner (1997) explains in her analysis of Xena, "she neither denies nor exploits her own sexuality" (p. 13).

Somehow by seizing their own licenses to rescript the Black female body to be able to inflict torment while appearing impervious to pain, thug misses accomplish a subversive politic of corporeal representation and see themselves as having arisen as heroines in their own right among rap audiences, rather than forgotten shadows of the thug or simply objects of sexual commodification. Thug misses are modern hybrids of the Sapphire, Jezebel, and brute. They are self-assured, independent, sexy, bad girls who supposedly do not tolerate nonsense. Unfortunately, this inversion of a codified patriarchy is underwhelming at times and so slippery that it can be easily be read as unimaginative and counterproductive. Although it is perhaps initially exciting to hear female rappers "rock mics" using the same formula of taunting the competition, exposing bravado, and skillfully rhyming about familiar themes, that does not take away from the fact that the formula is not inventive. Nonetheless, innovative capitalization and enhancement of the thug image become the principal claim of female thug rappers. By eroticizing a hegemonic thug fantasy and embodying it with a female standpoint, thug misses may have only divested themselves of any possibility of reclaiming true agency. Instead, they put themselves at risk to become lost once again in the shadows, but this time in their own poisoned reinvention of Black female bodies' sexual mystique. To put it plainly, in many ways, the scripting of the Black female body in hip-hop as a thug is derivative at best. It is merely emblematic of a master narrative—old-guard male representations of women as feisty, overreactive, sexualized mistresses. So, hip-hop women's counter-narrative occupies a space that simply aligns with the master narrative rather than running against it as we suspected it would.

Whether thugs or thug misses, the contemporary brute image remains well intact. It is pervasive throughout Black popular culture and is one of the most intricate images to be found because of its admirable resilience in the face of tribulation as well as its frequently demonstrative counteraffectionate, uncivil, unruly, and irresponsible inscriptions. For example, popular cultural images have taught consumers that the average thug does not see women as potential companions deserving of commitment and love; instead they are considered "bitches," and as such are mere commodities. Rap artists DMX & Sisquo (1999) articulate this point in the song "What These Bitches Want" on DMX's album ". . . and then there was X." The rap says:

> Aiyyo!! Dog, I meet bitches, discrete bitches. Street bitches, slash, Cocoa Puff sweet bitches (WHAT?) . . . I fuck with these hoes from a distance. The instant they start to catch feelings. I start to stealin they shit then I'm out just like a thief in the night. I sink my teeth in to bite. You thinkin life, I'm thinkin more like—whassup tonight? Come on ma, you know I got a wife.

Even while keeping in mind that "rap music is the contemporary stage for the theatre of the powerless" (Rose, 1994, p. 101), it can be easily argued that these artists and their producers are opportunists taking advantage of modern consumptive and voyeuristic audience impulses to witness violence and acquire pleasure from commodified sexual images that excite the senses. Puzzlingly, Dyson (1996) is not so severe in his appraisal of these images; he seems to extol them, suggesting that there is an evangelical call to arms afoot via thug rap. In fact, he nimbly apprehends the critical practice of contextualizing and unraveling thugs' motivations for thuggery. In the same breath in which he admits that gangsta rap music has been rightfully criticized for its vulgarity, commodification, and paralysis of Black women's bodies, he rationalizes that the complexity of these rappers' despondent backgrounds leads them to filter these images to the public so they can feed their families and monetarily uplift their communities. Essentially, all they want to do is escape and give back to the ghetto enclaves from which they emerged. Though true for some artists, I am afraid that Dyson's sonorous critical deconstruction is potentially more damaging than assistive. I agree that all texts should be considered within context and by virtue of pretext, but it is entirely too uncritical to release gangsta and thug rappers' sexual perniciousness from social critique and intellectual scrutiny. In my reading of his analysis, Dyson appears to have concocted an intellectual elixir that conveniently relieves gangsta rappers and the newer breed/genre of hip-hop thugs from any responsibility.

It is not that the self-proclaimed thug artists' experiences are not real; and it is not that the telling of their experiences should be avoided. It is also not the case that thugs are without viable reason for their gangsta behavior. It is that the hyperfascination with this monolithic industry-driven inscription of blackness exposes many negatively scripted Black stereotypes. The fallout from this suggests a perhaps unintended artistic complicity. Both Dyson and Rose are correct in that thug rappers and their producers have mutually exploited one another and that their artistry is evolutive. The artists have cunningly duped the industry into buying a product that was initially thought to be uninteresting (Ross & Rose, 1994); however, their compliance has consensually granted producers the opportunity to commit an even larger grievance via the perpetuation of imagery that is considered far from fantastical in the inscriptive gaze of the guardians of patriarchy. The microcosm of thugs and thug misses as bad boys and bad girls is unfolded via sexually charged and violent hip-hop narratives, and these popularized elegies do not exist in a vacuum. Because of the wide appeal of Black cultural expression, they dramatically affect and abet the deleterious inscriptions of Black bodies everywhere.

Rap and hip-hop have become their own combined enterprise. This industry is a multibillion dollar institution that does generate positive outlets for personal expression, wonderful alternatives for struggling youth, and ameliorative psychological conditions for Black community well-being. It accomplishes this with the music of artists who function on the edge of the genre like Alicia Keys, Mary J. Blige, Erykha Badu, Indie Arie, as well as Jill Scott, and more centrally Sister Souljah, Lauryn Hill, Queen Latifah, Mos Def, Will Smith, Common, The Fugees, Wyclef, and others. However, these artists and their most important "conscious rap" are a relatively small faction composed of the exceptions, rather than the rule (Cummings & Roy, 2002). Thug elegists primarily occupy the contemporary landscape of hip-hop music— they are the rule, considered the most authentic rap storytellers in the present era (Neal, 2002; Watkins, 1998).

## THE CONTEMPORARY STOCK
## MINSTREL THUG IN BLACK FILM

The buck, brute, or thug image, in all its manifestations, has also seized a distinct sphere of cultural production that serendipitously has been perpetuated in Hollywood blockbuster movies like *New Jack City*, *Harlem Nights*, *Boyz in the 'Hood*, *Crooklyn*, *Friday*, *Next Friday*, *Set It Off*, *The Wash*, *Baby Boy*, and a whole slew of Black popular and independent films. At one time, this was thought to be a most unfortunate predicament because "minority [sic] actors . . . are often faced with limited choices: pimps, prostitutes, movies with thin scripts and low budgets, projects with tight shooting schedules and minimum pay" (Farley, 2002, p. 128). Nonetheless, it is another matter altogether when actors, directors, or producers willingly participate in the perpetuation of stereotypical Black images.

The thug's sometimes maniacal, perennially dystopic "penis-as-animal" (Bordo, 1994, p. 270) behaviors only recapitulate and exacerbate the public paranoia about the beast-like nature of the Black male as brute. The silver screen is exploding with these iconographic images, preoccupied with a Black representational gaze fixated on almost nothing but the ugly aspects of Black existence that celebrate trifling ghetto living and poverty, neither of which are indicative of a composite Black culture, but pretend to be (Kelley, 1997; Morrison, 2002; Watkins, 1998).

Here, it would be easy to cite devastating or optimistic statistics concerning the well-being of African Americans in order to illustrate by comparison actual versus depicted African American life (Pinar, 2001; Smelser, Wilson, & Mitchell, 2001; Wilson, 1998). Additionally, the spectacular consumption of rap music is another avenue of discussion that would permit segue into conversation about the commodification of Black bodies (Fenster, 1995; Watts, 1997). It might even be intriguing to talk about the ironies of capitalism and Black youth (Watkins, 1998) or expound on the parallel of thug life to the self-inflicted and painfully disengaging experience and physical bodily inscriptions imposed via tattooing and body piercing (Morrison, 2002). However, as the citations foretell, this work has already been done, and accomplished exceedingly well I must add. Instead, I have chosen to analyze next a heuristic as well as intriguing extension of the discussion of thug-related hip-hop artistry—the thug-induced "pimp–whore complex" (Scott & Stewart, 1989) in Black pimp films.

## AN ANALYSIS OF *AMERICAN PIMP*: MINSTREL BRUTE PERSONIFIED

The recent proliferation of pimp-related films remarkably reproduces grotesque dialectics between subject and object as well as historical and contemporary corporeal representations. In consonance with the minstrel brute, the Black stud, playa, mack, and pimp images are all Black bucks trying to come to terms with masculinity. A common scapegoat used to justify these roles is emasculation. According to Staples (1982), Black men incurred psychological damage from enslavement, which left them as undignified expatriates in their own homes, removed from familial responsibilities except as breadwinner, and in some severe cases castrated. As a result, they were emasculated, dethroned if you will. Anxious to recapture the ultimate attribute and sign of a man—control—their only recourse was to seize reckless control over and in every visible aspect of their life from women to materialistic resources.

Cose (1993) counters Staples' redemption logic and contends, "those with a sense of history know that the stud image did not spring from the Black community but originated with Whites searching for signs that Blacks were intellectually inferior and morally degenerate—and therefore suitable for use as slaves" (p. 158). There is little relief resulting from either assertion or rationale, especially when Black filmmakers facilitate the perpetuation of the stud, thereby reproducing Black male subjectivity and substituting white hegemony for Black hegemony. The truth is that the stud is like the playa and the pimp, both of which are embodiments of masculine representation and regulation. The male pimp, mack, playa, and stud unscrupulously seek out and secure sexual liaisons with multiple consenting, but still very emotionally vulnerable partners. Hence, as in *American Pimp*, it is highly unlikely that two playas will be sexually engaged by one another. That destroys the power-driven sensation, the libidinal thrill, and the rush that the playa experiences when he is able to accumulate multiple partners, then emotionally destabilize and objectify them so that he remains psychically detached from the activity. For him, it is a pimp game, nothing more than a leisurely activity composed of paternally bound rules and objectives. He chooses to become the master gamesman, rhetorically recasting the dangerous act of prostitution as play. The idea of play, as signified in the commonly used phrase "pimp game," has powerful resonance with sex and pleasure as entertainment devices. It is severely beyond the range of conventional tropes related to men "scoring" with women (Borisoff & Hahn, 1993). Women are treated as mere game pieces, chips, or tokens on the region-bound game boards thugs use within the game of survival. Metaphorically, thugs are the players who mobilize and control the movements of the game pieces. The thugs set the rules and revise them; they also often play the role of banker. Sometimes thugs play for large cash rewards and sometimes they do "nickel pimping" (Scott & Stewart, 1989, p. 57), which involves mooching off of women for favors, money, shelter, or some other material resource. Thugs are selfish; the primary concern of a thug is his own survival, so he will do whatever it takes to make that happen. This is evidenced in several pimp films of the late twentieth century.

With the release of White filmmaker Beeban Kidron's *Hookers, Hustlers, Pimps and Their Johns* (1993)[7] came a spate of copycat films directed by Blacks who were convinced their depiction of prostitution as a "pimp game" was even more authentic than the last. These movies included Dre Robinson's *Pimps* (1997), Brent Owens's *Pimps Up, Hos Down* (1999), and the Hughes Brothers' (Albert and Allen) more noted film and documentary *American Pimp* (2000), for which motion picture studio executives competed. Common to all these films is a celebration of unmediated misogyny and pandering. With this surge of epics, there is also an energetic embrace of profound masculine anxieties associated with control and domination of women. Rather than systematically and intelligently interrogate the abrupt interception of Black agency in defining Black bodies, films like these suggest that many Black artists including filmmakers and musicians are vying for elitist subjectivity over portions of the composite community. In centering the masculine *subject* as pimp and marginalizing the female *object* as prostitute, any collective sense of the Black body is fractured.

Aware of this, the Hughes brothers explained to an audience of moviegoers why they chose to present the film as they did. One of the bonus tracks of the DVD version of *American Pimp* showed this live interview and discussion with Albert and Allen Hughes, the directors of the documentary. They explained that they purposefully presented the film with a nonjudgmental tone. They also noted that they were fully aware of the negative consequences a film like this could have, so they chose a documentary mode that would allow the pimps and prostitutes to speak for themselves while exonerating the directors from responsibility for what was said. The Hughes brothers' interest in directing this film was intricately tied to their childhood during which they witnessed pimping firsthand by a close relative. They wanted to expand the audience's imagination to capture the reality that there are rampant occurrences of prostitution across the United States and this activity often goes unchecked. However, they also wanted to invite outgroup audiences into a world they would probably never come to know. Defying the directorial urge to tidy up filmic endings, the Hughes brothers reveal their conscious choice to leave a resentfully painful denouement with the audience. They intended for the audience to feel as though this situation was unresolved, and it is, especially with each revitalized repetition of pimp imagery.

Just as Black slaves functioned as devices of labor for their master, the reproduction of the machinery of enslavement is exemplified in several pimp films in which the Black male is owner and the Black female is property. Her body and mind are summarily exploited, abused, and treated as instrument. She is treated inhumanely, denigrated with slurs like "bitch"and "ho," though as the Hughes brothers show us in *American Pimp*, these are allegedly considered affectionate nicknames in the "pimp game."

It does not require a sophisticated analysis to lay testimony to such a transparent straw argument. Just as "nigger" and "boy" were affixed derogatory labels used to describe, besmirch, and refer to Black men during slavery, "bitch" and "ho" function to sabotage and subjugate Black women's bodies, minds, spirits, and hence their identities. The more sophisticated question, however, is what does this signify about the economy of the gaze—to name and see her as a female dog or whore? In response to a larger project concerning the dismissal of women's standpoints within a limited range of patriarchal epistemologies, Butler (1990) indirectly ruminates on this question and surmises:

> Women are the "sex" which is not "one." Within a language pervasively masculinist, a phallogocentric language, women constitute the *unrepresentable*. In other words, women represent the sex that cannot be thought, a

linguistic absence and opacity. Within a language that rests on univocal signification, the female sex constitutes the unrestrainable and undesignat-
able. . . . This association of the body with the female works along magical
relations of reciprocity whereby the female sex becomes restricted to its
body, and the male body, fully disavowed becomes paradoxically the incor-
poreal instrument of an ostensibly radical freedom. (pp. 9–12)

Consequently, the paradoxically autonomous male body grants itself permission to name and, out of functional necessity, he initiates controlling and per-
secutory practices that complement his derogative linguistic rendering of the
female body. Remember, in the pimp game, she is merely a token.

Giving credit to the novel *Iceburg Slim, American Pimp* is interspersed
with excerpts from blaxploitation films like *Willie Dynamite, Slaughter's Big
Rip Off,* and *The Mack. The Mack* (1973) has a title character explicating the
"game" as follows: "Anybody can control a woman's body, but the key is to
control her mind." In fact, in the documentary *American Pimp,* each of the
thirty pimps and prostitutes interviewed suggested that the pimping "game"
is properly "played" only when the female prostitute understands she is simply sexual apparatus. As noted with the thug, the pimp's hallmark characteristic is desensitization or emotional paralysis. He does not feel, and as hook
(2003) asserts with respect to adolescent boys, there is violence in this "abusive insistence . . . that they not feel" (p. 195). In allowing the pimp to control her perceptions and self-esteem, she forces herself into a precarious position in which she is unable to experience unconditional and unselfish love.
Love only complicates the situation. In excusing the behaviors of pimps, several prostitutes explained the pimp's role as a protector, an overseer, suggesting that prostitutes could choose to be free of this enterprise, but then they
would be unsafe, especially if they stayed in this profession. One pimp
described the archetypal pimp's duty as follows: "I supply the food. I supply
the shelter, and I supply the medical bills. I supply everything. All she gotta
supply is the money." In this tragicomical synopsis of pimp responsibilities, we
return to the Black male's dependency on women to facilitate his survival.
All he has to do to fulfill his obligations is be a ruthless, cold-hearted, mind-
controlling, objectifying, hypermasculine mack of emotionally and psychologically vulnerable women. On closer examination though, this complicit
behavior carries with it an implicit interposition of identity negotiation,
which suggests a connection between the thug's anxiety about his socially
subjugated masculinity, his maintenance of the pimp image/style, and his psychological investiture in the pimp–whore complex. The disquieting reality, as
Cornel West (2001) puts it, is

For most young Black men, power is acquired by styling their bodies over
space and time in such a way that their bodies reflect a uniqueness and pro-
voke fear in others. To be "bad" is good not simply because it subverts the

language of the dominant White culture but also because it imposes a unique kind of order for young Black men on their own distinctive chaos and solicits an attention that makes others pull back with some trepidation. This young Black male style is a form of self-identification and resistance in a hostile culture; it also is an instance of machismo identity ready for violent encounters. Yet in a patriarchal society, machismo identity is expected and even exalted—as with Rambo and Reagan. In this way, the Black male search for power often reinforces the myth of Black male sexual prowess—a myth that tends to subordinate Black and White women as objects of sexual pleasure. (pp. 305–306)

West is absolutely correct to suggest that Black macho rigidity is entangled in Black men's quest to be acknowledged, valued, and emotionally secure. He is only secure when he is able to reconstruct knowledge-forms and narratives that fit his fantasies about retrieving custody over his own social and ontological agency. This is evidenced during *American Pimp* with the pimp–whore relationship creation narratives.

The documentary shows pimps who mouth platitudes concerning the origins of and their participation in pimping. These wide-ranging narratives glorified pimping. One "genesis of pimping" story was told of Black male slavehands directing enslaved girls to have sex with the White slavemaster in order to get physically close enough to him to retaliate by stabbing or trying to hurt him. Another pimp suggested pimping began in ghettos as a way to escape the financial ruins of ghetto life while plunging into entrepreneurial endeavors. One pimp from Atlanta named Sir Captain opined that pimping must have evolved from a need to overcome the street life by mastering it. He audaciously remarked, "The street game is the Black man's game. . . . It's the only game he [the White man] can't control. He can control all the dope dealers in the world. He can't control the pimp." These prefatory ruminations lead to a discussion of how pimps were introduced to and how they "play" the "game." Some claimed an innate capacity and drive to be a pimp, while others suggested they learned about it later in life and worked hard to secure respect as a pimp. It should be mentioned that some pimps, like one named "Bishop" from Chicago, who was a pimp for over twenty years before he was ordained as a minister, would take some of their profits and give back to their communities by purchasing and distributing free school supplies to the children and generally ensuring the safety of the families and children in the community. Though his pimping was well known, his charitable and altruistic acts of kindness salved his relationship with the community and permitted a sort of redemption of his image. Respect is a term that reverberated throughout the documentary—respect from prostitutes, from the pimp's family, from the surrounding community, and from other pimps who validated and uplifted him. As viewers, we play witness to a "Players Ball" in Milwaukee in which hundreds of well-manicured men dressed in fur coats, long hats, and snakeskin shoes attend a gala where they would compete (by showcasing their scantily clad, booty-shaking prostitutes) for trophies as rewards for acquiring and managing a bevy of prostitutes. It is suggested that these balls take place throughout the United States each year, from San Francisco and Las Vegas to Milwaukee and New York. The predominant tropes presented in *American Pimp* are disquieting. The reality is that sexual deviancy, inherent in the pimp–whore complex as exhibited professionally with a pimp and his prostitutes or via interpersonal relationships, robs the transformative potential and liberatory possibilities of vulnerable Black bodies.

## SUMMARY AND IMPLICATIONS

Jerry Watts (1994) poignantly remarks,

> The victim status is an inherently unequal relationship, one premised on the fact that the victimized is necessary for the existence of the victimizer. The victimizer is able to enjoy the life he or she lives in part because of his or her exploitation of the victimized. As a result, the best moral posture one can expect from a victimizer locked into a victim status relationship with the victimized is paternalism. Through paternalism, the victimized can often receive material benefits and economic improvement. *Paternalism cannot grant the subjugated emancipation* [italics added]. (p. 17)

To cast it another way, polysemous hegemonic inscriptions of Black bodies, no matter whether at the hands of White or Black producers, are still tragic. We, the populace of moviegoers, hip-hop fans, and general consumers of Black popular culture, are still debilitated with the emergence of each reinvented minstrel figure and each recreated and lauded act of misogyny. Indeed, even at its best in popular culture, when paternalism was supposed to make the public feel safe, protected, and affirmed, it has instead shown us hyper-vigilant, narcissistic, and exploitative metanarratives that contravene any attempt at liberation (Awkward, 2002). It is not that we are doomed, but that we are survivors of epistemic and cosmological violence; yet the incipient healing from the scars inflicted on us is being routinely interrupted by inscriptive regimes of truth and authenticity in popular culture. We masochistically return to popular culture to be pleasured by its modernized romanticization of heterosexual men's misogyny, hegemony, and colonization. Hence, there is a mutual dependence on one another that may be explained as the I–Other, victimizer–victim, scripter-inscribed dialectics. Audiences' penchant to accept these images is akin to saying, as singer Bill Withers croons, "if it feels this good gettin' used, then use me up." This involution should stimulate hyper-awareness of the emotive conditions in which the panoptic aesthetic is confined; however, we are seemingly apathetic or blinded by the motives, or perhaps just forgiving of the scripters who have exposed us to the destructive mythoforms we now accept as real and verifiable inscriptions.

We also forget about how our sexuality is confounded by this discussion of sex. For heterosexuals, it is easy to overlook the heterosexual tendencies unitarily displayed in filmic depictions of sexuality. This is certainly parallel to Whites overlooking the privileges granted to them and being stupefied by any assertion that others are not equally privileged. Heterosexual experiences possess privileged space in popular culture, and homoerotic experiences are relegated to secondary or tertiary levels of importance. Increasingly, this is changing, but the incontrovertible reality is these ontic relations and their economies are still fairly new to consumers of mass media. We devour the nude when it is presented heterosexually, and we voyeuristically embrace it when it is presented to us in shocking ways, such as with the 2 Live Crew or in *Pimps Up, Hos Down*. It directly affects our memory and desire, our fascinations about the sexual object, and potentially our treatment of women. Without our conscious volition, we find ourselves seeing women as objects, gazing at them sexually even when there is no mediated device to stimulate such an observation. We then comply with the hegemonic inscriptions of women's bodies. Again, it is what we do with the inscriptions that is potentially endangering.

We need only look at the sexually raunchy musical antics of rap artists like Luke Campbell and the 2 Live Crew on their album *As Nasty as They Wanna Be* to gain a semblance of this voyeuristic brouhaha. His pornographic music videos and adult-only concerts have made him a millionaire artist and producer. DeCurtis (1999) notes, "Luther Campbell, former leader of 2 Live Crew, label head, and rising skin-industry baron, realized that flesh made controversy. Eventually, he became controversy made flesh" (p. 269). Indeed, he paved the way for the current slew of disempowering videos depicting women in compromising positions with cameras with tight shots focusing in on women's breasts, buttocks, and sexually pulsating dance moves.

There must be a rewriting of Black male and female bodies in popular media. In seeking this desiderate agency to corporeally reinscribe culturally progressive meanings, particular attention must especially be paid to patriarchal effacement and materialization of these bodies in the consumptive interests of market values like competition, greed, money, and power. It is hardly enough for artists like N.W.A., Luther Campbell, Lil Kim, Foxy Brown, P. Diddy, and Master P to own their own record companies and labels. Hip-hop music of the ilk described in this chapter is readily accessible to American youth, youth who sometimes are searching for acceptance. This image is popular, and, when embraced, often comes with a certain degree of respect (Watkins, 1998). Yet, the temperament of thug-related hip-hop music disengages audiences who are not enchanted by the misogynistic impulses of the genre. Consequently, there is a moral, social, and cultural estrangement experienced by those who first hear hip-hop music and wonder if its nihilism, sexual perversion, and apolitical tenor is simply the result of a generational shift or if this genre of music really does offer poison to our youth.

Invariably, we are left with romanticized depictions of ghetto life that only seem attractive because of the ghetto dwellers resilience, perseverance, and down-to-earth dispositions. From this menagerie, we come to understand from a middle-class perspective that we can expect a chilling candor that bespeaks courage and fear at the same time—courage to sustain and fear of never being treated as capable, competent, normal human beings. This dialectic emerges and centers around commodified Black bodies that have been scripted as pathological.

W. E. B. DuBois once stated, "It is a peculiar sensation, this double consciousness, this sense of always looking at ourselves through the eyes of others. Of measuring one's soul by the tape of the world who looks on in an amused contempt and pity" (p. 3). For too long, Blacks have looked at themselves through the eyes of others. Historically, Blacks have had to detach themselves from the scripted stereotypes about them that are presented in popular media and elsewhere. As I have explored throughout this book, two conspicuous effects have surfaced as a result of negative scripts in the popular media: distancing and complicity.

One result has been that Blacks have distanced themselves from the images they see portrayed on film. Yet, collectively, we are so intrigued by these plastic inscriptions that we support them. Many Blacks still find humor in *Bringing Down the House* and *Head of State*. Furthermore, we are entertained by movies like *Baby Boy* despite their formulaic typecasting, harmful implications, and stereotypical portrayals of Black bodies. In fact, we are left with few filmic alternatives that depict Black lives. The sad message we are sending the entertainment industry, when we support these films with our dollars, is that we are prepared to be degraded. When films and music yield millions of dollars in profit, the only way to read this is as a measure of success; hence this leads to even more degrading images.

Another result has been complicity. Producers of negative scripts about Black bodies, some of whom are Black, have constructed a unifocal perspective of blackness that sees it in its most pathologized form. When criticized for having done this, typical responses are that the product is simply for entertainment purposes or that it is representative of a very real and vivid portrait of Black life. They often fail to comment on how this one-dimensional portraiture debilitates Black identities by scripting Black bodies as deviant, criminal, aloof, degenerate, depraved, and deprived. No one takes responsibility for the negative effects these images have on Black lives and American race relations. In fact, there appears to be complicity with these images, which only serves to isolate and polarize Black bodies from what can be understood as normal unless we define normal Black identities as universally ghettoized. The result has been Black entertainers and producers who are trading consciousness for profit, and this is not the sole conundrum or fault of hip-hop music or Black films. This is endemic to the entire entertainment industry where we witness pockets of responsible entertainment between debilitating discourses that disprivilege impressionable minds and succumb to consumerist impulses.

We need positive, healthy, productive, and liberatory discourses to accompany agency. It is not enough to have a hip-hop clothing line or record label. Perhaps our saving grace is that although inscribed bodies appear intractable, they can be transformed. What I have sought to illustrate in this chapter is that transfigurations of Black bodies have essentially rotated hegemony, flipping it on its side; hence the reinventive, or subletting, Black corporeal scripts discussed here have maintained the same posture as the previously inscribed White ones; they have moved in place, but not forward. Yet the powerful will and resilience of thug rappers to be appreciated for their indigenous experiences are encouraging. There is no salvation in losing connection with one's cultural self. What is most needed is a popular cultural transformation that will couple retrieved agency and potent discourse with emancipatory will.

# FIVE

# Toward an Integrated Theory of Black Masculinity

It is important to see than an overreliance on ideology critique has limited our inability to understand how people actively participate in the dominant culture through processes of accommodation, negotiation, and even resistance.

—Giroux, 1992

Throughout the book until this point, I have problematized representations of Black bodies in popular culture. I have presented the origins, history, politics, and stereotypes of Black bodies in the United States. I have also assessed damage to Black representations as caused by Black popular culture. We are now in desperate need of remedies and paradigmatic resolutions that will assist in recuperating Black bodies and offering corrective insights about how Black bodies function. Rather than attempt to theorize Black women's identities and hence speak for and about experiences with which I am not fully familiar, I will restrict my theorizing to Black men and Black masculinities.

Theory, by its very nature, is something that can be proven wrong. It has voids because no one theory can possibly characterize all aspects of a given phenomenon. Communication scholar Stanley Deetz (1992) explains, "A theory is a way of seeing and thinking about the world. As such, it is better seen as the 'lens' one uses in observation rather than as the 'mirror' of nature" (p. 66). The existing lenses used to explore Black masculinity, as a communicative aspect of gendered lives, require correction. Any time a body of theory, set of discoveries or range of conceptualizations are no longer effective in explaining the phenomena or behaviors they purport to describe, a paradigm shift is needed. Presently, there is no body of theory that is specifically designed to examine Black masculinities as communication-driven aspect of identities. I have stated elsewhere: "Black masculinist scholarship cannot afford to accept, approve, and adopt the same cultural, social and political agendas as traditional White masculinist scholarship. The two areas of gender theory share some commonalities, however there is a distinction that emerges at the intersection where gender meets culture" (Jackson, 1997, p. 731).

After having reviewed the existing interdisciplinary literatures and conceptualizations of Black masculinity, I feel I have read a set of foreign autobiographies, few of which pertain to me, a Black male. Married, middle-class, educated spiritual Black men, who are goal-driven, employed, competent, and noncriminal are missing from both the vast amount of literature and the constellation of media representations of Black males. We are in desperate need of radical progressive paradigms of Black masculinity, ones focused on liberation, on agency to define the self. The present model is an attempt to present one such paradigm.

The indisputable and tragic reality is that Black males have been pathologized and labeled as violent/criminal, sexual and incompetent/uneducated individuals. It is this prevalent set of stereotypical depictions of Black masculinity as a stigmatized condition or of Black males as an "endangered species" that makes it extremely difficult to theorize Black masculinities in the same ways as White or other marginalized group masculinities. Black masculinities are first and foremost cultural property communicated in everyday interaction as manifestations of Black identities.[1]

Traditionally, the impulse among gender theorists in many disciplines including communication has been to interpret the incendiary nature of masculinity studies in the specter of the European American experience. The assumption made is that all masculine persons function in homogeneous ways.[2] However, a growing contingent of Black writers, including bell hooks, Clyde Franklin III, Patricia Hill Collins, Richard Majors, Michelle Wallace, Philip Brian Harper, Na'im Akbar, Haki Madhubuti, Earl Ofari Hutchinson, and others, have proposed that Black masculinities are cultural property, and that they are ritualistically, explicitly, and implicitly validated by communities within everyday interactions. I agree with bell hooks's (1992) assertion about scholarship pertaining to Black masculinities. She writes:

> [the literature on black masculinity] does not interrogate the conventional construction of patriarchal masculinity or question the extent to which Black men have internalized this norm. It never assumes the existence of black men whose creative agency has enabled them to subvert norms and develop ways of thinking about masculinity that challenge patriarchy. (p. 89)

Essentially, the literature presupposes complicity with hegemony, and never questions whether Black men have been affected by their own exclusion from the mainstream to the extent that they have constructed their masculinities differently. In assuming that all masculinities are the same, one presupposes that all men should completely share the burden of U.S. White male patriarchal allegations without sharing the licenses to White male privilege, access, inclusion, and power. It seems that there are few instances in which Black men as "endangered species" still function in a position of privilege, hence with the same sensibilities as White men. So, I am persuaded by hooks's argument that social depictions of Black masculinities as dominant are "fantastical" and "narrow" (p. 89). While introducing a Black masculine paradigm, this chapter issues a challenge to rethink how cultural particularity influences the existing range of Black masculinities, which significantly diverge from culture-generic characterizations of what it means to be masculine.

Feminist thinkers, who encapsulate and hold liable negative masculine tendencies for the American fixation on power, competition, greed, control, and institutionalized exclusion, have inspired a large segment of critical masculinity scholarship. Consequently, the versions of masculinity that are described are often culturally generic, fragmented, and aloof. There are very few gender studies that depict masculinities as positive, healthy, mature, productive, and balanced identities, but these masculinities do exist. The gender descriptors "masculinity" or "masculinist" usually refer to antagonistic, puerile, insecure, very unaware, and chaotic male identities. It is true that masculine, like feminine persons enact a wide range of behaviors on a daily basis, from dysfunctional to quite functional. So, theorizing masculinities, in terms of a gendered continuum ranging from healthy to unhealthy and positive to negative self-definitions, is both necessary and revolutionary. As mentioned previously, the everyday existence of healthy and productive human beings is not so new, which means that there has been slippage in some gender theories with respect to how they account for healthy masculinities. This dearth of critical gender commentary on cultural masculinities only accents the inseparable link between power, ideology, and the politics of representation. It is the intent of this chapter to address this void in gender thinking and offer a paradigm that may serve as some basis for explaining productive and counterproductive masculine behaviors, while accenting culture as a means of understanding masculine realities.

This chapter is organized into three parts. First, it begins by defining the terms "masculinity" and "femininity" and then discussing male and female sex and gender role stereotypes. Second, a theoretic paradigm of Black masculine identities is introduced. Finally, the chapter concludes with implications of Black masculinity studies and suggestions for future research.

DEFINING MASCULINITY AND FEMININITY

Clearly, there are masculine and feminine mystiques that socially dominate how we see the world. It only takes a quick survey of childrearing practices among parents and mass-mediated reinforcements of sex and gender role stereotypes to see how these images are sharply divided.

Often, when writers speak of masculinities and femininities, we assume we know what the terms mean, and we also presume that these universal categories are reasonable ways to conceptualize lived realities. Rather than totally discard the terms, I recommend that the terms be redefined as perceptual categories in flux. In order to discuss definitions of masculinity and femininity, it is appropriate to return to the distinctions between sex and gender. The contemporary conversation concerning sex and gender is similar to that of race and ethnicity. The first term in each pair refers to biologically conceived characteristics of an individual, while the latter pertains to social ascriptions and prescriptions. This is not to suggest an innate set of characteristics that predestine an individual because of his or her race, but that race is often marked by physical attributes like skin color. The concept of race is also accompanied by socially constructed meanings (Hecht, Jackson, & Ribeau, 2003).

## Sex Roles

Just as one may be able to determine another's sex and/or race by observing optic markers, such as hair, skin, lips, eyes, musculature, and so on, one may also be able to determine one's sex by the same means. This is what I call "preverbal communication," the communication that begins via physiognomic markers before the talk begins, and continues as an undercurrent of all interaction. When I speak of sex roles rather than sex, expectations emerge. Sex roles are the behaviors associated with males and females. It is what they do with their bodies. For example, one female role is to procreate. Males are expected to talk with a deep voice. Although it is generally easier to visually identify a male or a female, gender identities are more intricate.

## Gender Roles

Gender roles refer to the ways women and men are socially and culturally assigned feminine and masculine behaviors. For instance, one stereotypical role expectation is that men will actively pursue women for a dating and mating relationship. Women are socially expected to be more nurturing and affectionate than men. For many, these stereotypical gender roles are socialized, beginning at birth. Family and friends often purchase products that are blue for newborn boys, and pink for girls. If you don't know the sex of the baby, green is appropriate. Many families would find it insulting to receive a baby boy's gift that is pink. Another stereotypical gender role is apparent with boys, who are normally socialized to play with trucks or action figures while girls are typically encouraged to play with dolls. This supposedly keeps the presumptions of what constitutes masculinity and femininity intact.

It is this social logic that inspired both Toys R Us and FAO Schwarz to come up with "Boys' World" and "Girls' World" in 1999. It must have sounded like a great idea at the time, until Toys R Us received negative feedback about their discriminatory and sexist toy lines in the "Girls' World" section. Toys like dolls, cookware, cleaning supplies, and phones were placed in "Girls' World," and trucks, cars, tools, monsters, race tracks, and video games were put in "Boys' World." This arrangement lasted for all of about two days as consumers complained that Toys R Us was promoting stereotypes by suggesting that boys should have all the fun while girls stay in the house, cook, clean, and talk on the phone. This short-lived fiasco with Toys R Us escaped much of the national media's attention. FAO Schwarz was a bit more strategic in their toy placement. They divided toys by color. So, both sections had almost the same toys, except that the girls' section had pink, orange, yellow, and green toys and the boys' had blue, black, purple, and green toys. They have somehow managed to reduce the negative feedback level significantly. The description of the "FAO Girl" is still stereotypical. It reads:

> Introducing FAO Girl. Because girls just wanna have fun. And fun stuff. This great new line will take your FAO Girl from homeroom to her room in style with a huge selection of hair accessories and jewelry, plush toys and pillows and cool gadgets—everything every girl can't do without. FAO Girls are filled with glamour, giggles and guts! (www.fao.com)

Body politics theorist Moira Gatens (1996) provides a valuable commentary concerning this problem of social stereotyping. She states,

> Masculinity and femininity as forms of sex-appropriate behaviors are manifestations of a historically based, culturally shared phantasy about male and female biologies, and as such sex and gender are not arbitrarily connected. The connection between the female body and femininity is not arbitrary in the same way that the symptom is not arbitrarily related to its etiology. Hence, to treat gender, the symptom, as the problem is to misread its genesis. (p. 13)

Gatens conceptualization is insightful regarding the dual functions of gender—body and role. Majors and Billson (1992) contend that gendered beings are not merely socially characterized. In the case of males, they are also forced to "attain masculinity" by "being responsible and being a good provider for the self and family" (p. 30). In other words, masculinity is earned and achieved, rather than socially prescribed. I concur with Majors and Billson that masculinity is not necessarily natural or innate as implied by Gatens's references to biologies; rather, it is learned.

Clearly, the intellectual analysis of the link between sex roles and gender stereotypes is non-unique. Sigmund Freud explored this issue in the early 1900s and countless gender theoreticians are commenting on this phenomenon on a daily basis. But are these academic assessments parochial? Have we redefined masculinities in such a way that they are no longer recognizable to the general population? It seems that socially understood conventions about masculinity include the medieval image of the "man as protector of his woman and family" to the more commonplace "man as the head of the household" and "primary breadwinner" motifs. Often, gender scholars' discussions of sex role orientations and gender stereotypes are antiquated conceptualizations that have outlived their epistemological utility. This is not to say that social discourse has completely discarded these notions, but that we must move forward because the analyses are stale. In an effort to do so, I recommend analyses of gendered relationships as behavioral institutions confined by people's own contextualized realities. With this in mind, masculinities are not to be understood as a singular or unitary reality, but as multiple masculinities, pluralized to accent an anti-essentialist perspective, which accounts for variegations due to culture, class, sexual preference, religion, and other axes of difference.

For the purposes of this chapter, masculinity is defined as a perceptual and cosmological category in flux. It is composed and validated by culturally particular behavioral tendencies that are consonant with personal, social, and communal expectations (Hecht, Jackson, & Ribeau, 2003). Although women may have masculine tendencies, I will discuss masculinity as a perceptual category that is male-centered.

Thus far, I have discussed the voids and inconsistencies in masculinity research and provided some insights about sex and gender-role stereotyping. Stereotypes are important information as indicators of problems within a given social context. Moreover, stereotypes inhibit social relationships and often offer inaccurate and damaging perspectives about others. Because stereotypes of all kinds are dangerous yet instructive, I would be remiss in discussing Black masculine identities without some discussion of the social stereotypes that problematize and inhibit them.

## PRECEPTS TO THE PARADIGM:
## BLACK MASCULINE IDENTITIES

I choose to theorize Black masculinities rather than cultural generic or universal masculinities because the latter are foreign to me. One's behaviors are potent enactments of one's worldview coupled with cultural sensibilities. Additionally, it is the cosmological trivium of communication, history, and identity that is culturally inscribed on the canvas I call the Self. Human beings are informed and transformed by the intricate *labyrinth* of agony, desire, pleasure, power, and difference. This labyrinth is literally the means by which we gauge self-efficacy and attachment to our personal and relational histories.

However, as masculine persons, we establish positions that grant agency to the self and limit access to "Others." To have agency is to operate in a subject rather than object position. It suggests that I have some say in how I define myself rather than having an institution or group define it for me. But it is difficult to become agent without being validated. Agency is a power-laden term that presupposes that people are defensive about how they will control their lives. It is about authority, permission, boundaries, and rules, and by establishing these things, it enables the self to make choices and explore the world without inhibitions. But since identities are co-defined in everyday interactions with others, agency is some times negotiated and ends up resting externally with the "Other." This is the juncture at which the labyrinth becomes heightened, and therefore most visible. As Audre Lorde (1984) cautions, "For Black women as well as Black men, it is axiomatic that if we do not define ourselves for ourselves, we will be defined by others—for their use and to our detriment" (p. 45). The frustration of a displaced agency causes the "I" (i.e., masculine person) to struggle to reacquire stability and control over his choices, worldview, and life possibilities. The "Other," in the previously described scenario, can be anyone from another Black masculine person to another cultural feminine person. Incidentally, both may be males.

CAN MANHOOD BE REVOKED?

The entire process of removing the agency of masculine persons is often referred to as emasculation or "revoking one's manhood." Three obvious assumptions are being made with this reference. The first is that men are the only ones who qualify as masculine, which of course is false. The second is that all men are masculine and all masculine persons are *men*; yet some may be males or boys.[3] Masculinity is a perceptual category that attends each stage of self-development—boyhood, maleness, and manhood. Third, another assumption is that manhood can be revoked. Manhood is a category of being. Rationally, it does not seem possible to revoke a person's sense of being, but because being a man is highly significant among masculine persons, boys and males must define in it as something that is "achievable." In addition, boys and males define "manhood" as a subconscious extension of the self that is externally presented and licensed. Being on the exterior, "manhood" is available to be seized. When defined this way, it is worn like paraphernalia; consequently, it can be undressed relatively easily. Manhood, in its purest manifestation as defined by men, cannot be revoked, partly because it is internalized. It is not a standpoint or position that is defined solely or even primarily by a "way of knowing," but rather a way of being. It is a life-force that is achieved after reaching a level of spiritual, emotional, mental, and ontological maturity, consciousness, and balance and having one's manhood coextensively and relationally validated by one's community. One who has achieved manhood is aware of the ontological spatial boundaries, and functions along the borders between himself and others to achieve desired ends, but is conscious of not "losing himself" in the identity negotiation process. "Losing himself" is always a threat because of the exhaustive code-switching mandate as he attempts to coordinate his actions with others, as well as the possibility that his masculine identity may become anonymous, silenced, suppressed, and accessorized. So, he must always be cognizant of the effects of identity negotiation; this is accomplished through policing and maintaining surveillance over his identity. Keeping oneself in balance is the goal of masculine behaviors. It is also what defines struggle, the centerpiece of Black masculine identities.

## BLACK MASCULINE IDENTITIES PARADIGM

Masculinities in general are perceptual categories in flux; therefore, defining black masculine identities requires that black masculine perceptions are taken into account. Stuart Hall (1997) asserts that identities are the labels given to the different ways interactants are positioned by and position themselves in past and present social narratives. Essentially, all definitions of masculinity are a matter of positionality.

Black masculine social positionings are primarily communication phenomena. Positioning is the axis of ontological difference among separate, but often overlapping masculine identities. That is, positions facilitate how masculinity is understood and enacted at any given moment. If any of the following factors is threatened, the perceptual position can shift from positive to negative as an instinctive protective response; hence, masculinities are not stable, predictable forces. They are as fluid as one's perceptions.

There are five sensitizing constructs that reappear throughout the literature on Black masculinity and are indicative of Black masculine positionality: struggle, community, achievement, independence, and recognition. These factors offer some explanation for how masculinities are selected and enacted. It is important to remember that masculinities vary with respect to conditions, maturity, and positionality. Masculinity, as with all behavioral manifestations, can be conceptualized along the twin registers of self-efficacy and symbiosis. Self-efficacy is a common psychological term that refers to the degree to which an individual feels he has control over his life. It is a primary aspect of any existence that requires affirmation and agency. Symbiosis is a common biological term that refers to the attachment one has to a certain life-space and/or relational history. It is reconceptualized here to indicate a social attachment that is partly defined or affirmed by a different, foreign, or asymmetrical cultural experience, such as the case with the term "African Americans" that implies a link to African ancestry rather than a word like "Black" that links people by their common color, then by collective experience. These are not unique to Blacks or Black males. Everyone has a need for self-efficacy and symbiosis.

To illustrate symbiosis, imagine that a person who has a strong Black cultural identification and is militant may hate Whites because of what he has learned about slavery, yet he is forced to interact with Whites if he wants to be employed. He becomes unavoidably attached to an American culture that has become synonymous with whiteness, while attempting to maintain a commitment to an African ancestral heritage. This historical symbiosis may cause him to behave negatively toward anyone who looks White. On the other hand, a Black person who has a strong Black identification may feel self-efficacious, and therefore have little problem initiating and maintaining relationships with Whites despite what he knows about slavery. Both persons function this way for a variety of reasons. The factors of positionality offer some explanation for how masculinities are selected and enacted. There are certainly many commonalities between general conceptions of masculinity and Black masculinities. This is sometimes apparent in the following paradigm. However, it is important to remember that masculinities vary with respect to ontological condition, maturity, and positionality.

## ASSUMPTIONS OF BLACK MASCULINE IDENTITY THEORY

There are several assumptions on which the Black Masculine Identity Theory is founded:

1. Struggle is a human activity that solidifies one's sense of community.
2. Struggle is defined by group experiences (i.e., it is not that struggle is unique to Black males but that racial and gender group experiences of Black males contextualize struggle).
3. Struggle is the centerpiece of the Black masculine identity model because of the complexity of defining and negotiating Black masculine identity.
4. All identity theories in some way call for dialectics. In this case, Black masculine identities are enwrapped in an I–Other dialectic involving politics of recognition.
5. Black masculine persons are usually preoccupied with a sense of self-efficacy, which, when achieved, offers a sense of life satisfaction, autonomy, and stability.
6. Black masculine persons' motivation to achieve is culturally, historically, and socially founded.
7. Without struggle, recognition, independence, and achievement, commitment to community is virtually impossible.

These seven assumptions are based on thematic patterns in the literature on Black masculinity and on pilot study thirty-minute interviews with thirty-five Black males residing in the western, southern, central, and eastern regions of the country who vary in educational levels and are ages 15 to 73.

This pilot study confirms much of what the literature teaches us about Black masculine identities as noted throughout this book. In many ways, these assumptions are cumulative and inextricable. It is just as difficult to have achievement without someone to recognize it as such as it is to be independent without some sense of struggle over social space and place. Each of these constituent parts is necessary for establishing any sense of community. Although it is possible to achieve and think you did it independently, which would exclude community, that is why struggle and recognition are important aspects of this model of Black masculine identities.

## Struggle and the Mandala

Psychoanalyst Carl Jung contended that the self, as an archetype, is naturally motivated to move toward growth, perfection, and completion. The ultimate symbol of the self, he argues, is the mandala, a diagram that contains a circle inside of a square or vice versa. The dialectic between the shapes is consistent with the conscious, subconscious, and unconscious elements of the self; hence, the combination of the three represents the total self, which is in constant pursuit of balance and wholeness. It is particularly interesting that Jung applies the second law of thermodynamics, the principle of entropy, to explain his interpretations of dreams.

The actual principle states that when hot and cold objects merge, the hotter flows into the colder to create a sense of equilibrium. No matter what conceptual label is used to describe entropic behavior, it refers to the degree to which disorder in a human or object-centered system may be managed. Since we, as human beings, are naturally incomplete, we often strive toward perfection and balance, and some times this is done on a most subconscious level. So, although it may appear on the surface that one may be stagnated or polarized in a certain life-stage, we are often behaving in ways that are meant to evoke recognition, approval, and validation.

Black masculine persons do this by taking agency in defining the "spaces" where they live. Place, space, home, and territory are metaphors often used in postmodern research to describe positions of the self in society. Home is a particularly useful metaphor because of its implicit properties of privacy, self-protection, shelter, and comfort. Place, space, and territory are much more public terms that fuse the constitutive features of adjacency, interconnectedness, isolation, possession, yet fragmentation. In both cases, there is clearly something that accents a void that needs to be filled. The motivation to do so characterizes struggle, but the behavioral quest is about human possibility and growth. This is why struggle is at the center of the mandala. To speak of achievement and independence, for instance, one must at some point address the issue of potentiality, and ask, "what are the possibilities of my achievement, or of my being independent?"

On a psychic level, struggle can be understood as the effort to seek out portions to fulfill our (self-observed) conscious needs and desires. The peculiar operation of conscious behavior in the social domain is that it nourishes and reproduces subconscious motivations . But it is the social domain that initially constitutes these self-understandings. Consciousness, by nature, is fragmentary, and is an enactment of self-recognition. The fascinating dimension of consciousness is how it gets perpetuated on a daily basis via communicated identities.

*Recognition.* It is quite apparent that human beings coexist, and consequently we coordinate our behaviors so that human activity is somewhat synthesized and rule-governed. Michael Walzer (1997) offers an interesting approach to managing social diversity by rethinking coordination as toleration. His central thesis is that difference can be tolerated if humans can recognize how we are basically alike and dissolve commitments to group localities. He supports his thesis by expounding on what he names "regimes of toleration," which are multinational instances of submerged difference for the sake of human totality. Though intriguing, Walzer's analysis oversimplifies human difference, and proposes an alternative that mimics "the melting pot" concept. This is not to mention that "toleration" suggests that people have to put up with others and that something must be done to overlook some part of their identity. Nonetheless, Walzer is correct in suggesting that human difference problematizes social coordination for those who find the activity of recognition to be a hassle.

The discourse humans use to capture the thoughts we have about the Other is significant. As Chandra Mohanty (1994) points out, "The central issue, then, is not one of merely acknowledging difference; rather, the more difficult question concerns the kind of difference that is acknowledged and engaged" (p. 146).

Personhood is founded on what the Canadian philosopher Charles Taylor (1992) coins the "politics of recognition." The entire concept of masculinity is predicated on recognition. Therefore, the natural progression of gender relationships is dependent on this social process. Taylor asserts that a politics of recognition requires that "Others" recognize and identify the authentic "I" and offer it permission to proceed with a given behavior. So, self-authenticity is discovered within the dynamics of human interaction; meanwhile, the "Other" serves the function of recognizing and validating that construction (Bordo, 1989; Fanon, 1967; Grosz, 1994; hooks, 2003). In cases when the "Other" fails to recognize or refuses to validate masculine behavior, then either the masculine person discontinues the behavior, or suffers social penalty, which is some times more punitive than any other kind. Certainly, people can and often do present themselves differently to different people. This is but another facet of recognition politics. This perceptual factor, which affects positionality, is explained by Ribeau, Baldwin, and Hecht (1997) as understanding—"the feeling that there was a genuine exchange of thinking, feeling and caring" (p. 150).

*Independence*. Independence is about self-authorization, autonomy, and freedom of self-expression. All human beings seek it at some point in their lives, often as teenagers. As one matures, the manner and mode of self-expression often become more sophisticated. It is then more about transformation of the self. Frequently, when scholars merge Black masculinities and independence in their conversations, they evoke notions of resistance to dependence, control of situations, and ultimately deviancy. Independence does begin with self-assertion, but does not need to end with abnormality or repudiations of the law. Perhaps the best method of pursuing this phenomenon is to theorize male masculinities as spaces that are attached to behavioral modes of existence, so that a male's (based on Akbar's distinctions) masculinity will be perceived quite differently from a boy's or a man's. Akbar (1991) suggests, "A male is a biological entity. . . . Maleness is also a mentality . . . dictated by appetite and physical determinants. This mentality is one guided by instincts, urges, desires, and feelings" (p. 3). A male, by this definition, may be an adult who still lives at home with his healthy parents or may cohabitate with a girlfriend who pays all of the bills while he remains unemployed. Essentially, the male is undisciplined. Akbar maintains, "Once the mind has become disciplined, the boy is in a position to grow into reasoning. . . . When the primary use of your reason is for the purpose of scheming or lying then you are fixated in the boyish mentality. . . . The thing that transforms a boy into becoming a man is knowledge" (pp. 4–12). Each will view independence differently.

For example, a male's masculine quest for independence may be read as an unwillingness to commit himself to a relational partner, while a man's masculine assertion of independence may be related to self-development. That is, he may find it necessary to separate himself in order to understand himself better, as a separate entity rather than a dependent pair. The most healthy relationships are interdependent; in these exchanges, there is some balance between autonomy and dependence.

*Achievement*. At first glance, achievement may appear to reflect only acquisition, but its real concern is with accomplishment of personal and collective goals. Personal goals may range from materialistic items such as owning a BMW to the spiritual goal of being at peace and one with God. The personal impinges directly on the collective. The content of and progress toward one's aspirations of achievement automatically affect the success and survival of the collective. This is reflected in the African American affirmation "I am because we are, and because we are; therefore I am." This is much different from the quote representing the individualist, competitive, survival-of-the-fittest" nature of Cartesian thought—"I think therefore I am." Masculine behavior cannot be substantiated as an intricate identity matrix if the only achievement concerns are with an individual's materialistic bread-winning capabilities. The cultural community to which one belongs is also critical. The commitment to the preservation of African American culture is critical.

The discussion of achievement cannot ignore the reality of cultural identity negotiation among Black males. Roberts (1994) maintains,

> African American men must negotiate two cultural models of human relationships. . . . The Euro-American model emphasizes values such as competition, individualism, and domination as central to the human condition. The African model for human relationships, conversely, stresses the importance of group and community needs over individual aspirations, cooperation over competitive relationships, as well as interconnectedness among people. (p. 384)

In seeking to achieve one's goals, both cultural modes of behavior may be enacted in rapid succession such that they appear to be simultaneously engaged. The real danger is when Black masculine persons cease from embracing indigenous African-centered values, hence negotiating African cultural aspects of their identities. Staying grounded in one's cultural worldview, while functioning within a "Euro-American model," is difficult when switching back and forth between two modes of consciousness; however, this activity is important. This is what is meant by the popular phrases in the Black community—"stay Black" and "keep it real." They are admonitions to remain aligned with one's culture as one pursues one's aspirations rather than relinquishing or negotiating aspects of the cultural self in the process.

*Community.* It is impossible to define one's self alone while living in a community of persons who must validate one's presence. Here, Black manhood is achieved ritualistically and behaviorally, while Black masculinity is perceptually reaffirmed. So, Black manhood is the behavioral category and Black masculinity is the perceptual category. Essentially, by this definition, manhood is relationally discovered via one's actions. The community not only affirms, but also contractualizes the behaviors of Black men via interaction. The value of Black manhood is what it gives to the rest of the community. If one is unproductive, then the community must question his value. Manhood is both an agreement and social, political, and/or cultural assignment contractually arranged. And, as a result of the contract, Black men are figuratively bound to the community, which is the co-author of normative masculine behavior.

Black manhood is a behavioral category in flux developing with age, experience, stability, cultural consciousness, self-comfort, and spiritual awareness, and affirmed by the community. The "community" can be defined broadly as in a global or diasporic "family" and/or locally as in the neighborhood in which one lives. This is why it is increasingly difficult to agree on universal criteria for Black manhood because communities are often diverse. Nonetheless, the community affirms one's masculinity, no matter whether one is homosexual or heterosexual, fatherless or not, employed or unemployed, male or female. The composite cultural community may not be the adjudicates of masculinity or manhood; sometimes, those who affirm are persons who function similarly to the adjudicated individual. Nonetheless, the community plays a viable role in how masculinities are constituted and positioned.

These five factors that affect Black masculine positionality—struggle, community, achievement, independence, and recognition—are important aspects of repositioning Black masculinities to counter their pathological depictions. These factors offer some explanation for how masculinities are selected and enacted, but also facilitate the redefinition of Black masculinity as cultural property.

## IMPLICATIONS OF BLACK MASCULINIST RESEARCH

I have recently become increasingly more concerned (perhaps even idyllic) about the end product of Black masculine corporeal inscriptions, constantly asking myself what all this really means, and where we need to go next. I have become extra cautious about those with whom I align myself, since it has become apparent that everyone isn't devoted to liberation. And liberation is key among Black masculine persons whose discursive behaviors are constant representations of a racial script. Theorizing masculinity as nonpathological, cultural, communicative, and gendered is one progressive formula to achieve this goal.

Recognition, independence, achievement, and community are four factors that affect masculine positioning. So, you might ask, what are the implications for females or homosexuals? In conceptualizing masculinities, it is my attempt to be critical, yet inclusive. Both sets of persons can be masculine based on the definition of masculinity given in this chapter. Nonetheless, I have diverged at times from a unitary gender framework to a heterosexual male conception of masculinity in order to accent unique concerns of that group of masculine persons. We are aware that class is a dominant and interceding factor of masculine realities as well. It is not discussed here due to the scope and nature of this book. Clearly, many scholars have combined race, class, and gender, rationalizing that these terms are inseparable, especially as I write about the intersection of power and social formations. Likewise, it could be argued that sexual preference, physical ability, and a host of other ontological facets cannot be disjoined. Difference as a pillar of identity must be constituted, grounded in critical examinations of everyday experiences. These experiences and personal histories are numerous, and must be deconstructed to better understand the formation and maturation of self-definitions.

The study of Black masculinities is an effort to recombine the African American gender community. That should remain the goal to stay consistent with an African American cosmology centered on community and collective identity. Theorizing masculinity as cultural, ontological, historical, communicative, and gendered is one progressive formula to achieve this goal. Extant gender research purviews the communicative, sociological, and psychological dimensions of male behavior. That should continue, and it should be culturally specific. If Black masculine theory is described as a set of explanations that stipulates a defining relationship between Black males and their environment, then certainly communication scholars should continue to create, develop, and sustain this circuit of inquiry. Empirical studies should explore this barren terrain. However, if its primary function is to illustrate its opposition to feminine ways of knowing, then the venture is counterproductive. There are truly unique concerns that Black men share about their masculinities. This chapter begins that interdisciplinary dialogue from a communicative approach.

# EPILOGUE

# "The Revolution Will Not Be Televised"

There is no law that is not inscribed on bodies. Every law has a hold on the body.

—De Certeau, 1984

The body is a most peculiar "thing," for it is never quite reducible to being merely a thing; nor does it ever quite manage to rise above the status of thing. . . . If bodies are objects or things, they are like no others, for they are the centers of perspective, insight, reflection, desire, agency.

—Grosz, 1994

A piece of work that will make sick men whole. But are not some whole that we must make sick?

—Shakespeare, *Julius Caesar*

It is my hope that this book offers instructive insights about how Black masculine bodies have been historically situated and are contemporarily scripted. I chose to introduce discussion of *various* sites where this occurs rather than writing a monograph that emphasizes a single media type or a single type of inscription. I believe the scripting paradigm has emancipatory potential for what it reveals about producer intentionality and audience consumption across the multiple spaces in our everyday lives. American citizens are inundated with negative stereotypical images within commercial and print advertising, news outlets, the Internet, television programs, and films. Many of us consume these images within each of these venues on a daily basis, and have become anesthetized to the effects of these mostly implicit and sometimes explicit daily racial assaults.

Scripting is a deconstructive paradigm that problematizes stereotypes and attempts to restore hope. As famed poet Gil Scott Heron suggests in his album *The Revolution Will Not be Televised*, liberation is constantly countered by implicit (and explicit) forms of oppression that are not always immediately identifiable. While we are busy launching activistic movements against the obvious forms, the more latent forms often go unnoticed; hence, the idea that if there is a revolution leading to radical progressive change, it will have to take place on multiple levels and must be wary of subversive attempts to undermine liberatory progress. It seems what we are missing, as hooks contends, is "sustained programs for education for critical consciousness that would continually engage black folks of all classes in a process of radical politicization" (p. 251). This does not suggest that Black people must bear the full burden of racial reconciliation or unproblematizing negatively scripted representations of themselves in popular media. We did not invent race and certainly cannot be solely responsible for the dissolution of its diseased end product, racism. What is more significant about hooks's observation is that popular media have the remarkable opportunity to provide a *sustained* pedagogy that is salvational rather than toxic. When media fail us in this regard we, as consumers, are left alone to become immediately responsible for our own critical consciousness. Ultimately, we as consumers are left with a hodgepodge of scripts, some of which we co-produced, some that simply mimic "real life," some that try to imagine another life, and some that impoverish the conditions of our daily lives. It is likely that, for some readers, the term "scripts" seems sanitized or sterile. It does not evoke the same kind of emotion that racist stereotypes produce. It is used here to suggest that, although rendered this way in popular media, Black bodies are more than flesh. They are more than signs and symbols of an objectified text where racism and sexism are deployed. They have become mnemonic instruments reminding consumers of a larger social agenda, one that feeds off of our learned desire to be competitive, individualistic, independent, and generally dismissive of the Other.

We would like to believe that popular media (including, but not limited to, television) leave us with no negative cultivation effects (Gerbner, 1999), that the stories told through music, television, and film are mere entertainment. In fact, according to the progenitor of cultivation theory George Gerbner (1999), decades of research have informed us that these "stories socialize us into roles of gender, age, class, vocation, and lifestyle, and offer models of conformity or targets of rebellion. They weave the seamless web of the cultural environment that cultivates most of what we think, what we do, and how we conduct our affairs" (p. ix).

As we sort through these scripts, we are perhaps naturally inclined to resist those that are unaligned with our interests and select those that we feel may improve our ways of seeing the world. The point is that *scripts about*

*Black and other bodies in popular media affect us,* whether we are conscious of it or not. What these scripts teach us needs to be understood. If we passively watch blockbuster films and the only time we see Asian protagonists is when they are practicing martial arts, then the film's pedagogy is aligned with a stereotypical script about Asians. If we watch movies like *Rules of Engagement* where Yemeni people are depicted as savages and terrorists and these images become commonplace in other mass-mediated scripts, then we will see all Arabs this way and begin to preverbally determine how and who they are. The question is: "What do you do with these scripts psychologically, socially, and culturally?"

The effect is deleterious if viewers subconsciously or consciously develop a stereotype based on these implicit memories about Asians and Arabs. The film has already begun or sustained the process of socially categorizing Asians or Arabs as an ethnic group that is foreign, exotic, strange, or heathen. Consequently, it has initiated automatic social cognitions. As Schacter's (1992, 1996) studies have revealed, it gets lodged in one's implicit memory and may lead to relational fragmentation or interrupted social relations. Of course, this is not always the case, but there is potential danger even in disavowing the significance of racialized scripts.

In chapter 1, I quote DuBois as having asked, "How does it feel to be a problem?" This final chapter, which follows an in-depth analysis of the crucible of race and body politics, the collapse of moral representation, and the abandonment of nonmarket values like love, offers solutions and poses challenges to reconsider our consumption of popular cultural images that potentially damage how we see and relate to one another.

I remain resolute that there are three foundational premises of racial and corporeal politics: (1) bodies are inscriptive surfaces that are discursive texts, which can be rewritten after acts of struggle toward emancipation, though still not fully divested of prior inscriptions; (2) body politics are the lifeline for race and racism; and (3) corporeal inscriptions stimulate the negotiation of racial identities. I have explored each of these throughout the book and argued that the politics of racial representation must be deconstructed, and one way of doing so with respect to Blacks is to analyze scripts about Black bodies.

The body is not inherently political; it is socially constructed and disciplined as such. Much of what extant studies tell us about race and racialized bodies tries to convincingly suggest that human beings are innately endowed with a set of encoded messages. Furthermore, we are informed that men and women behave in certain ways because it is their nature. We are told heterosexuality is predetermined and homosexuality is an abominable aberration of the natural order. These are all myths enwrapped in ideologies, which preserve norm-centering White Anglo-Saxon, heterosexual males and marginalize everyone else. Some of these myths fail to survive public scrutiny, while others are so believable that they merge with social norms and practices; hence, they become camouflaged as a natural part of everyday life and are said to be "just the way it is."

So, the problem with concluding a critical theoretic book of this nature is trying to figure out directions in which to proceed. If an occurrence such as the scripting of the Black body in popular culture is seen as "just the way it is," but does not recognize its sickness, then how does one prescribe a solution without first working to unravel and refute the emplaced ideology? Said another way, if a whole society is sick, how do you devise a cure? One must first convince the populace that they are sick, though the recurring implication will be that maybe everyone else is well and you are sick. Any attempt to subvert the normalized negative inscriptions of Black bodies will be resisted until ignorance and passive acceptance of the myths are expunged.

When examining popular cultural inscriptions of Black bodies in the United States, we are really dealing with a question of media integrity and taciturn public morality. The conundrum is that popular culture is there to inform and entertain us. It is like a novel that is half fiction and half non-fiction, and it is up to the audience to figure out which is which. Passive audiences will look at the images on film and television or hear the aural renditions of the same themes and figure it is all mythologized entertainment, except for the images that have been deeply ingrained via patterned repetition, which are considered true. The rest of the imagistic representations are presented as half-truths, which dazzle us with technological innovations, narcotize us with their spine-chilling visual effects, and numb us with compelling narratives so that we do not have to think about our daily worries. So, essentially for these audiences, it is functionally out-of-bounds to criticize media practices because, as critics, we appear to be complaining about the very reason why we engage the media in the first place. The media's intention is to relax its audiences. It is a multidimensional entertainment utility that uses myth, ideology, signification, metonymy, synecdoche, and a host of rhetorical devices to lull audiences asleep and help them escape reality. If that is the media's function as an aesthetically pleasing set of venues, then why change it at a time when it seems irreplaceable as is in American life?

The essentialist scripting of U.S. Black bodies in popular culture remains as it is at our own peril. Producers, writers, artists, and audiences are each responsible for the ongoing cycle of negative inscriptions we are currently witnessing in popular culture. In a capitalist society, music and film producers only support products that will sell. If audiences do not invest in these products, they will disappear from the marketplace. So, the question is: are audiences willing to monitor their viewing and listening habits and eliminate negative inscriptions such as pimp and thug images from their range of visual pleasures? Certainly, there are many individuals who do not see these images as problematic. Even when given the opportunity and power to reconstruct and rewrite how Black bodies are inscribed or will be historically understood in the future, too few Blacks and too few non-Blacks have chosen to resist further exploitation of the Black body. With each new exploitative image, we add to the existing damage caused by previous negative inscriptions.

## PERSONAL AND CRITICAL REFLECTIONS

Unfortunately, Black corporeal scripts promulgated by popular media have reconditioned North Americans to think of Blacks in the most vile ways. The media does very little toward relieving us of the stereotypes associated with blackness in the United States, and perhaps that is not their job. In my most self-critical moments, I have to remind myself that everyone is not concerned about liberation. Everyone does not care that Black children and other children of color are forced to bear the brunt of socially constructed notions of race founded on epistemic violence and wreaked on consumers of popular media. They are an "abandoned generation" that are told they need not be nihilistic when the state apparatus and media reinforcement of stifled progress reinvents cycles of oppression right before their eyes on a daily basis (Giroux, 2004). I agree that our youth should not be nihilistic, but I also believe we have to balance the scale of representations. It is difficult for a young, impressionable mind to be deluged with negative representations of their selves and be impervious to these painful images.

I have to remember that the teleology of the television, film, and music industries is that of a consumerist vehicle and not an agency responsible for radical progressive social change. I also must remember that just because one is Black and shares a collective history (with other Blacks) of oppression, disenfranchisement, and devaluation neither means that this has affected us in the same way nor does it mean we are all aware of the social exigency, political predicates, and cultural meanings that gave rise to the social movements and political action initiatives that shaped the privilege this hip-hop generation enjoys. So, at times, I take pause and wonder whether I am the one with the problem because I expect too much.

As a lifelong fan of positive hip-hop music and message rap, I expect seemingly conscious rap artists-turned-actors like Queen Latifah to not appear in or co-produce movies like *Bringing Down the House* that exploit a pre-scripted and poverty-enhanced blackness for material gain. As a fan of progressive comics, I expect comedian Chris Rock, in his directorial debut *Head of State*, would do more than make a few politically astute assertions while designating himself as the film's Black protagonist the president of the United States. Although his moral convictions were impressive, the stereotypical loud-mouth dee-jaying part of his persona did nothing for the current image and perceptions of Black presidential hopefuls or Black people as social participants. To date, one exemplary popular cultural representation of a Black U.S. president that is salvational is the role of David Palmer (Dennis Haysbert) within the first season of Fox Television's primetime show *24*. This show depicts a morally righteous, politically savvy, thoughtful individual who is not scripted to be a jiving, shucking, foot-shuffling, bufoonic minstrel resurrection, but instead a man of conviction and character whose blackness is not pathologized. In my opinion, this is partly what makes it an exceptional and remarkable show. It is remarkable because it presents a Black person as another human being who has faults, but is not inherently faulty.

Perhaps the positive representations in film, music, or television series like *24* and even the television series *Soul Food* and *Living Single* will become contagious and inspire more producers to develop a range of Black images. Presently, that range is limited in the entertainment industry. The average television viewer or cinemagoer has to wait years between projects before a wholly positive show or set of Black images appears, although we can channel surf on any given day and find positive images of Whites on every other station. Biographer Christopher John Farley (2002) points to film industry leaders as the source of this persistent problem of negative Black representation and explains the dilemma this way:

> With few women, and almost no minorities, calling the shots in Hollywood, women and minorities often tend to get overlooked in terms of casting and script development. The major filmmaking guilds (actors, directors, producers and writers) are 80 to 90 percent white. Only about 10 percent of the board members or partners on the biggest talent agencies are women and there are, at the time of this writing, no minorities. There is no minority, in Hollywood, at the time of this writing, with the power to green-light a major movie. That means if you want to get a Black movie made, a white executive has to okay it—and that executive is in most cases going to be male. (pp. 131–132)

We can watch movies where sane, non-criminal, non-savage images of Whites appear quite frequently. As an individual who is sane, non-criminal, and non-savage, I am then forced to see myself vis-à-vis these shows because I am hard pressed to find frequent representations of this nature that look like me.

It is not that I am taking aim at these shows and music artists, but that they have taken aim at Blacks and Black communities, and their pathologized representation are leading to the detriment of our collective and local communities. Individual consumers must gather as a collective just to address and redress the damage caused by negative scripts, otherwise we are left with an indelible psychological, cultural, social, and political residue poisoned by hopelessness, despair, criminality, lustfulness, incompetence, ignorance, and voicelessness.

WHAT NOW?

As Wiegman (1995) reminds us, Blacks frequently have not been allowed to write their own cultural histories into the ledgers of popular culture. The result has been a sedimentation of plastic inscriptions that ritualistically externalizes Black bodies. That is why hip-hop music is so extremely important and such a serious endeavor when unblemished by the subgenre that objectifies women, debases the composite African American community, and steeps itself in material gain with little regard for the lessons it teaches its consumers. Indeed, hip-hop music artists have become the leading popular-cultural voice of underrepresented and marginalized youth in the United States. As a counterpublic, rap and hip-hop have always been about the "shifting terms of black marginality in contemporary American culture" (Rose, 1994, p. 3). One need only examine the ever-changing lingo of hip-hop artists like Snoop Doggy Dog, P. Diddy, and others to determine that hip-hop music is claiming its own voice. Moreover, hip-hop mogul Russell Simmons has served as a spokesperson for the youthful generations that so adore hip-hop music via "Rap-the-vote" and other political and charitable initiatives. Meanwhile, admired artist KRS-One has been on the college lecture circuit and has written a book entitled *Ruminations*. There are several artists who are messengers of the underclass via hip-hop music, even when the artist him or herself is not part of the underclass; and there are others who know that resistance has always been the cornerstone of what rap and hip-hop represent, yet they employ that undercurrent at times as a utility for launching creative, but derogatory and abusive music careers. Poet Bridget Gray brilliantly makes this point in an excerpt of her poem "My Letter to Hip Hop":

Dear Hip Hop,

I'm writing to inform you I'm going to have to end our relationship. I know in the beginning I was down to work my hips, but I was tricked. Seduced by your beat. You had me for three minutes and forty-six seconds. I was suspended in time, but when I snapped out of it I had to ask "Did I hear what I thought I did in that last rhyme?" Now forgive me, maybe I'm getting old or maybe I'm just slow, but I didn't even know you could say "bitch" on the radio, yet I was entranced by your beat I heard somewhere before, oh, I remember that was the original score. Now unless I'm dreaming I could have swore, right after you called me a "bitch" you called someone else a whore, and at this point I'm trying to process a few things. What were the original words to that song and you want me to do WHAT with my thong? I'm trippin' cause nobody is acting like anything is wrong. After all the anthem for the new millennium was "big Pimpin." . . . I thought Hip Hop was a way to poetically express yourself but it seems you'd say anything to get your C.D. off the shelf. So let's toast with champagne and blunts to your health but first tell me why, "Every other video, brotha gotta be a gigolo," and you show your respect by pouring beer for the homie who's dead. Then pour the rest of the forty over some female's head. And what's crazier than that is she doesn't seem to mind. But if you look past her ass deep into her eyes you might find a hint of surprise, cause she didn't realize, the camera shot would be between her thighs. And she furthers the lie as she tries to deny pretending its okay. She just gave a piece of her self-esteem away, and it aired nine times on MTV today, and all that for little to no pay, but "He's a hustler baby and he told you so, and when he's through you're a video ho." (http://www.bridgetgray.com/)

What Bridget Gray piercingly describes is a tragic predicament in which all hip-hop enthusiasts find themselves, although some do not see this situation as tragic. In fact, many are enticed by the voyeurism that drives videos and other visual displays of hip-hop music.

Despite the disempowering voices of thug and gangsta rappers, Black bodies are still retrievable. Nonetheless, it is critical to note that narratives about Black bodies in popular culture, generally, and thug rap in particular have been tenuous. This phantasmagoria has left us with little more than signifying practices and reshaped truths. However, there are strategies that may be useful for overcoming this predicament. Butler (1990) ingeniously offers one:

> The subject is not *determined* by the rules through which it is generated, because signification is *not a founding act, but rather a regulated process of repetition* that both conceals itself and enforces its rules precisely through the production of substantializing effects. In a sense, all signification takes place within the orbit of the compulsion to repeat; "agency," then is to be located within the possibility of a variation on that repetition. If the rules governing signification not only restrict, but enable the assertion of alternative domains of cultural intelligibility . . . then it is only *within* the practice of repetitive signifying that a subversion of identity becomes possible. (p. 145)

Film director Spike Lee has long understood this logic and has initiated a series of racially political films such as *School Daze, Mississippi Masala, Do the Right Thing, D.R.O.P. Squad,* and most recently *Bamboozled.* Through his own cinematic approach and style, Lee both constructs and reports the intricacies of racially contrived inscriptions. He is not the only one. Several avant-garde filmmakers like Haille Gerima and Julie Dash have done the same. Also, in an effort to strengthen the cultural consciousness of music listeners, artists like KRS-One, Wyclef Jean, Common, Stevie Wonder, U2, The Black-Eyed Peas, Indie Arie, Lauryn Hill, Chuck D, Jill Scott, Alicia Keys, and others have discussed human suffering and the entrenchment of racial ideologies in everyday public life.

Alongside these revolutionary aesthetic perspectives, there must be continued radical progressive social change that is initiated from community activists and intellectuals (Giroux, 2000). For example, Byrd (2001) offers a redemptive critique of Black masculinity and manhood in which he explores the character of John the High Conqueror as a antihegemonic mode of masculinity that replaces homophobic gender "traps" in favor of a more savvy and aware masculine persona, which embraces spirituality and consciousness. Even still, there needs to be a clear admission and embrace of multiple Black masculinities rather than an essentialist, unifocal Black masculinity. Houston and Davis (2001) also present a recuperative set of essays that reenvision Black women's standpoints, grounding them in cultural, spiritual, and emotional consciousness. The model produced in this book is another conceptual frame that reintroduces Black masculinities in healthy, nonhegemonic terms.

There must be emically produced paradigmatic shifts that move away from seeing Black bodily inscriptions, male or female, as spectacles (Giroux, 1998). Debord (1994) asserts, "The spectacle is the self-portrait of power in the age of power's totalitarian rule over the conditions of existence" (p. 19). The inscriptions and images of Black bodies are the spectacles that often mirror the interests of others and lead to more stereotypes and hampered race relations. It is important to understand that the bodies themselves are not the spectacles, but rather the canvases on which the spectacle is written. As explored in this book, there are multiple cues that function as spectatorial significations written on the body. Skin color is one such cue. Doane reminds us, "Skin becomes the locus of an alienation more acute to the extent that it is inescapable—at first sight, racial identity is ineluctably established and the Manichean polarity of black/white with all its metaphysical implications is activated" (Doane, 1999, p. 452). Skin color is one among several preverbal cues that automatically trigger personal antecedents and social ascriptions to be applied wholecloth to others, and, as a Manichean dialectic, race continually signifies social dualism between Whites and non-Whites in the United States.

Future research will need to account for how hair, body image, and weight rhetorically resist negative Black corporeal inscriptions, symbolically suggest cultural consciousness, and creatively resituate racial perspectives in varying contexts including mass media and popular culture. Also, future studies will need to offer viable and innovative concepts and strategies that will attempt to relieve us from the patriarchal prerogatives and mimetic representations of essentialized Blackness with which too many audiences have become comfortable. I agree with hooks (1995), who asserts:

> To recover radical political equilibrium, Black folks must collectively seek self-determination. Yet, that seeking cannot happen as long as most folks are either brainwashed so that they passively internalize white supremacist

attitudes and values. . . . It should be obvious that the process of decolo-
nization and radical politicization requires literacy. Without critical literacy,
black folks cannot assume responsibility for ourselves. (p. 257)

The challenge is to firmly stand by moral convictions that patriarchal
apparatus as manifested in contemporary minstrelsy, thuggery, pimping, and
misogyny in all their reinvented forms is still exploitative and unacceptable.
Only through what hooks calls "critical literacy" can we fully come to terms
with this moral position. These images are not representative of all Black
lives; thus, a fuller and more accurate composite of Black bodies that presents
the positive and negative rather than the often unidimensionally negative
filmic, televisual, and aural portrayals that have become so commonplace
must be introduced to the range of epistemological and axiological interpretations of Black corporeality.

Throughout this book, I spend a considerable amount of time assessing
the state of negative racial representations in the media. It is conspicuous
that I lend little time to acknowledging positive representations. I do this
intentionally. I think we are in an existential crisis and, when one is in a crisis, it is most important to figure out what the dimensions of the crisis are
before strategizing its elimination. There is much work to be done. Clearly,
movies like *Daughters of the Dust*, television shows like *24*, music like that of
Common, and writers like bell hooks, Cornel West, and others offer liberatory representations of Black bodies; however, images and discourses like
these are too infrequent. Only when we are able to see full representations of
Black bodies rather than primarily pathologized ones in the media will we be
able to witness significant racial progress and restored hope for children of
color as mass media consumers (Giroux, 2004). Until then, we can only hope
audiences will begin to see Black bodies for who they really are—human
beings who are just as normal as Whites, yet in their own cultural habitat
behaving in non-White ways. Then and only then will we restore Black bodies and blackness to their rightful place alongside other relatively normal,
healthy, and functional representations of American public life.

# Notes

## INTRODUCTION

1. I refer intentionally to the Black body as a singular entity. It is very important to understand that Black bodies are frequently treated as an incorrigible public monument in popular culture. The fact that the vast majority of mass-mediated representations of the Black body stereotypically present it as a morally decrepit, socially debased, and sexually charged object of public fascination is haunting. To discuss "the Black body" pluralistically, as it should be if it were emancipated from a consumer and producer-driven labyrinth of negative inscriptions, is to dismiss the point that U. S. popular culture has yet to mature enough to recognize the inherent polysemy of Black bodies, the fact that they cannot be captured unitarily in a momentary representational gaze. We only witness salvatory justice to images of blackness with the few sprinklings of television shows like *The Cosby Show, Soul Food, My Wife and Kids*, and the *Bernie Mac Show*. Many of the other televisual and cinematic inscriptions of blackness dispense representational dreams, collective fantasies, and out-of-control depictions of love that leave us the myth that we are bereft of liberatory possibilities.

## CHAPTER ONE. ORIGINS OF BLACK BODY POLITICS

1. When referring to *the* Black body, I am discussing the full composite of Black bodies, not an essential, singular, unitary entity that describes or fails to notice diversity among Blacks. I am also speaking most specifically of Blacks in the United States. Although I am suggesting that the reader understands my reference to Blacks as reference to African Americans in particular, in order to make the necessary arguments about skin color politics, it is critical to note that Blacks throughout the diaspora may be scripted similarly due to social constructions of race and common racial features shared with African Americans in the United States.

2. See Donald Bogle's four companion volumes: *Toms, Coons, Mulattoes, Mammies & Bucks* (1973), *Brown Sugar: Eighty years of America's Black Female Superstars* (1980), *Blacks in American Films and Television* (1988), and *Primetime Blues* (2000). See also Joseph Boskin's *Sambo: The Rise and Demise of an American Jester* (1986),

Patricia Turner's *Ceramic Uncles & Celluloid Mammies* (1994), and Robin Means Coleman's *African American Viewers and the Black Situation Comedy* (2000). I do not intend to discuss vaudeville either, which gave rise to well-known entertainers such as Bill Bojangles Robinson and Sammy Davis Jr., and eventually led to actor-dancers like Gregory Hines.

3. I purposefully label this racial rather than cultural representation because it was not their values, norms, beliefs, or customs that were portrayed on stage, it was their physicality accompanied by projections of racial humor via saturated use of malapropisms and gibberish. Even with later depictions of characters like Sappho or Sapphire, who were uppity, intelligent characters perpetually equipped with repartee, these racial representations lay side-by-side with the more stereotypical ones.

4. See Jackson (2000) and Jackson and Heckman (2002) for a description of corporeal zones. Both articles essentially suggest that traditional explanations of verbal and nonverbal communication depict the two as a dichotomy rather than points on a continuum from preverbal to epiverbal communication.

5. See bell hooks's (1992) *Black Looks*, in which she explains that Sarah Bartmann's naked African body was placed on exhibit in 1810 and dubbed "Hottentot Venus," a term that became derogatorily associated with enlarged buttocks and a fantasy about what was imagined to be her unique genitalia. In fact, as Anderson (1997) explains, "In Bartmann's case, this (the physical look of her genitalia) was due to the tribal practice of lengthening the labia. In her culture, this was a mark of beauty, but Europeans viewed these physical anomalies to be natural in Blacks and thought Bartmann's genitalia were deformed from birth" (p. 86).

6. Br'er was a contraction for brother.

7. According to drama theorist Lisa Anderson (1997), the predecessor of the film was a play written by the eventual director of the film, Dion Boucicault. The play appeared on stage in 1859, just four years prior to President Abraham Lincoln's signing of the Emancipation Proclamation.

8. For more discussion about skin color politics, see Russell, Wilson, and Hall (1992) *The Color Complex*.

9. As an aside, her sister Isabel, also an actress who portrayed the tragic mulatto, later married light-skinned politician Adam Clayton Powell, Jr.

## CHAPTER TWO. SCRIPTING THE BLACK BODY
## IN POPULAR MEDIA: EXPLORING PROCESS

1. Tray is an abbreviation for his character name "Ashtray."

## CHAPTER FOUR. "IF IT FEELS THIS GOOD GETTIN' USED":
## EXPLORING THE HYPERTEXT OF SEXUALITY
## IN HIP-HOP MUSIC AND PIMP MOVIES

1. I use the terms rap and hip-hop synonymously, though there have certainly been compelling arguments for isolating the two.

2. One of many laudatory and complimentary words referring to the greatness or splendor of something being described.

3. "Playa" is the same as player—someone who plays the field, alternating positions. The metaphor implies the relational activity of a polygamous male. "Dog" is a term one would think would be considered despicable, but the term, when used among some males, has been altered to mean someone who is cool and part of a posse of males who share similar interests. Playa and dog are used pretty much interchangeably in hip-hop music, just as thug and ruffneck are.

4. Stagolee is the muscular, mythic hero in Black folktales who, armed with rhythmic skill and profanity, intimidates all would-be foes. See Hecht, Jackson, and Ribeau (2003) and Lester (1991) for more details.

5. *Thug Misses* is the title of female rap artist and Tampa, Florida, native Khia's 2002 album. The instant hit "My Neck, My Back" is a song filled with sexual innuendo.

6. Ruff Ryders is a rap artist syndicate composed of about a dozen rappers like Eve, Swizz Beats (the producer), Chivon, Wah Dean, Timbaland, Bubba Sparxxx, and JadaKiss.

7. This is the only one in the list that is produced and directed by Whites.

## CHAPTER FIVE. TOWARD AN INTEGRATED THEORY OF BLACK MASCULINITY

1. We purposefully use the term "Black" instead of African American for two reasons: to accent the body politic inherent in seeing the color black during interracial interaction and to make the point that "Black" refers to peoples throughout the diaspora who are Black, from Brazil to Trinidad to the United States and beyond. These Black masculinities share the common positionalities and overall struggle discussed in the Black Masculine Identity Theory.

2. Incidentally, these are often the same people who believe that all humans share the same desires, interests, needs, and motivations.

3. According to Na'im Akbar (1991): "A male is a biological entity. . . . One need not look beyond the observable anatomical characteristics to determine that he is a male. . . . Maleness is also a mentality that operates with the same principles as biology. It is a mentality dictated by appetite and physical determinants. This mentality is one guided by instincts, urges, desires, and feelings. He is in this mentality a whining, crying, hungry, and dependent little leech. . . . The next stage in the transformation from the biologically bound definition of "male is the development of the "boy." The movement is determined by the development of discipline. Once the mind has become disciplined, the boy is in a position to grow into reasoning. . . . When the primary use of your reason is for the purpose of scheming or lying then you are fixated in the boyish mentality. . . . The thing that transforms a boy into becoming a man is knowledge" (pp. 3–12).

# References

Akbar, N. (1991). *Visions for black men*. Tallahassee, FL: Mind Productions.

Allen, J., Als, H., Lewis, J., & Litwack, L. (2000). *Without sanctuary: Lynching photography in America*. Santa Fe, NM: Twin Palms Press.

Althusser, L. (1994). Ideology and ideological state apparatuses (notes towards an investigation). In S. Zizek (Ed.), *Mapping ideology* (pp. 100–140). London: Verso.

Anderson, L. M. (1997). *Mammies no more*. Lanham, MD: Rowman & Littlefield.

Appiah, K. A., & Gates, H. L. (2003). Slavery in North America. In K. Appiah & H. Gates (Eds.), *Africana: The encyclopedia of the African and African American experience* (pp. 849–851). Philadelphia: Running Press.

Asante, M. (1974). Theoretical and research issues in black communication. In J. L. Daniel (Ed.), *Black communication: Dimensions of research and instruction*. New York: Speech Communication Association.

Asante, M. K. (1999). Foreword. In R. L. Jackson, *Negotiation of cultural identity*. Westport, CT: Praeger.

Awkward, M. (2002). Black male trouble. In J. K. Gardiner (Ed.), *Masculinity studies and feminist theory* (pp. 290–304). New York: Columbia University Press.

Baker-Fletcher, G. (1996). Black bodies, whose body?: African American men in XODUS. In B. Krondorfer (Ed.), *Men's bodies, men's gods: Male identities in a postchristian culture*. New York: New York University Press.

Bakhtin, M. (Eds.). (1981). *Dialogic imagination: Four essays*. Austin, TX: University of Texas Press.

Barthes, R. (1977). The death of the author. In S. Heath (Trans.), *Image, music, text: Essays*. New York: Hill & Wang.

Barthes, R. (1991). *Grain of the voice, 1962–1980: Interviews*. Berkeley: University of California Press.

Barthes, R. (1999). Myth today. In J. Evans & S. Hall (Eds.), *Visual culture: The reader* (pp. 33–40). Thousand Oaks, CA: Sage.

Bates, B., & Garner, T. (2001). Can you dig it? Audiences, archetypes and John Shaft. *Howard Journal of Communications, 12*, 137–157.

Bell, K. (1999). The more they change, the more they remain the same. In T. McDonald & T. Ford-Ahmed (Eds.), *Nature of a sistuh: Black women's lived experiences in contemporary culture* (pp.197–222). Durham: Carolina Academic Press.

Belton, D. (Ed.). (1996). *Speak my name: Black men on masculinity and the American dream*. Boston: Beacon Press.

Bem, S. L. (1993). *The lenses of gender: Transforming the debate on sexual inequality*. New Haven: Yale University Press.

Best, S. M. (1996). "Stand by your man": Richard Wright, lynch pedagogy, and rethinking black male agency. In M. Blount & G. P. Cunningham (Eds.), *Representing black men* (pp. 131–154). New York: Routledge.

Bhabha, H. (1986). Remembering Fanon: A foreword. In F. Fanon, *Black skin, white mask* (p. xv). London: Pluto Press.

Bhabha, H. (1992). Postcolonial authority and postmodern guilt. In L. Grossberg, C. Nelson, & P. Treichler (Eds.), *Cultural Studies* (pp. 56–68). New York: Routledge.

Blank, R. (2001). An overview of trends of socioeconomic well-being, by race. In N. Smelser, W. Wilson, & F. Mitchell (Eds.), *American becoming: Racial trends and their consequences* (Vol. 1, pp. 21–39). Washington: National Academy Press.

Blount, M., & Cunningham, G. (1996). *Representing black men*. New York: Tavistock Publications.

Bogle, D. (1989). *Blacks in American film and television: An illustrated encyclopedia*. New York: Fireside.

Bogle, D. (1996). *Toms, coons, mulattoes, mammies and bucks: An interpretive history of blacks in American films* (4th ed.). New York: Continuum.

Bogle, D. (2001). *Primetime blues: African Americans on network television*. New York: Farar, Straus, & Giroux.

Booker, C. B. (2000). *"I will wear no chains": A social history of African American males*. Westport, CT: Praeger.

Bordo, S. (1989). The body and the reproduction of femininity: A feminist appropriation of Foucault. In A. Jaggar & S. Bordo (Eds.), *Gender/body/knowledge*. New Brunswick, NJ: Rutgers University Press.

Bordo, S. (1994). Reading the male body. In L. Goldstein (Ed.), *The male body: Features, destinies, exposures*. Ann Arbor: University of Michigan Press.

Borisoff, D., & Hahn, D. (1993). Thinking with the body: Sexual metaphors. *Communication Quarterly, 41*(3), 253–260.

Boyd, H., & Allen, R. (Ed.). (1996). *Brotherman: The odyssey of black men in America*. New York: Fawcett Books.

Boyd, T. (1997). *Am I black enough for you?: Popular culture from the 'hood and beyond*. Bloomington: Indiana University Press.

BridgetGray.Com. (2004, April 30). An excerpt of my letter to hip-hop. Retrieved from http://www.bridgetgray.com/

Butler, J. (1990). *Gender trouble: Feminism and the subversion of identity*. New York: Routledge.

Byrd, R. (2001). Prologue: The tradition of John, a mode of black masculinity. In R. Byrd & B. Guy-Sheftall (Eds.), *Traps: African American men on gender and sexuality* (pp. 1–26). Bloomington: Indiana University Press.

Cameron, K. (1990). Paul Robeson, Eddie Murphy, and the film text of "Africa." *Text and Performance Quarterly, 10*, 282–293.

Campbell, C. (1995). *Race, myth, and the news*. Thousand Oaks, CA: Sage.

Chase-Riboud, B. (2003). *Hottentot venus: A novel*. New York: Doubleday.

Chideya, F. (1995). *Don't believe the hype: Fighting cultural misinformation about African Americans*. New York: Plume.

Collins, P. H. (1991). *Black feminist thought: Knowledge, consciousness and the politics of empowerment*. New York: Routledge.

Connor, M.K. (1995). *What is cool?: Understanding black manhood in America*. Berkeley, CA: Crown Publications.

Cose, E. (1993). *The rage of a privileged class*. New York: Harper.

Costello, M., & Wallace, D. F. (1990). *Signifying rappers: Rap and race in the urban present*. Hopewell, NJ: Ecco Press.

Crenshaw, K. (1988). Race, reform and retrenchment: Transformation and legitimation in antidiscrimination law. *Harvard Law Review, 101*(7), 1331–1387.

Cripps, T. (1977). *Slow fade to black: The Negro in American film, 1900–1942*. New York: Oxford University Press.

Cripps, T. (1993). *Making movies black*. New York: Oxford University Press.

Cummings, M. S. (1988). The changing image of the African American family on television. *Journal of Popular Culture, 22*, 75–85.

Cummings, M., & Roy, A. (2002). Manifestations of afrocentricity in rap music. *The Howard Journal of Communications, 13*, 56–79.

Cunningham, G. P. (1996). Body politics: Race, gender, and the captive body. In M. Blount & G. P. Cunningham (Eds.), *Representing black men* (pp. 131–154). New York: Routledge.

Darwin, C. (1859). *The origin of species*. London: Penguin Books.

Dates, J., & Barlow, W. (Eds.). (1993). *Split image: African Americans in the mass media*. Washington, DC: Howard University Press.

Dates, J., & Pease, E. (1997). Warping the world—media's mangled images of race. In E. Dennis & E. Pease (Eds.), *The media in Black and White* (pp. 77–82). New Brunswick, NJ: Transaction Publishers.

Davis, F. J. (1996). *Who is black?: One nation's definition*. University Park: Penn State University Press.

Davis, K. R. (2001). *Driving while black: Coverup*. Cincinnati: Interstate International Publishing of Cincinnati.

De Beauvoir, S. (1974). *The second sex* (H. M. Parshley, Trans.). New York: Vintage.

Debord, G. (1994). *The society of the spectacle*. New York: Zone Books.

De Certeau, M. (1984). *The practice of everyday life*. Berkeley: University of California Press.

Decoy, R. (1987). *The Nigger Bible*. Los Angeles: Holloway House.

DeCurtis, A. (1999). 2 Live Crew Trial. In A Light (Ed.), *The vibe history of hip hop* (pp. 268–276). New York: Three Rivers Press.

Deetz, S. (1992). *Democracy in an age of corporate colonialization: Developments in communication and the politics of everyday life*. Albany: State University of New York Press.

Dent, G. (Ed.). (1992). *Black popular culture* (a project by Michelle Wallace). Seattle: Bay Press.

Diawartha, M. (1993). *Black American cinema*. New York: Routledge.

Diop, C. A. (1991). *Civilization or barbarism*. New York: Lawrence Hill Books.

Dixon, T., & Linz, D. (2000). Overrepresentation and underrepresentation of African Americans and Latinos as lawbreakers on television news. *Journal of Communication, 50*(2), 131–154.

Doane, M. A. (1999). Dark continents: Epistemologies of racial and sexual difference in psychoanalysis and the cinema. In J. Evans and S. Hall (Eds.), *Visual culture: The reader* (448–456). London: Sage.

Drudge Report. (2004, February 1). Outrage at CBS after Janet bares breast during dinner hour: Super bowl show pushes limits. Retrieved February 24, 2004, from www.drudgereport.com/mattjj.htm.

DuBois, W. E. B. (1903). *Souls or black folk*. Chicago: A. C. McClung & Co.

Dyson, M. E. (1994). Be like Mike?: Michael Jordan and the pedagogy of desire. In H. Giroux & P. McLaren (Eds.), *Between borders: Pedagogy and the politics of cultural studies* (pp. 119–126). New York: Routledge.

Dyson, M. E. (1996). *Between God and gangsta rap: Bearing witness to black culture*. New York: Oxford University Press.

Dyson, M. E. (2001). When you divide body and soul, problems multiply: The black church and sex. In R. Byrd & B. Guy-Sheftall (Eds.), *Traps: African American men on gender and sexuality* (pp. 308–326). Bloomington: Indiana University Press.

Ebert, R. (2000). Loving Jezebel. *Chicago Sun Times*. Retrieved August 1, 2002, from www.suntimes.com/ebert/evert_reviews/2000/10/102705.html.

Ellis, J. (1982). *Visible fictions: Cinema, television, video*. New York: Routledge & Kegan-Paul.

Ellison, R. (1952). *Invisible man*. New York: Vintage.

Ellison, R. (1972). *Shadow and act*. New York: Vintage.

Entman, R. M. (1992) Blacks in the news: Television, modern racism and cultural change. *Journalism Quarterly, 69*(2), 341–361.

Entman, R. M., and Rojecki, A. (2000). *The black image in the white mind: Media and race in America.* Chicago: University of Chicago.

Euell, K. (1997). Signifyin(g) ritual: Subverting stereotypes, salvaging icons. *African American Review, 31*(4), 667–675.

Evans, J. (1999). Introduction. In J. Evans & S. Hall (Eds.), *Visual culture: The reader* (pp. 11–20). Thousand Oaks, CA: Sage.

Fanon, F. (1967). *Black skin, white masks.* New York: Grove.

Fao Girl. (2000). Available: www.fao.com.

Farley, C. J. (2002). *Introducing Halle Berry: A biography.* New York: Pocket Books.

Fenster, M. (1995). Understanding and incorporating rap: The articulation of alternative popular musical practices within dominant cultural practices and institutions. *The Howard Journal of Communications, 5*(3), 223–244.

Fisher, G. (1998). *The mindsets factor in ethnic conflict.* Yarmouth, ME: Intercultural Press.

Foster-Dixon, G. (1993). Troping the body: Etiquette texts and performance. *Text and Performance Quarterly, 13*, 79–96.

Foucault, M. (1972). *Discipline and punish: The birth of the prison.* New York: Vintage.

Foucault, M. (1980). Two lectures. In C. Gordon (Ed.), *Power/knowledge: Selected interviews and other writings.* New York: Pantheon.

Foucault, M. (1984). Nietzsche, genealogy, history. In P. Rabinow (Ed.), *The Foucault reader.* New York: Penguin.

Franklin, J. H., & Moss, A. A. (1988). *From slavery to freedom: A history of Negro Americans* (6th ed.). New York: Knopf.

Gaines, J. M. (2001). *Fire and desire.* Chicago: University of Chicago Press.

Gandy, O. (1999). *Communication and race.* London: Oxford.

Gardiner, J. K. (Ed.). (2002). *Masculinity studies and feminist theory.* New York: Columbia University Press.

Gatens, M. (1996). *Imaginary bodies: Ethics, power, and corporeality.* New York: Routledge.

George, N. (1992). *Buppies, b-boys, baps & bohos: Notes on post-soul black culture.* New York: HarperCollins.

George, N. (1998). *Hip hop America.* New York: Penguin.

Gerbner, G. (1999). Foreword: What do we know? In J. Shanahan & M. Morgan, *Television and its viewers: Cultivation theory and research* (pp. ix–xiii). New York: Cambridge University Press.

Gilroy, P. (1990). Sounds authentic: Black music, ethnicity, and the challenge of the changing same. *Black Music Research Journal, 10*(2), 128–131.

Gilroy, P. (1992). It's a family affair. In G. Dent (Ed.), *Black Popular Culture* (pp. 302–316). Seattle: Bay Press.

Giroux, H. (1992). *Border crossing: Cultural workers and the politics of education*. New York: Routledge.

Giroux, H. (1998). *Channel surfing: Racism, the media, and the destruction of today's youth*. New York: St. Martin's Press

Giroux, H. (2000). *Impure acts: Practical politics of cultural studies*. New York: Routledge.

Giroux, H. (2001). *Breaking in to the movies: Film and the culture of politics*. Williston, VT: Blackwell Publishers.

Giroux, H. (2004). *The abandoned generation*. New York: Palgrave Macmillan.

Gould, S. (1981). *The mismeasure of man*. New York: Norton.

Gray, H. (1989). Television, black Americans and the American dream. *Critical Studies in Mass Communication, 6*(4), 376–386.

Gray, H. (1997). *Watching race: Television and the struggle for the sign of blackness*. Minneapolis: University of Minnesota Press.

Grosz, E. (1994). *Volatile bodies: Toward a corporeal feminism*. Bloomington: Indiana University Press.

Guerrero, E. (1993). *Framing blackness: The African American image in film*. Philadelphia: Temple University Press.

Hall, E. T. (1983). *The dance of life*. New York: Anchor Books.

Hall, S. (1992). What is this black in black popular culture? In G. Dent (Ed.), *Black popular culture* (pp. 21–36). Seattle: Bay Press.

Hall, S. (1997). *Representation: Cultural representations and signifying practices (culture, media and identities)*. Thousand Oaks, CA: Sage.

Hamera, J. (1994). The ambivalent, knowing male body in the Pasadena Dance Theatre. *Text and Performance Quarterly, 14*, 197–209.

Harper, P. B. (1996). *Are we not mean: Masculine anxiety and the problem of African American identity*. New York: Oxford.

Harris, C. (1993). Whiteness as property. *Harvard Law Review, 106*(7), 1709–1791.

Harris, T. (1999). Interrogating the representation of African American female identity in the films "Waiting to Exhale" and "Set It Off." *Popular Culture Review, 10*(2), 43–53.

Hawes, L. (October 1998). Becoming other-wise: Conversational performance and the politics of experience. *Text and Performance Quarterly 18*(4), 273–299.

Hecht, M., Jackson, R., & Ribeau, S. (2003). *African American communication: Exploring identity and culture*. Mahwah, NJ: Lawrence Erlbaum.

Heider, D. (2000). *White news: Why local news programs don't cover people of color*. Mahwah, NJ: Lawrence Erlbaum Associates.

Henley, N. (1977). *Body politics: Power, sex, and nonverbal communication*. New York: Macmillan.

Hitchcock, P. (1993). *Dialogics of the oppressed*. Minneapolis: University of Minnesota Press.

Holiday, B. (1939). *Strange fruit*. New York: Commodore Records.

hooks, b. (1992). *Black looks: Race and representation*. Boston: South End Press.

hooks, b. (1994). *Outlaw culture: Resisting representations*. New York: Routledge.

hooks, b. (1995a). *Art on my mind*. New York: The New Press.

hooks, b. (1995b). *Killing rage: Ending racism*. New York: Henry Holt & Co.

hooks, b. (2003). *Rock my soul: Black people and self-esteem*. New York: Atria Books.

Houston, M., & Davis, O. (Eds.). (2001). *Centering ourselves: African-American feminist and womanist studies of discourse*. Cresskill, NJ: Hampton Press.

Hutchinson, E. (1994). *The assassination of the black male image*. New York: Middle Passage Press.

Jackson, R. L. (1997). Black manhood as xenophobe: An ontological exploration of the Hegelian dialectic. *Journal of Black Studies, 27*(6), 731–750.

Jackson, R. L. (1999). *The negotiation of cultural identity*. Westport, CT: Praeger.

Jackson, R. L. (February 2000). So real illusions of black intellectualism: Exploring race, roles, and gender in the academy. *Communication Theory, 10*(1), 48–63.

Jackson, R. L. (2000). Africalogical theory building: Positioning the discourse. *International and Intercultural Communication Annual, 22*, 31–41.

Jackson, R. L. (2002). Exploring African American identity negotiation in the academy: Toward a transformative vision of African American communication scholarship. *Howard Journal of Communication, 12*(4), 38–54.

Jackson, R. L., & Dangerfield, C. (2002). Defining black masculinity as cultural property: An identity negotiation paradigm. In L. Samovar & R. Porter (Eds.), *Intercultural Communication: A Reader* (pp. 120–130). Belmont, CA: Wadsworth.

Jackson, R. L., & Richardson, E. (Eds.). (2003). *Understanding African American rhetoric: Classical origins to contemporary innovations*. New York: Routledge

Jhally, S., & Lewis, J. (1992). *Enlightened racism: The Cosby Show, audiences and the myth of the American dream*. Boulder, CO: Westview Press.

Johnson, C. (1994). A phenomenology of the black body. In L. Goldstein (Ed.), *The male body* (pp. 121–136). Ann Arbor: University of Michigan Press.

Jones, J. (1991). The new ghetto aesthetic. *Wide Angle, 13*(3), 32–43.

Julien, I. (1996). Filmmakers' dialogue. In A. Read (Ed.), *The fact of blackness: Frantz Fanon and visual representation* (pp. 166–179). Seattle: Bay Press.

Kandi, K. (2002). Rah Digga: Harriett Thugman. *YRB*, 20–23.

Karenga, M. (2002). *Introduction to black studies* (3rd ed.). Sankore Press.

Katz, J. (Writer/Director). (2002). *Strange fruit* [Film]. California Newsreel.

Keating, A. (1995). Interrogating "whiteness," (de)constructing "race." *College English, 57,* 901–918.

Kelley, R. D. G. (1997). Playing for keeps: Pleasure and profit on the post-industrial playground. In W. Lubiano (Ed.), *The house that race built: Black Americans, U.S. terrain.* New York: Pantheon.

Khamit-Kush, I. (1999). *What they never told you in history class.* New York: A & B Publishers.

Kincheloe, J., Steinberg, S., & Gresson, A. (1997). *Measured lies: The bell curve examined.* New York: St. Martins Press.

Kitwana, B. (2002). *The hip hop generation: Young blacks and the crisis in African American culture.* New York: BasicCivitas Books.

Klein, M. (1959). Our adult world and its roots in infancy. *Human Relations, 12,* 291–303.

Krims, A. (2000). *Rap music and the poetics of identity.* New York: Cambridge University Press.

KRS-One (2003). *Ruminations.* New York: Welcome Rain Publishers.

Lehman, P. (2001). In an imperfect world, men with small penises are forgiven: The presentation of the penis/phallus in American films of the 1990s. In M. Kimmel & M. Messner (Eds.), *Men's lives.* (5th ed., pp. 494–504). Boston: Allyn & Bacon.

Lester, J. (1991). *Black folktales.* New York: Grove.

Levinas, E. (1969). *Totality and infinity: An essay on exteriority* (A. Lingis, Trans.). Pittsburgh: Duquesne University Press.

Looby, C. (1997). As thoroughly black as the most faithful philanthropist could desire. In H. Stecopoulos & M. Uebel (Eds.), *Race and the subject of masculinities* (pp. 71–115). Durham, NC: Duke.

Lorde, A. (1984). *Sister outsider: Essays and speeches.* Freedom, CA: Crossing Press.

Lott, T. (1999). *The invention of race: Black culture and the politics of representation.* Oxford: Blackwell.

Lovejoy, A. (1960). *The great chain of being.* New York: Harper & Row.

MacCabe, C. (1999). *The eloquence of the vulgar.* London: British Film Institute.

MacDonald, H. (2003). *Are cops racist?* New York: Ivan R. Dee.

Madhubuti, H. (1990). *Black men: Obsolete, single, dangerous?* Chicago: Third World Press.

Majors, R., and Billson, J. (1992). *Cool pose: The dilemmas of black manhood in America.* New York: Lexington Books.

Marable, M. (2001). The black male: Searching beyond stereotypes. In M. Kimmel and M. Messner (Eds.), *Men's lives* (5th ed.). Boston: Allyn & Bacon.

Mapp, E. (1972). *Blacks in American films: Today and yesterday*. Mestuchen, NJ: Scarecrow Press.

Mapplethorpe, R. (1983). *Black males*. Amsterdam: Gallerie Jurka.

Marable, M. (1995). *Beyond black and white: Rethinking race in American politics and society*. New York: Verso.

Marriott, D. (2000). *On black men*. New York: Columbia University Press.

McCall, N. (1995). *Makes me wanna holler: A young black man in America*. New York: Random House.

McIntosh, P. (1994). White privilege and male privilege: A personal account of coming to see correspondence through work in women's studies. In M. Andersen and P. Collins (Eds.), *Race, class, and gender: An anthology* (pp. 76–87). Belmont, CA: Wadsworth.

McPhail, M. (1991). Complicity: The theory of negative difference. *Howard Journal of Communication, 3*, 1–13.

McPhail, M. (1994a). *The rhetoric of racism*. Lanham, MD: University Press of America.

McPhail, M. (1994b). The politics of complicity: Second thoughts about the social construction of racial equality. *Quarterly Journal of Speech, 80*, 343–357.

McPhail, M. (1996). *Zen in the art of rhetoric: An inquiry into coherence*. Albany: State University of New York Press.

McPhail, M. (1998). From complicity to coherence: Rereading the rhetoric of afrocentricity. *Western Journal of Communication, 62*(2), 114–140.

McWhorter, J. (2000). *Losing the race: Self-sabotage in black America*. New York: The Free Press.

Means-Coleman, R. (2000). *African American viewers and the black situation comedy*. New York: Garland.

Meeks, K. (2000). *Driving while black: What to do if you are a victim of racial profiling*. New York: Broadway Press.

Mercer, K. (1988). Diaspora, culture, and the dialogic imagination: The aesthetics of black independent film in Britain. In M. B. Cham & C. Andrade-Watkins (Eds.), *Critical perspectives on black independent cinema* (pp. 50–61). Cambridge: MIT Press.

Mercer, K. (1999). Reading racial fetishism: The photographs of Robert Mapplethorpe. In J. Evans & S. Hall (Eds.), *Visual culture: The reader* (pp. 435–447). Thousand Oaks, CA: Sage.

Meyers, M. (2004). African American women and violence: Gender, race and class in the news. *Critical Studies in Media Communication, 21*(2), 95–118.

Miller, J. (1993). The case of early black cinema. *Critical Studies in Mass Communication, 10*(2), 181–184.

Miller, M., Alberts, J., Hecht, M., Trost, M., & Krizek, R. (2000). *Adolescent relationships and drug use*. Mahwah, NJ: Lawrence Erlbaum.

Mohanty, C. (1994). On race and violence: Challenges for liberal education in the 1990s. In H. Giroux & P. McLaren (Eds.), *Between borders: Pedagogy and the politics of cultural studies*. New York: Routledge.

Morrison, C. D. (2002). Reading the black male body: Tupac Shakur as text(s). In R. L. Jackson & E. B. Richardson (Eds.), *Understanding African American rhetoric* (pp. 187–203). New York: Routledge.

Moses, W. (1993). *Black messiahs and Uncle Toms: Social and literary manipulations of a religious myth*. University Park: Penn State University Press.

Neal, M. A. (2002). *Soul babies: Black popular culture and the post-soul aesthetic*. New York: Routledge.

Nesteby, J. R. (1982). *Black images in American films, 1896–1954*. Lanham, MD: University Press of America.

Ogg, A., & Upshall, D. (2001). *The hip hop years: A history of rap*. London: Channel 4 Books.

Oliver, M. B., Jackson, R. L., Moses, N., & Dangerfield, C. (2004). The face of crime: Viewers' memory of black and white facial features of individuals pictured in the news. *Journal of Communication, 54*(1), 88–104.

Oliver, W. (1989). Black males and social problems: Prevention through Afrocentric socialization. *Journal of Black Studies, 20*(1), 15–39.

Orbe, M. (1998). Construction of reality on MTV's The Real World: An analysis of the restrictive coding of black masculinity. *Southern Communication Journal, 64*(1), 32–47.

Orbe, M., & Hopson, M. (2002). Looking at the front door: Exploring images of the black male on MTV's The Real World. In J. N. Martin, T. K. Nakayama, & J. A. Flores (Eds.), *Readings in cultural contexts* (pp. 157–166). Mountain View, CA: Mayfield Press.

Orbe, M., & Strother, K. (1996). Signifying the tragic mulatto: A semiotic analysis of Alex Haley's *Queen*. *Howard Journal of Communications, 7*, 113–126.

Perkins, W. E. (1996). *Droppin' science: Critical essays on rap music and hip-hop culture*. Philadelphia: Temple University Press.

Pinar, W. (2001). *The gender of racial politics and violence in America: Lynching, prison rape and crisis of masculinity*. New York: Peter Lang.

Pozner, E. (1997). Not your mother's heroines. *Sojourner: The women's forum*, 12–13.

Ribeau, S., Baldwin, J., & Hecht, M. (1997). An African American communication perspective. In L. Samovar & R. Porter (Eds.), *Intercultural communication: A reader* (8th ed., pp. 147–153). Belmont, CA: Wadsworth.

Roberts, D. (1997). *Killing the black body*. New York: Pantheon.

Roberts, G. (1994). Brother to brother: African American modes of relating among men. *Journal of Black Studies, 24*(1), 379–390.

Rocchio, V. F. (2000). *Reel racism: Confronting Hollywood's construction of Afro-American culture*. Boulder, CO: Westview.

Rogin, M. (1996). *Blackface, white noise: Jewish immigrants in the Hollywood melting pot.* Berkeley: University of California Press.

Rose, T. (1994). *Black noise: Rap music and black popular culture in contemporary America.* Hanover, NH: Wesleyan University Press.

Ross, A., & Rose, T. (Eds.). (1994). *Microphone fiends: Youth music and youth culture.* New York: Routledge.

Russell, K., Wilson, M., & Hall, R. (1992). *The color complex: The politics of skin color among African Americans.* New York: Doubleday.

Schacter, D. (1992). Implicit knowledge: New perspectives on unconscious processes. *Proceedings of the National Academy of Science, 89,* pp. 1113–1117.

Schacter, D. (1996). *Searching for memory.* New York: HarperCollins.

Scott, J., & Stewart, J. (1989). The pimp-whore complex in everyday life. In N. Hare & J. Hare (Eds.), *Crisis in black sexual politics* (pp. 57–62). San Francisco: Black Think Tank.

Shelton, M. (1997). Can't touch this! Representations of the African American female body in urban rap videos. *Popular Music & Society, 21*(3), 107–116.

Shilling, C. (1993). *The body and social theory.* Newbury Park, CA: Sage.

Silk, C., & Silk, J. (1990). *Racism and anti-racism in American popular culture.* New York: Manchester University Press.

Silverman, K. (1992). *Male subjectivity at the margins.* New York: Routledge.

Smelser, M., Wilson, W., & Mitchell, F. (2001). *America becoming: Racial trends and their consequences.* Washington, DC: National Academy Press.

Smith, F. (1998). *American body politics.* Athens: University of Georgia Press.

Smythe, M. J. (1995). Talking bodies: Body talk at Bodyworks. *Communication Studies, 46,* 245–260.

Snead, J., MacCabe, C., & West, C. (1994). *White screens/black images: Hollywood from the dark side.* New York: Routledge.

Southern, E. (1983). *The music of black Americans.* New York: Norton.

Spaulding, H. (1990). *Encyclopedia of black folklore and humor.* Middle Village, NY: Jonathan David Publisher.

Spellers, R. (2003). The kink factor: A womanist discourse analysis of African American mother/daughter perspectives on negotiating hair/body politics. In R. L. Jackson & E. Richardson (Eds.), *Understanding African American rhetoric: Classical origins to contemporary innovations.* New York: Routledge.

Speziale-Bagliacca, R. (1991). *On the shoulders of Freud: Freud, Lacan and the psychoanalysis of phallic ideology.* New Brunswick, NJ: Transaction.

Spivak, G. (1988). Can the subaltern speak? In C. Nelson & L. Grossberg (Eds.), *Marxism and the interpretation of culture* (pp. 217–313). Urbana: University of Illinois Press.

Staples, B. (1995). *Parallel time: Growing up in black and white*. New York: Harper-Collins.

Staples, R. (1982). *Black masculinity: The black male's role in American society*. San Francisco: Black Scholar Press.

Stecopoulos, H., & Uebel, M. (Eds.). (1997). *Race and the subject of masculinities*. Durham: Duke.

Tate, G. (1992). *Flyboy in the buttermilk*. New York: Simon & Schuster.

Taylor, C. (1992). *Multiculturalism and the politics of recognition*. Princeton, NJ: Princeton University Press.

Tierney, S., & Jackson, R. L. (2002). Deconstructing whiteness ideology as a set of rhetorical fantasy themes: Implications for interracial alliance building in the United States. In M. J. Collier (Ed.), *Building intercultural alliances* (Vol. 25) (pp. 81–106). Newbury Park, CA: Sage.

Todorov, T. (1984). *Mikhail Bakhtin: The dialogical principle* (Wlad Godzich, Trans.). Minneapolis: University of Minnesota Press.

Toll, R. C. (1974). *Blacking up: The minstrel show in nineteenth century America*. New York: Oxford University Press.

Toop, D. (1984). *The rap attack*. Boston: South End Press.

Trend, D. (1994). Nationalities, pedagogies and media. In H. Giroux & P. McLaren (Eds.), *Between borders: Pedagogy and the politics of cultural studies* (pp. 225–241). New York: Routledge.

Turner, P. (2002). *Ceramic uncles and celluloid mammies: Black images and their influence on culture*. Richmond, VA: University of Virginia Press.

*Unbreakable:* The official website. Retrieved on October 2, 2002. Available: http://video.go.com/unbreakable/html/making/production.html.

Vivian, B. (2002). Jefferson's other. *Quarterly Journal of Speech, 88*(3), 284–302.

Walzer, M. (1997). *On toleration*. New Haven: Yale University Press.

Watkins, M. (1994). *On the real side*. New York: Simon & Schuster.

Watkins, S. C. (1998). *Representing: Hip hop culture and the production of black cinema*. Chicago: University of Chicago Press.

Watts, E. K. (1997). An exploration of spectacular consumption: Gangsta rap as cultural commodity. *Communication Studies, 6*, 42–58.

Watts, E., & Orbe, M. (2002). The spectacular consumption of "true" African American culture: "Whassup!" with the Budweiser guys? *Critical Studies in Media Communication, 19*, 1–20.

Watts, J. G. (1994). *Heroism and the black intellectual: Ralph Ellison, politics and Afro-American intellectual life*. Chapel Hill: University of North Carolina Press.

Webster, Y. (1992). *The racialization of America*. New York: St. Martin's Press.

Welsing, F. C. (1991). *The Isis papers*. Chicago: Third World Press.

West, C. (1982). *Prophesy deliverance: An Afro-American revolutionary Christianity.* Louisville, KY: Presbyterian Publishing Corporation.

West, C. (1993). *Race matters.* New York: Vintage.

West, C. (1993). *Keeping faith: Philosophy and race in America.* New York: Routledge.

West, C. (2001). *Cornel West reader.* New York: Basic Civitar Books.

Wiegman, R. (1990). Black bodies/American commodities: Gender, race and the bourgeois ideal in contemporary film. In L. Friedman (Ed.), *Unspeakable images: Ethnicity and American cinema.* Urbana: University of Illinois Press.

Wiegman, R. (1993). The anatomy of lynching. *Journal of the History of Sexuality, 3*(3), 445–467.

Wiegman, R. (1995). *American anatomies: Theorizing race and gender.* Durham, NC: Duke University Press.

Wilson, A. (1990). *Black-on-black violence: The psychodynamics of black self-annihilation in service of white domination.* New York: Afrikan World InfoSystems.

Wilson, A. (1998). *Blueprint for black power: A moral, political, and economic imperative for the twenty-first century.* New York: Afrikan World Infosystems.

Wilson, K. (2000). Predicting vocational rehabilitation eligibility based on race, education, work status, and source of support at application. *Rehabilitation Counseling Bulletin, 43,* 97–105.

# Index

subjugation p7
pejorative p7
prostylization p5
promulgated p7
presupposition p4
semiological p4
complicity p4
corporeal politics p4
concomitant p5